Louis Jouin

Evidences of Religion

Louis Jouin

Evidences of Religion

ISBN/EAN: 9783741163838

Manufactured in Europe, USA, Canada, Australia, Japa

Cover: Foto ©Lupo / pixelio.de

Manufactured and distributed by brebook publishing software (www.brebook.com)

Louis Jouin

Evidences of Religion

EVIDENCES OF RELIGION.

BY

LOUIS JOUIN,

PRIEST OF THE SOCIETY OF JESUS,

AUTHOR OF

"*Elementa Philosophiæ Moralis*," "*Compendium Logicæ et Metaphysicæ*," *etc.*

NEW YORK:
P. O'SHEA, 37 BARCLAY ST.
MDCCCLXXVII.

Imprimatur.

John Card. McCloskey,
Archbishop of New York.

NEW YORK, October 3, 1877.

CONTENTS.

PREFACE iii

INTRODUCTION.

1. Difficulty of refuting the Attacks of modern Unbelievers against Religion.—2. They deny the first Principles of Reason, in order to deny the Existence of Religion.—3. Proof of the Existence of God, taken from the common Consent of Mankind.—4. The Idea of the Divinity is not the Result of Ignorance or Fear.—5. Proof of the Existence of God from contingent Being.—6. The Cause of the Universe is intelligent.—7. The Universe cannot be the Result of Chance.—8. It is not unscientific to seek the Cause of the Universe beyond the physical Order.—9. Matter is not self-existing.—10. Absurdity of an infinite Number.—11. The Principle of Causality is objectively real.—12. God is not the "Unknowable."—13. Absurdity of Pantheism.—14. Pantheism does not establish the Unity of Science.—15. Creation is both possible and a Fact.—16. How God contains all Perfections.—17. Principal Attributes of God.—18. Life is not the Result of mechanical Forces.—19. The Principle of Life is distinct from the Organism of the Body.—20. Simplicity of the Soul of Man.—21. Its Spirituality.—22. Difference between the Soul of Man and the Soul of the Brute.—23. The Freedom of the Will.—24. Why this Introduction was needed. 1

PART I.

ON THE NECESSITY AND EXISTENCE OF REVEALED RELIGION.

CHAPTER I.

ON THE NECESSITY OF WORSHIPPING GOD.

1. In what Religion consists.—2. What Worship is.—3. Necessity of internal Worship.—4. Necessity of external Worship.—5. God does not need our Worship, but on our Part it is necessary.—6. Not Religion, but the Abuse of Religion, has caused many Evils.—7. Religion does not unfit Man for the Duties of this Life. 37

CHAPTER II.

THE SUPERNATURAL.

1. Great Aversion of modern Unbelievers to the Supernatural.—2. Definition of the Natural and the Supernatural.—3. The natural State of Man.—4. The supernatural State.—5. Necessity of embracing revealed Religion, if given by God. . 42

CHAPTER III.

THE POSSIBILITY OF REVEALED RELIGION.

1. The Possibility of Revelation cannot be denied save by Atheists.—2. Proof of this Possibility.—3. Definition of Mysteries Natural and Supernatural.—4. Possibility of the Revelation of supernatural Mysteries.—5. Mysteries are not altogether unintelligible.—6. The Difficulties raised against Mysteries are not insoluble.—7. Their Revelation is not useless. 51

CONTENTS.

CHAPTER IV.

MEANS OF KNOWING TRUE REVELATION.—MIRACLES.

1. Immediate and mediate Revelation.—2. Definition of Miracles.—3. Possibility of Miracles.—4. The Constancy of the Order of Nature does not exclude the Possibility of Miracles.—5. Physical Certainty is not opposed to moral Certainty.—6. The Illiterate may be competent Witnesses to a miraculous Fact.—7. All the Laws of Nature need not be known, in order to judge whether a Fact is miraculous.—8. Miracles are a certain Proof of Revelation.—9. Necessity of a Criterion to distinguish true Miracles from false Ones.—10. The Criterion to be used for this Purpose.—11. Mesmerism.—12. Spiritism not opposed to Miracles.—13. Its Phenomena not new Inventions.—14. The Explanation given of these Phenomena is not unscientific. 57

CHAPTER V.

ON PROPHECIES.

1. Definition of Prophecy.—2. Possibility of Prophecy, and its validity as a proof of revealed Truth.—3. Pagan Oracles are no valid Objection against Prophecy. 73

CHAPTER VI.

NECESSITY OF REVELATION.

1. Distinction between physical and moral Necessity.—2. The moral Necessity proved from the Fact that all Nations deprived of Revelation fell into Idolatry.—3. Paganism was Demon-worship.—4. Paganism a School of Vice.—5. The same Effects manifested where revealed Religion is discarded.—6. The Perfectibility of Man insufficient to do away with Revelation.—7. Man did not progress from total Ignorance to higher Knowledge.—8. Idol-worship not the primitive Religion of Mankind.—9. Pagan Philosophers never reached a sufficient Knowledge of Truth.—10. Even had they attained its full Knowledge, still Revelation is necessary.

—11. An external Rule necessary to keep down Man's Passions.—12. Without Revelation Sinners not sure of Pardon.—13. Revelation necessary for social Worship.—14. Would Revelation have been necessary, had Man been created in a purely natural State.—15. The primitive Revelation lost through Man's Fault. 76

CHAPTER VII.

ON THE EXISTENCE OF REVELATION.

1. The Existence of Revelation proved from its Necessity.—2. From the common Consent of Mankind.—3. From the national Traditions of Antiquity.—4. From the Rite of Sacrifice.—5. How this Rite originated. 94

CHAPTER VIII.

ON MAHOMETANISM.

1.—There is no Need of passing in Review all religious Beliefs.—2. Idolatry evidently absurd.—3. Mahomet's Want of Credentials, and his Contradictions.—4. The Koran full of Fables. Immorality of the false Prophet.—5. Ignorance of Mahomet.—6. Recommends only external Observances.—7. Baneful Effects of Islamism.—8. Its rapid Spreading no Proof in its Favor. 98

CHAPTER IX.

ON THE JEWISH RELIGION. THE GENUINENESS OF THE PENTATEUCH.

1. Genuineness of the Pentateuch proved from the Jewish Traditions.—2. The Pentateuch existed before the Schism of the Ten Tribes.—3. It is anterior to the Time of the Judges.—4. Its Author contemporaneous with the Exodus.—5. His Legislation bears the Impress of the Desert.—6. He is perfectly acquainted with Egypt.—7. The objection against the genuineness of the Pentateuch has no Weight.—8. Solution of Objections. Facts not in accordance with the Existence

of the Mosaic Law.—9. The Author did not live after the Conquest of Palestine. 103

CHAPTER X.

AUTHENTICITY OF THE PENTATEUCH.

1. Its Authenticity rejected by Infidels, on Account of the Miracles contained in it.—2. The Pentateuch underwent no Change.—3. That Moses is a trustworthy Author is proved from his Style.—4. He could not be an Impostor.—5. The Miracles related by him are intimately connected with the History of the Jews.—6. The Jews were convinced of their Reality.—7. The Jews could not have been deceived by Moses.—8. They considered themselves bound by the Law of Moses, even after his Death.—9. The Worship of the Jews a standing Memorial of those Miracles.—10. The Sabbatic Year a constant Miracle.—11. Mention made of Mosaic Miracles by pagan Authors. 114

CHAPTER XI.

PRINCIPAL EVENTS RELATED IN GENESIS.

1. Moses a competent Witness of the Events related in Genesis.—2. The Words *Elohim* and *Jehovah* do not point to two different Authors.—3. The six Days of Creation do not furnish a valid Objection against Genesis.—4. Objections taken from ancient Chronologies and geological Facts.—5. Age of the human Race according to Genesis.—6. Chaldean Chronology.—7. Egyptian Chronology.—8. Egyptian Monuments no Argument for the great Antiquity of the human Race.—9. Chinese Chronology.—10. Prehistoric Times.—11. Quaternary Formations of comparatively recent Date.—12. Stone Ages no Proof of the high Antiquity of Man.—13. Fossil Remains of Man found together with extinct Species of Animals.—14. Peat Formations and Lake Dwellings.—15.

The State of Civilization of ancient Nations no Proof of the Antiquity of the human Race.—16. Traditions regarding the Deluge.—17. Unity of the human Race.—18. Tower of Babel. 126

CHAPTER XII.

THE JEWISH RELIGION, AS TO ITS CEREMONIAL, WAS TO BE PERFECTED BY A NEW REVELATION.

1. The Jewish Religion, in its Ceremonial, typical of the Messiah.—2. Promise of a Messiah.—3. The Messiah believed in by the Jews.—4. Expected by the Generality of Mankind.—5. The Messiah was to give a new Law.—6. To establish a new Sacrifice and a new Priesthood.—7. The Religion established by the Messiah a Perfection of the Mosaic One. 154

CHAPTER XIII.

THE MESSIAH PROMISED TO THE JEWS IS ALREADY COME.

1. The Advent of the Messiah proved from the Prophecy of Jacob.—2. Of Daniel.—3. Authenticity of Daniel's Prophecy. —4. Proof from the Prophecies of Aggeus and Malachias. . 162

CHAPTER XIV.

JESUS CHRIST IS THE MESSIAH PROMISED TO THE JEWS.

1. Christ alone realized what was foretold by the Prophets.— 2. All the Prophecies are fulfilled in Him.—3. Dispersion of the Jews after His Death. 169

CHAPTER XV.

THE GENUINENESS AND AUTHENTICITY OF THE GOSPELS.

1. Genuineness of the Gospels proved by the Testimony of the Writers of the first Centuries of the Church.—2. They could not have been Forgeries.—3 They were acknowledged by the Heretics of the earliest Ages.—4. The Jews admitted their Genuineness.—5. So did pagan Writers.—6. The

Gospels have undergone no Change.—7. Authenticity of
the Gospels.—8. Christ's Miracles admitted by the Talmud.—
9. Also by pagan Writers.—10. Testimony of Josephus.—
11. Genealogy of St. Matthew.—12. Assertions of modern
Critics of the Rationalistic School. 172

CHAPTER XVI.

THE RESURRECTION OF CHRIST ATTESTS HIS DIVINE MISSION.

1. Christ foretold His Death and Resurrection.—2. His Death
was real.—3. Christ rose from the Dead : how His Enemies
account for this Fact.—4. The Apostles were not deceived.—
5. Did not deceive.—6. Could not deceive, even had they
wished.—7. Testimony of the Apostles confirmed by the
Behavior of the Jewish Authorities.—8. They confirmed
their Testimony with their Blood.—9. Why the Jews refused
to believe.—10. Apparent Contradiction between St. Mark
and St. John.—11. Spread of the Gospel throughout the
whole World. 184

PART II.

ON THE CHURCH ESTABLISHED BY CHRIST.

CHAPTER I.

DIVINITY OF CHRIST.

1. Importance of the Dogma of the Divinity of Christ.—2.
Exposition of the Dogma.—3. Divinity of Christ supposed by
the Economy of the Christian Religion.—4. Traditions of
pagan Nations.—5. Prophecies of the Old Testament proving
the Divinity of the Messiah.—6. Assertions of Rationalists.—
7. Divinity of Christ not invented either by St. Paul or by
St. John.—8. Testimony from St. Matthew, St. Luke, and St.
John.—9. From St. Paul.—10. Traditions of the first Ages of

the Church before the Heresy of Arius.—11. Solution of some Difficulties. 207

CHAPTER II.

Figures by which the Church is Expressed in the New Testament.

1. The Church is a Kingdom.—2. A City.—3. A House.—4. A Temple.—5. Meaning of these Figures.—6. The Church is a Body.—7. What this Figure implies.—8. The Church a Sheepfold.—9. A Bride.—10. Parables referring to the Church. 227

CHAPTER III.

Institution of the Church as Related in the Gospels.

1. The Calling of the Apostles and their Election.—2. Promises made to St. Peter alone.—3. To all the Apostles.—4. Fulfilment of these Promises.—5. The Mission of the Holy Ghost.—6. Presence of the Holy Ghost in the Church as a Body, and in the individual Members.—7. Corollaries: the Church is one.—8. The sole Teacher of Truth.—9. She is indefectible and infallible in her Teaching.—10. Catholic.—11. Holy.—12. Apostolic. 236

CHAPTER IV.

Unity of the Church.

1. Christ willed the Church to be one.—2. She is one in Faith.—3. This Unity is indispensable.—4. The Apostles insisted on it.—5. The Church always asserted it.—6. Unity of Charity without Unity of Faith insufficient.—7. Absurdity of Unity in fundamental Articles only.—8. It cannot be determined.—9. Unity in Sacraments.—10. In Government.—11. Unity of Government required by Unity of Faith. . . 247

CHAPTER V.

CATHOLICITY OF THE CHURCH.

1. Foretold in the Old Testament and willed by Christ.—2. The End Christ had in View requires it.—3. It is simultaneous.—4. How it is simultaneous. 258

CHAPTER VI.

SANCTITY OF THE CHURCH.

1. In what consists the Holiness of the Church?—2. The Unworthiness of some of her Members no Obstacle to her Holiness.—3. This Holiness must be made visible.—4. Proved by the Gift of Miracles. 262

CHAPTER VII.

APOSTOLICITY OF THE CHURCH.

1. The Church apostolic.—2. Material Succession alone not sufficient.—3. Apostolicity required by all ancient Writers.—4. No extraordinary Mission to teach new Dogmas, or reform old Ones.—5. No Break in the Apostolic Succession to be feared.—6. The four Properties of the Church based on Unity.—7. The Church can never fail.—8. No dogmatical Reform needed in the Church.—9. The Promises made to the Church not conditional.—10. Reform of individual Members may at times be required. 268

CHAPTER VIII.

THE ROMAN CATHOLIC CHURCH ALONE HAS THE PROPERTIES OF CHRIST'S CHURCH.

1. Unity of the Roman Catholic Church.—2. She has always held the same Doctrines.—3: The Catholic Church could not vary in her Doctrines.—4. Definitions of Doctrine argue no Change.—5. Catholicity of the Roman Catholic Church.—6. Her Sanctity: she makes her Children holy.—7. Converts

pagan Nations.—8. Fosters Virginity.—9. Produces Saints.—10. Whose Sancfity is confirmed by Miracles.—11. Her Stability.—12. Sects constantly lose Ground.—13. Calumnies against the Church refuted.—14. Apostolicity of the Church.—15. Antipopes no Break in the Apostolic Succession.—16. Nor is the great Schism of the West a Break.—17. Neither the Greek Schismatics—18. Nor Protestants can claim to be the Church of Christ. 275

CHAPTER IX.

Teaching Authority of the Church.

1. The Church must have an Authority.—2. Different from that of civil Society.—3. Not confided to the Faithful.—4. An external Teacher required in the Church.—5. The teaching Body must be infallible, because it must be authoritative.—6. Without infallible Teaching no Faith possible.—7. Christ willed the Church to be infallible.—8. The Church always claimed Infallibility.—9. Infallibility not opposed to Science.—10. Galileo.—11. The Church not opposed to Civilization.—12. The Church may be known even to the Unlettered.—13. How Children and the Ignorant come under the Teaching of the Church.—14. Infallibility does not give rise to civil Intolerance.—15. The Inquisition. 292

CHAPTER X.

The Bible not Sufficient to Constitute the Infallible Teaching of the Church.

1. The Authority of the Church necessary to know that we have the whole Bible.—2. Its Inspiration can be proved only by the Church.—3. Vain attempts of Protestants to prove its Inspiration.—4. The Authority of the Church required for the Understanding of the Bible.—5. And for knowing whether the vernacular Copy is conformable to the Original.—6. The first Christians had no Bible.—7. With

CONTENTS. xiii.

the Bible alone, Christ would have poorly provided for his
Church.—8. Objections from Scripture. 310

CHAPTER XI.

PRIMACY OF ST. PETER.

1. The Church must have a supreme visible Authority.—2. Independent of the civil Power.—3. The Government of the Church not aristocratic.—4. The Church a Monarchy.—5. The supreme Power vested in St. Peter and his Successors.—6. Primacy promised to St. Peter by Christ.—7. The Church built on St. Peter.—8. The Keys of Heaven promised to him.—9. Fulfilment of the promise.—10. St. Peter exercised this Primacy. 324

CHAPTER XII.

THE SUCCESSOR OF ST. PETER IN THE PRIMACY.

1. St. Peter's Privilege permanent in the Church.—2. The Bishop of Rome the Successor of St. Peter.—3. Proved by History.—4. False Decretals.—5. St. Peter was Bishop of Rome, and died there. 340

CHAPTER XIII.

INFALLIBILITY OF THE POPE AS HEAD OF THE CHURCH.

1. All must agree in Faith with the Pope.—2. What is meant by Infallibility of the Pope.—3. Proofs. The Foundation of the Church.—4. The Centre of Unity.—5. This Doctrine held by the Church.—6. Gallicanism false.—7. The Pope's Dogmatical Decrees cannot be reformed by the Church.—8. Unity of Faith demands this Infallibility.—9. Objections: St. Cyprian.—10. Liberius.—11. Honorius.—12. Councils examined the Decisions of the Popes.—13. Bad Popes.—14. Usefulness of General Councils.—15. The Decrees of the Vatican Council did not change the Relations between Church and State. 350

CHAPTER XIV.

Relations of Church and State.

1. The Church superior to the State.—2. The normal Condition of a State requires Union between Church and State.—3. No Encroachment to be feared on the Part of the Church.—4. The Deposing Power of the Popes.—5. The State cannot impose any Religion.—6. When the State has, by a social Act, embraced the true Religion, it has a Right and is bound to protect and defend the Unity of Religion.—7. Toleration, and its Limits.—8. The Laws of Marriage not to be interfered with by the State.—9. The State cannot educate Children.—10. Has no Right to impose a Tax for the Support of mere secular Schools.—11. Liberalism.—12. So-called Catholic Liberalism.—13. Absurdity of this Theory.—14. Its Fundamental Error.   363

INDEX.   381

PREFACE.

This little treatise on the Evidences of Religion has been designed more especially for students who pursue a full course of philosophy, to afford them an insight into the grounds on which our holy religion rests, and to place in their hands the weapons necessary for warding off attacks of the enemies of the Church. Being intended for a text-book, it is, of necessity, concise in the exposition of arguments, and in the solution of the many difficulties raised by the adversaries of religion. Although the several subjects it treats of might have been developed more at length, and strengthened with other arguments, I think nothing essential has been omitted. It was impossible, in a short work of this kind, to bring forward all the difficulties raised by modern infidels; yet the chief ones have been touched upon, and those principles laid down which may serve as a solution to other objections not mentioned here.

As irreligion is spreading every day more and more, it is highly important that our Catholic young men, who, by education and position in society, may acquire influence with their fellow-citizens, should be well instructed, not only in the teachings of faith, but also in the motives of credibility which establish scientifically the truth of our holy religion. This will, on the one hand, enable them to avoid embracing principles in opposition to our faith, while, on the other, it will give them arms wherewith successfully to rebut the calumnies uttered against the Church. Still it must be remarked that, though the study of the Evidences of Religion is very useful, and, we may even add, almost indispensable for the educated classes, it is by no means necessary that every Catholic should go through such a course of studies, in order to be able to make an act of faith; for the authority of the Church is quite sufficient to afford all men a rational ground for their belief. Even the dullest intellect cannot help seeing that the Catholic Church is not a human, but a divine institution. The admirable unity binding her members into one compact body, though they be spread over the entire earth, and belong to every nation under heaven; her vigorous life, which enables her, in spite of every opposition, to enlarge her fold daily more and more; her success in converting the fiercest tribes; her continued existence through countless persecutions raised against her at all times,—are more than sufficient to show that she is guided and protected from on high.

This work has two Parts. In the first, we shall show the necessity and existence of a revealed religion, which is none other than that which Jesus Christ preached; in the second, we shall prove that the Catholic Church is the only one which Christ founded on earth.

A. M. D. G.

INTRODUCTION.

1. Difficulty of refuting the Attacks of modern Unbelievers against Religion.—2. They deny the first Principles of Reason, in Order to deny the Existence of Religion.—3. Proof of the Existence of God, taken from the common Consent of Mankind.—4. The Idea of the Divinity is not the Result of Ignorance or Fear.—5. Proof of the Existence of God from contingent Being.—6. The Cause of the Universe is intelligent.—7. The Universe cannot be the Result of Chance.—8. It is not unscientific to seek the Cause of the Universe beyond the physical Order.—9. Matter is not self-existing.—10. Absurdity of an infinite Number.—11. The Principle of Causality is objectively real.—12. God is not the "Unknowable."—13. Absurdity of Pantheism.—14. Pantheism does not establish the Unity of Science.—15. Creation is both possible and a Fact.—16. How God contains all Perfections.—17. Principal Attributes of God.—18. Life is not the Result of mechanical Forces.—19. The Principle of Life is distinct from the Organism of the Body.—20. Simplicity of the Soul of Man.—21. Its Spirituality.—22. Difference between the Soul of Man and the Soul of the Brute.—23. The Freedom of the Will.—24. Why this Introduction was needed.

1. IT is at present far more difficult to grapple with the adversaries of our holy faith than it was at the beginning of Christianity. There was then at least some common ground on which the battle could be begun; Pagans admitted some principles of reason which might form the basis of an argument. Nowadays most of our opponents deny the very first principles of reason, and

yet look with disdain upon those who refuse to bow down before their unreasonable and absurd affirmations. They gravely assert that we have no other cognitions save such as are afforded us by the senses. Nay, even these cognitions they strip of their objective reality; since, according to their theory, we can know only that we have sensations, but we are unable to ascertain whether the objects to which our sensations refer are really such as we perceive them. What, then, is the amount of our knowledge? Very little indeed; at most, we know simply that we are, and that we feel something, but we cannot say what we are, nor what we feel: this must ever lie beyond the reach of our cognizance.

It is utterly impossible to enter the lists with such persons—we must leave them to their ignorance; but they should, at least, refrain from boasting of their science. Yet they pretend to reason, to investigate the external phenomena of which they profess to know nothing. They even establish general principles; but these principles are not first principles of reason, known to every one who has the use of his reasoning faculties,— principles which, being evident of themselves, need no proof. The only principles which they admit are generalizations of facts observed by the senses, and which are arrived at by induction. But, as the facts themselves have no objective reality, the principles based on these facts are likewise bereft of objective reality. Moreover, these men do not perceive that they are in contradiction with themselves. Induction cannot be applied to facts, unless the mind already possesses several principles of reason, evidently known, and which cannot be the result of a previous induction. Indeed, induction is based on this principle, "The order of nature is constant." How do we know this? Is it the result of previous induction? No; for induction itself presupposes this principle. To go through the process of induction, we must make use of our senses, in order to observe the facts from which general principles are to be gathered. We must, therefore, grant that we may rely on the testimony of our senses; but this we can do only inasmuch as we know already that the order of nature is constant. We must, besides, admit the two principles of contradiction and causality. Hence, to deny the first principles of reason is tantamount to denying the possibility of any knowledge whatever, and declaring our utter ignorance of everything.

2. But why do they advocate such a theory of ignorance? Because they aim at discarding all cognitions which lie beyond the domain of the senses; they wish to come to the denial of whatever cannot be seen, nor touched, nor weighed in the chemical balance. From this they would infer that there is no God, no soul; consequently, neither religion nor moral duties.

It will not, therefore, be amiss to say some words, at least, on these subjects and on these objections which are raised by infidels against these truths.

3. The existence of a Primary Cause and a Supreme Ruler of the universe is a truth which no man who has attained the use of reasoning faculties can possibly deny. It has been universally acknowledged by all nations; for, though many were ignorant of the true nature and attributes of the Deity, they, nevertheless, admitted His existence. No people, no savage tribe, has been found without some form of religious rite.

This truth is, moreover, confirmed by the universal consent of mankind, in acknowledging an essential difference between virtue and vice. All admit that there are actions which are intrinsically good and praiseworthy, and that others, on the contrary, are essentially wrong and blameworthy. All agree on certain general principles of morality, though they may differ most widely in the application of the same, or in the deductions drawn therefrom. They admit, therefore, the existence of a natural law, binding on all men, irrespective of any sanction imposed by human laws: for they feel the upbraidings of conscience when they have violated it, even though their deeds were unseen by human eye, and there be no fear whatever of detection. Now, as a law necessarily supposes a lawgiver, this natural law points to a lawgiver superior to the human race, to whom all must render an account of their actions.

This constant and universal voice of mankind cannot be disregarded, because it must be based on truth. It must have a cause: and no other cause but the evident perception of the truth of the existence of God can account for it. All other causes assigned to explain this fact, such as passions, prejudices, education, the fraud of human legislators, are insufficient. The passions of men would rather prompt them to reject the existence of a Being who takes cognizance of even their most secret crimes, and who is to pass judgment on them. Prejudice and education, not being everywhere identical, could not have given rise to the same conceptions among the different nations of the earth, living as they were without mutual intercourse. Lawgivers could never have persuaded their subjects that the laws imposed upon them came from, and were sanctioned by, the Deity, unless the people had been convinced beforehand, as of a fact, that God existed.

4. Modern atheists assert that the idea of a Divinity arose from ignorance and fear. Mankind, unable to investigate the cause of natural phenomena, attributed them to unseen agencies, whom they conceived to be superior to man, and thus arose the idea of divinities; and, as every material thing was supposed to be governed by

a special divinity, the primitive religion of the human race was Polytheism, or the worship of many gods. This assertion is entirely groundless. It rests upon the theory that the primitive condition of mankind was a state of utter ignorance and savage life—that man is but the result of the gradual development of some simian family. This supposition is in contradiction with all the traditions of the human race. The study of these traditions shows unmistakably that the primitive religion of mankind was a pure Monotheism, and that idolatry was introduced afterward. The condition of savages is, therefore, a state of degeneracy. The assumed fact of man's descent from apes is based upon mere suppositions. The fixity of species, the well-known sterility of hybrids, contradict it. The fossil remains of species long since extinct show that, even during the geological ages, the law of the fixity of species prevailed; no intermediate forms, indicating the gradual transition from one species to the other, have ever been discovered. All fossil remains belong to some determined species of plants or animals. No gradual development can ever change a plant into a sentient being; much less can a mere sentient animal be transformed by natural or sexual selection into an intellectual being, such as man: because, how much soever the senses may be perfected, they must always depend in their action on the organs of the body, whereas

PROOF OF THE EXISTENCE OF GOD.

the act of intelligence is entirely independent of these organs, as we shall prove hereafter.

This common belief of mankind in the existence of a Supreme Ruler of the universe cannot possibly be false: to suppose it so, were to assert that the human mind is absolutely incapable of distinguishing truth from error.

5. Moreover, this conviction is founded on evident principles of reason. It is a fact beyond dispute that there exists contingent being, viz.: being which was not always, which begins its existence, and afterward ceases to be. We ourselves are conscious of the fact that we did not always exist, and that the span of our life here upon earth is but short. Now, the existence of contingent being supposes the existence of necessary, self-existing being. The contingent, not existing necessarily, being indifferent as to its existence or non-existence, depends for its being upon a cause, since it could not produce itself. This cause is either contingent or self-existing. If it be contingent, it must likewise owe its existence to another: we must, therefore, come to an ultimate cause which is necessary and self-existing, and this ultimate cause of all contingent being is God.

To evade the cogency of this reasoning, some have imagined an infinite series of beings producing one another; but such an infinite series is absurd, as will be shown further on. Every series of successive terms must have a first term or a beginning, and hence no series can be truly infinite. But, were we even to allow the possibility of an infinite series of contingent beings, we should still be forced to admit the existence of a necessary and self-existing being; for this series, being composed of contingent beings only, must needs be itself entirely contingent, and cannot, therefore, exist without a cause. A collection of beings may no doubt produce effects, to the production of which each single individual of the collection is not equal; but in this case every individual possesses already an initial aptitude to produce the effect: thus one man may be incapable of raising a great weight, which many men, by uniting their efforts, may easily lift. But the mere collection of many beings cannot change their nature; a collection of many blind men can never form a multitude endowed with sight, nor can the gathering of many fools constitute an assembly of wise men. If, therefore, all the individuals composing the assumed infinite series be essentially contingent, the whole series must remain contingent.

6. The self-existing cause of the universe is an intelligent Being. This is evidenced by the admirable order which reigns throughout the whole creation. Order supposes the apt disposition of the means necessary to attain an end, and this cannot be accomplished without intelligence; for,

though the immediate agent which produces a work with order be not always endowed with intelligence, as is the case in machines and animals, these agents must have been formed by an intelligent cause, which rendered them fit to attain the end for which they were destined. One must be wilfully blind not to see the order which pervades the whole universe. It is manifested in the regular forms of crystallization; in the determined proportions in which elements combine to form new bodies; in the great variety of the forms of life which constitute a gradual scale from the lowest to the highest organism; in the admirable construction of each organism for the attainment of its proper end, and in the mutual relations of different organisms. We may see it in the regular path pursued by the heavenly bodies; in the laws which regulate all motion, whether in the heavens or on earth; in the regular succession of seasons, etc. And this order is the more admirable, because, though each being is subject to continued change and corruption, the order remains ever constant.

7. Who can attribute the existence of this order to chance? Chance is a nonentity. Men are accustomed to say a thing happens by chance, when its occurrence is unexpected and its cause unknown, though all are aware that such a cause exists. It were, indeed, far less absurd to say that a watch was the work of chance, than to

attribute to such a cause the existence of the universe. When our adversaries find in the strata of the earth's crust some fragments of flint-stone bearing the form of an arrow or spearhead, of a knife or a scraper, they exclaim: "Behold the work of design; these weapons must have been shaped by the hand of man." Why, then, should they discover no trace of design in the admirable order which pervades the universe? Final causes, they contend, are an exploded theory; philosophers have to do with physical causes alone. If there be no final causes, why then do they assert that the flint-stones referred to above were fabricated by man for weapons or other useful implements? Can we deny that our eyes are made for the purpose of seeing, our ears for hearing, our tongues for tasting? But if, sometimes, we are unable to find the purpose to which certain things are made subservient, we must ascribe this ignorance to the narrow compass of our intellect; and it would be absurd to hold that such things were not designed for some purpose by the Almighty Ruler of the universe.

8. Infidels contend that science has to investigate physical causes only, which fall within the province of the senses. Metaphysical causes, which escape the power of the senses, are, they say, mere nonentities, unworthy of engaging the attention of scientific men. To have recourse to an invisible cause, in order to explain the

phenomena of nature, is unscientific. Yet they themselves do not adhere to this principle. To explain the phenomena of light, heat, electricity, they admit an imponderable fluid called ether, which pervades the whole universe; now this fluid, because imponderable, cannot be subject to chemical analysis, cannot be weighed in the chemical scales. They perceive its effects only; and yet from the effects it produces, they argue its existence. Why, then, should it be unscientific to argue from the visible effects in this universe the invisible cause of them all: God, the omnipotent Creator of all things? But we analyze light, we measure its velocity, as well as the strength of electrical currents; whereas the primary cause of all things cannot be subject to our analysis. Very true; yet this analysis, this measurement, reaches only the effects produced, not the cause itself; this latter escapes all attempts at being laid hold of by the senses: reason alone can take cognizance of it, and form some conjectures about its nature. The same may be said of every force with which matter is endowed: these forces we can neither see nor touch; we can only observe their effects; and yet our adversaries do not deem it unscientific to treat of their existence.

9. The necessity of admitting a primary cause for the universe is so evident that our opponents do not really deny it; they even seek to determine it. So true is it that the human mind can

never rest satisfied till it reaches the ultimate cause of things. But this ultimate cause, they say, is not an all-wise, almighty Creator, who called everything from nothing into being; no, it is the very matter out of which the universe is made. This matter is supposed to be self-existing from all eternity; it possesses a certain activity of its own, together with an inherent necessariness of development according to determined laws. To this development is due not only the material universe with all the order which reigns therein, but life itself is the result of its action. Some men flatter themselves that this supposition is sufficient to account for the universe, without any need of resorting to the hypothesis of a God, and that they have thus pointed out, within the physical world, a primary cause which is subject to our experience.

What amount of absurdities are they obliged to swallow who obstinately refuse to acknowledge God as the Creator of the universe! Do they know the physical constitution of the primary elements of matter? No chemical analysis is capable of reaching them. We may indeed obtain the molecules of the various substances, but no experiments can tell us what constitutes the intrinsic difference of these substances; by the effects they produce we see that they differ, but their intimate essence will ever be impervious to the senses. To determine the constitution of the last elements of matter does not belong to the domain of chemistry, but to that of metaphysics, discarded though this latter science be by our adversaries. The former may at most afford us some data on which to base our investigation; more it cannot do. And of all the suppositions philosophers have invented to explain the nature of the last elements of matter, the atomic theory advocated by our adversaries is the least tenable, because, as it deduces the variety of substances from the number, arrangement, and proportions of elements, the difference between substance and substance is only accidental, not essential; besides which, this theory cannot account for the activity proper to matter. Hence, after all, it follows that the ultimate cause, such as they establish it, cannot fall under the cognizance of the senses.

But it is far more extravagant still to assert that the elements of matter are self-existing from all eternity. It is vain to look for proofs of this strange doctrine in the writings of unbelievers: they give none; they merely affirm. The only attempt at a proof is this: matter is indestructible, therefore it is self-existing and eternal. The antecedent of this reasoning is true, if we speak of physical agency, for physical agents can only modify matter; but it is false if we consider matter itself. Matter is contingent; its nature does not necessarily imply existence; it may or may not exist: so that He who called it into existence may destroy it at His pleasure.

A self-existing being has within itself all that is necessary, both for being and action, because, owing its existence to none, it is independent of all other beings. It is, moreover, unchangeable; for, as it exists necessarily, not only its being, but its very mode of existing, is necessary: it cannot, therefore, lose it and acquire another, or, in other words, it is not subject to change. Besides this, it is from all eternity without beginning, so that no change is possible, since every change supposes a succession of terms: and what succession of terms can be imagined without a beginning? Therefore, whatever is subject to change must have begun, and cannot be self-existing. Now, the elements of matter are not independent, since in their action they depend one upon another; they are subject to constant change, since they enter into the composition of bodies. Moreover, every element of matter has, as our adversaries admit, its own size, figure, weight; it combines with other elements only in certain given proportions. The elements are, consequently, limited both in their being and in their action. What power assigned them their limits? Who determined their mode of action? Everything which has a limit might be conceived either greater or smaller: it might act in one way or in another. If, then, it has a determinateness of its own, it owes it, not to itself, but to another being; for, as it could not produce itself, so neither could it assign to itself a limit. It might be urged that its very nature requires this limit. Still this does not answer the question, but merely evades it, since we may yet ask why its nature requires such a limit and not another: in the nature of the element itself we can see no necessity of this kind. Every element, therefore, owes its existence to some cause, and hence no element can be self-existing.

10. Furthermore, the number of material elements is determined. Who determined their number? Why are there so many and no more? It might be said that their number is infinite: but an infinite number is an impossibility. Infinity cannot be measured; but every number, being a collection of units, is measured by them. The infinite can by no means be considered as the aggregate of finite beings; because the finite, however much it might be made to increase, is, and always must remain, a finite thing. Let us suppose an infinite number: every number is divisible. Conceive, therefore, this infinite number divided into halves; these halves are not infinite; these finites would, therefore, constitute the infinite: which is plainly absurd. Again, every number is either odd or even. To which of these two classes does the infinite belong? If to the former, we may conceive a unit added on to make

it even; if to the latter, we may make it odd by adding a unit: it could not, therefore, have been infinite. If, on the contrary, you say that it is neither odd nor even, or both together at the same time, you are propounding an absurdity. You cannot have one infinite number greater than the other, for the infinite must include every possible number. Let us therefore suppose the number of elements to be infinite. But every element has a certain extension; it may therefore be conceived as divided into several parts, and thus we should obtain another infinite greater than the first.

To these reasons we may add this further consideration. Our adversaries must admit an infinite space existing in fact. Now, the elements of matter either fill the whole space, so that there be no vacuum left between any of them, or they do not fill the whole space. In the first case, no movement is possible; in the second, the elements of matter cannot be infinite, since they do not fill the infinite space, and we may conceive other elements placed in the empty spaces left by the existing ones. If, then, the number of elements be limited, there must be a being who determined them; in other words, the elements of matter cannot be self-existing. Finally, the elements of matter, in their action, are subject to certain laws: but who gave them these laws? It is as impossible to admit a law without a lawgiver, as to suppose an effect without a cause.

THE PRINCIPLE OF CAUSALITY. 17

11. Our adversaries, to deprive us of the means of proving the existence of God, pretend that we cannot make use of the principle of causality, viz.: "There is no effect without a cause;" because either we have not the idea of causality, or the principle, if admitted, can be applied only to the phenomena which fall under the cognizance of the senses. The reason why we are said to lack the idea of causality is, that the phenomena we observe show us, not the influence of one on the existence of another, but a mere sequence of facts. This is absolutely untrue; for we know full well that we are ourselves the cause of many of our actions. By the very fact of attributing activity to matter, we admit causality, since we suppose that by means of its activity matter produces something. Besides, the reason alleged to show that we have no idea of causality proves the very opposite; indeed, it takes for granted that causality does not imply a mere sequence of facts, but an influence on the existence of effects, and that we can distinguish between the conditions required for the production of effects and the cause producing them. Now, what is this, if it is not grasping the meaning of causality?

We have, moreover, an absolute certainty of this principle. We know it *a priori;* we do not reach it by means of induction, for induction itself supposes the knowledge of causality. An effect is something which was not always, but which at some time began to exist. It could not give existence to itself; hence it received it from another: in a word, it has a cause. If, then, every effect must have a cause, the universe, which, as we have proved, is an effect, must have its cause: this cause cannot be a contingent one (§ 5). The universe must, therefore, owe its being to a necessary self-existing cause, distinct from it, independent in its existence and action, eternal, unchangeable and infinite.

But, we are told, this principle may be used only in the investigation of physical causes, and God is not a physical cause. If our opponents mean that God is not made up of matter, that, being a spirit, He cannot be apprehended by the senses, we grant their assertion; but, if they imply that He is not a cause really existing, we must deny such an assumption. Not every cause producing visible or tangible phenomena can be seen or touched, as we have already stated with regard to the cause of light, electricity, etc. If we may apply the principle of causality in this case, why should we be denied its use in searching out the First Cause of the universe? The universe, after all, is visible; a cause it must have, and this cause cannot be contained within the universe itself, since it would be both contingent and insufficient to account for the existence of things. True science claims not only to investigate the proximate causes of external phenomena, but to reach, if possible, the ultimate cause. When infidel writers assert that the motion of the heavenly bodies is sufficiently explained by the law of universal attraction, and that consequently there is no need of admitting, by way of hypothesis, the being of God, they proclaim an absurdity. This universal attraction has become nowadays somewhat problematical; but, granting its existence, there remain several other questions to be answered. Who impressed this law upon every particle of matter? Who projected these bodies into space, so that every star in the sky should follow its appointed path, without interfering with its fellows? Who produced this matter? Let us even suppose that all the heavenly bodies were at first mere nebulæ: the same questions still remain unanswered.

12. Our opponents might perhaps not find much difficulty in admitting the existence of an invisible First Cause of the universe, provided we allow them to consider it as unknowable; for then they could hold themselves freed from all duties toward God: a consummation which, at bottom, is the only object they have in view. But this we cannot grant them. Undoubtedly we do not possess a full knowledge of the infinite, absolute, eternal Being; yet He is by no means unknown to us. By the very fact that we can distinguish between the finite and the infinite, the conditioned

and the absolute, we have sufficient perception of what the infinite and absolute is. We predicate of Him many attributes, such as eternity, absolute simplicity and spirituality, unchangeableness, omnipotence, unlimited wisdom, etc., all of which we know to be incompatible with the finite. But this, they say, implies Anthropomorphism: for it is attributing to the infinite the properties which we ourselves possess, and the infinite, if it exist, must be totally different from the finite. We do not proceed thus. We do not conceive God to be a man raised to the highest expression of human perfection. The difference between God and man is infinite. But, as whatever perfections are found in the effect must likewise be found in the cause in a manner compatible with its nature, we are forced to attribute to God those perfections which, though limited in man, may still exist without any imperfection whatsoever; consequently, to God we attribute being, life, wisdom, will, holiness, justice, etc.: but we consider that these perfections are in Him unlimited, infinite. We do not give to Him a body, because a body must necessarily be limited, composed of many parts, subject to change. The life we attribute to God is a spiritual life, which does not manifest itself in a succession of acts; for in God there can be no change, but He possesses His life in one eternal infinite act. His knowledge is not derived from the objects existing out of

Himself. By one act, the same which constitutes His infinite life, God, contemplating Himself, knows every thing possible, past, present and future. He does not reason; for, though the reasoning powers in man be a great perfection, the previous ignorance of those things to which we attain by reasoning necessarily implies imperfection. We are, therefore, very far from deserving the reproach of Anthropomorphism.

13. Pantheists admit the infinite as the primary cause of all things; but this infinite is not the Almighty Creator of heaven and earth whom Christians adore. It is a vague, indefinite, impersonal something, the substratum of every existing finite, necessitated to incessant development, receiving a determinate existence only inasmuch as it "externalizes" itself in the finite: in stones it is matter, in plants life, in animals sensation, in man intelligence; nay, in man alone it becomes conscious. Pantheists have imagined various theories, to explain this process of development; some make it real, others ideal; but, at whatever point of view it be considered, it is a tissue of absurdities. It confounds the finite with the infinite; it makes the infinite a dependent, ever-changing being,—a being which in itself is nothing, and yet is everything; a most imperfect being, yet supposed to contain all perfections; it is unlimited, because infinite, and still limited, inasmuch as it becomes everything; in fine, a

being containing in itself every imaginable contradiction.

14. Yet these men are not satisfied with a mere assertion of such wretched views; they would allege some apparent reasons to substantiate them; nor do they, like our former adversaries, quite discard the principles of metaphysics.

They boast of having established the unity of science. They do, indeed, confound the subjective with the objective, the ideal order with the real. They do not show the bond which unites the finite to the infinite, they simply identify them. But unity can never be the result of confusion; the unity of science is based on the unity of God, who, distinct from, and infinitely superior to, all finite beings, is the source and pattern of all truth.

15. Pantheists assert that creation is impossible, because we can form no conception of it. This is entirely false. The idea of creation naturally arises from the consideration of contingent being. Contingent being, by the very fact that it does not exist of itself, must have a cause, and its ultimate cause must be itself necessary and self-existing. Now the self-existing Cause cannot produce the contingent, by drawing it out of Himself, or by dividing Himself; because the Infinite is a pure spirit, not subject to any change. Hence the contingent can owe its existence only to the omnipotent act of the will of the Infinite.

Pantheists likewise assert that God must necessarily be a cause. If they mean that God necessarily *is*, we grant the assertion; but, if they pretend that God necessarily *causes*, we must deny it. For God, being infinitely perfect and independent both in His being and in His action, stands in need of nothing. He may create the finite, or may not create it, as He wills and pleases.

God must be *active*, for our God is a living God; but His infinite act, inasmuch as it is necessary, is the immanent act by which He knows and loves Himself; and the mystery of the Holy Trinity, revealed to us by Him, shows us more fully what is the necessary act of God.

16. God, being infinite, must contain all perfections. This is beyond a doubt. But He cannot contain finite perfections *formally*, *i. e.*, just as they are found in finite creatures; for His infinite being would thus become a series of contradictions. He contains formally all those perfections which do not necessarily imply any imperfection, and these He possesses without limit. All other perfections which cannot exist without being limited, such as extension, sensation, reason, etc., He possesses *eminently* and *virtually; i. e.*, He possesses whatever is perfect in them, He is the pattern of all these perfections, and He has the power of creating beings endowed with them.

17. From what has been said, we may gather the principal attributes of the necessarily self-existing Being called God.

God is eternal, for His existence has neither beginning nor end; and, being unchangeable, He possesses His life in one infinite act, embracing all the past, the present, and the future. He is therefore infinite. He is a pure spirit, for body He cannot have. As He exists and acts independently of all things, and yet knows everything, because His intelligence has no limits, He must know everything possible, past, present and future, by contemplating Himself; otherwise He would depend in His knowledge on things out of Himself, and His knowledge would be successive: which cannot be, since He is subject to no change. He is, therefore, the source of all being, all perfection, all truth; and He is the only God. He is all-powerful, because unlimited and independent in His action. He is free with regard to all created things, because, being infinitely perfect, He does not stand in need of them, but may create them or not at His pleasure. He rules and governs all things, because He is the Supreme Master and Lord of the whole creation, and brings everything to its appointed end.

18. Materialists, in order to pave the way to the denial of the spirituality and immortality of the soul, maintain that life is merely the resultant of the mechanical and physical forces with which

the elements of matter are endowed. What are their proofs? None whatever. Mr. Tyndall, in his Address before the British Association, at Belfast, in the August of 1874, affirms that experiments to substantiate this assertion are nowhere; that life, as far as we know at present, can arise only from the development of some "demonstrable antecedent life." * He, as well as Mr. Huxley, does not admit the validity of the proofs which have been adduced in favor of spontaneous generation. Yet, at the same time, he contends that, going in thought beyond all experimental demonstration, he discerns in matter " the promise and potency of every form and quality of life;" † and, while maintaining that the only fair way of reasoning is the method based on experiments, he, without any experiments, even in spite of them, proclaims that matter alone is the origin of life. The motive of this strange conduct is evident; for, if matter be inadequate to the formation of life, we must have recourse to a Creator: and this our adversaries will not consent to admit. Mr. Tyndall, in the same Address, says:

---

* "Report of the Forty-fourth Meeting of the British Association," p. xciii. London: John Murray, 1875.

† *Nature*, Aug. 20, 1874, p. 318.—It will be observed that we quote from two different editions of this notorious Address. We could not refer the previous quotation to the columns of *Nature*, simply because the whole passage in question would be sought for in vain in this, the first edition of the Address. On the other hand, if Mr. Tyndall has thought proper to qualify, in more than one instance, the baldness of his expressions as they first appeared in *Nature*, we are not therefore obliged to follow him whenever he shifts his base.

"The Anthropomorphism,"—as he calls the doctrine of the existence of a personal god,—" which it seemed the object of Mr. Darwin to set aside, is as firmly associated with the creation of a few [primordial] forms as with the creation of a multitude."* Hence he wants the definition of matter to be changed, so as to include the power of generating life. The only attempts at an argument in favor of this assertion are the property which matter has of grouping itself into crystals, and the fact that chemists have succeeded in producing some substances which formerly were thought to be the product of vitality alone.

19. The principle of life is necessarily distinct from, and superior to, the forces with which material elements are endowed; for, not only does it give unity of being and action to the living organism, but it holds also in check all the chemical forces of the constitutive elements of the body, and makes them subserve the development and preservation of the organism. As soon as it ceases to act, the chemical forces get the upper hand, and the organism falls into decay. Nay, the principle of life is distinct from the organism, and can in no wise be identified with it, since after death the organism still remains for some time, although life is extinct. It is something intrinsic in the living body; in the life-germ the organism

---
* *Nature, Ibid.,* p. 317.

is already contained, but as yet undeveloped. The principle of life causes this development: it enables the organism to take in its nourishment, it elaborates the various substances, transforms them into the substance of the organism, eliminates whatever is unnecessary or injurious to it.

The principle of life is necessarily one, because it gives unity to the living body. It cannot, therefore, be the result of the various forces belonging to the elements which form the organism ; because it modifies them, controls them, and makes them subservient to the organism. Some have thought it possible to compare a living organism to a machine set in motion by the motive power, and in which the several parts tend to bring about certain results. But this comparison is not to the point. For the motive power of a machine is not intrinsic, but external to it ; its unity is not substantial, but artificial. Besides, the living body takes in the substances it needs, it elaborates them, to develop itself from its first germ ; it grows, repairs the losses it sustains, and produces germs from which spring other organisms like itself. Can any comparison be made between a machine or a crystal in formation and a living organism?

When materialistic scientists dissect an organized body to find the principle of life, they seem to forget that they have before them only a dead body, from which the principle of life has already fled. They believe they have discovered and accounted for the principle of life, when they have found the functions of certain organs; and they do not reflect that, besides these organs, there must be a motor to give them life, and without which they remain inactive. They might as well ascribe works of art to the instruments alone, leaving aside the artist who uses them.

Science has been able to reproduce certain substances which are a result of vital force, but they are nothing more than chemical components. Science has not produced the slightest organism: this it never can do; it may decompose the various parts of organized bodies, and determine their chemical components, but science cannot reproduce a single part, much less the whole, of an organized body. But, even granting that men of science were to succeed in the impossible task of reconstructing an organized frame, there would still remain a bridgeless gulf between a set of dead organs and the principle of life.

20. If the very principle of life is, in general, something distinct from the mechanical and chemcal forces of the body, and superior to them; if it is even distinct from the organism of the living body, it follows that the fact of the human soul can in no way be explained after the tenets of materialism. In plants and brutes the living principle, though distinct from, and superior to, the organism, is still united to it in such a way that it is incapable of acting without it. But

with man the case is by no means the same. The human soul, though depending for many of its acts on the organs, has also acts of its own quite independent of them.

That the thinking principle in man is a substance not only simple but spiritual, is shown by its operations. It works by thoughts, by judgments, by reasonings. Now, these acts are simple; therefore their principle must be simple. Thoughts or ideas may be perceived more or less distinctly, but they cannot be measured; they can neither be seen nor touched, they cannot be divided into parts, so as to take a half or a third of them. The object of thought may be a compound thing, the soul may consider either the whole at once, or each part separately; yet, whether it perceives the whole, or considers a part only, these perceptions are each of them a simple act of the mind which admits of no division.

Materialists, of course, put aside intellectual perceptions, in their wish to reduce every act of the mind to a mere sensation; still our very consciousness tells us that we not only feel and have in our imagination the sensible image of the object presented to our senses, but that we also understand the nature of the object perceived by the senses. This perception is not a sensation, but an intellectual act.

Now, a principle producing simple acts must be itself simple, *i. e.*, without extension, without physical parts. From our own consciousness we learn that the principle of thought is *one*. Let us now suppose that this principle has extension. In such a case either every part constituting the soul perceives the whole idea, and then we shall have as many principles of thought as there are parts: which is in contradiction with experience; or the idea is diffused through all the supposed parts of the soul, and thus the idea itself would suffer extension: which, as we have seen, is impossible; and moreover, as no part of the soul could contain the whole idea, there would be neither perception nor consciousness of it. If only one part of the soul perceive the whole idea, as this part is supposed to be extended, the same reasoning holds good. Therefore, the thinking principle, or the soul, can have no extension, and must be a simple substance.

It might be urged that the idea results from the action of all the parts of the soul. But then the thought could not be simple, for what is made up of many parts cannot be simple. And this resultant of all the actions cannot be self-conscious, since it is not a substance, but a mere effect of the parts which are said to constitute the soul. Again, all the parts cannot be conscious of the whole thought, for none has the entire perception of it; or else there would be as many thinking principles as there are parts.

Now, if this be true of objects perceived by

means of the senses, how much more is it true with regard to objects which cannot be attained by them. We have perceptions of truth, justice, right, law, etc.; we can form the ideas of simplicity, eternity, infinity. These ideas are undoubtedly simple; hence the thinking principle producing them must itself be simple. It may suit Materialists to deny the existence of these and other universal ideas; they may call them mere words expressing a certain class of individuals or acts; but their assertion has no weight, for it is in direct opposition to our own consciousness. Words are arbitrary signs, which cannot be understood unless we know their meaning, or have a conception of the objects they signify. When we predicate of an act that it is right or wrong, we not only perceive such an act, but we compare it with a standard present to the mind, viz., the idea of right and wrong; and we pronounce the act either good or bad, inasmuch as we perceive its agreement or disagreement with our mental standard.

We certainly recollect the past, and, though we cannot lift the veil which covers the future, we may often guess what lies beneath it. But, had we nothing but sensations, as Materialists pretend, neither the past nor the future could affect us. The senses can be acted upon only by objects present to them. Imagination may reproduce sensations experienced before; it may combine many sensations, so as to form a whole which never had any existence, but the imagination is actually present: the idea of past or future is not contained in it. For the knowledge of the past requires an act of comparison; and, though the senses or the imagination may furnish us with the terms of comparison, they cannot produce the comparison itself, since the perception of relation is an act purely intellectual. Cognition, therefore, not being merely an act of sensation, the thinking principle cannot be a material being, nor can thought be explained by the mere activity of brain force.

Nay, even the sentient principle must of necessity be simple; for the sentient being is likewise *one*—there must be one subject which feels the various sensations produced in its body. Were the sentient principle a compound being, either all its parts would perceive the whole sensation, and there would be in the animal as many sentient beings as there are parts; or each part would have a corresponding amount of sensation, and then none could experience the whole sensation.

21. But there is a wide difference between the mere sentient principle in animals, and that principle which in man is both thinking and sentient. The former depends in its every act on material organs; the latter, though requiring the bodily organs for all its sensible perceptions, has intellectual conceptions, has operations of judgment

and reason, in no wise dependent on organs. The senses cannot apprehend objects which have nothing sensible, as are ideas of justice, truth, and infinity. Even in material objects the mind grasps what the senses cannot reach. It understands mathematical figures, which cannot be the object of the senses, for no figure without depth or breadth can exist, nor can it even be imagined. How badly soever the figures on the blackboard are drawn, to illustrate geometrical demonstrations, we understand them, we perceive the properties of lines traced, *v. g.*, in a circle, we see their equality or inequality, their proportions, though no such equalities or proportions exist in the drawings offered to the senses. In like manner it is impossible for the senses to reach the connection in a reasoning between premises and conclusion.

22. Materialists have endeavored to endow animals with intellectual faculties, and they collect many facts which seem to indicate the powers of reason in animals. To man they allow, at best, a more highly developed reason. But all their facts prove nothing. Animals act by instinct, by the promptings of nature; and the reasoning functions we attribute to them are not theirs, but ours, who are analyzing their actions. Animals never improve; they always act in the same manner. Had they even the lowest degree of reasoning, they would be susceptible of improvement:

experience would show them how to ameliorate their dwellings, or how to capture their prey more easily. For several thousand years their habits have invariably remained the same. When animals are trained by man, they cannot teach their young what they have learnt themselves. At times change of climate, or other circumstances, may force them to modify somewhat their habits; but here again we see the work of nature, for the acquired habit is transmitted by generation. Mr. Darwin sees improvement in the bees; for some there are of the lowest order, whose cocoons serve both as a hive and as a reservoir to store their honey, whilst others not only build their cells in so perfect a manner that our best artists could not equal them, but they have solved a geometrical problem, till lately unsolved by our greatest mathematicians, viz.: what form to give to their little dwellings, so as to spend the least possible quantity of wax in their construction. If this were the result of intellect, reasoning powers in bees would be far superior to those of man. But Mr. Darwin's assumption is a pure fiction of his fervid imagination. These different kinds of bees were always distinct, and they always acted in the same manner. The same holds good of all similar instances brought forward to substantiate the supposed fact of perfectibility in animals.

23. Man is likewise endowed with free-will. Our own consciousness testifies to this fact: for

we know the difference between the feelings, emotions, acts which depend on ourselves, and those which are independent of our will. We may choose between objects presented to us, and even when we feel a strong inclination toward anything, we have the power to refrain from it. Never, indeed, do we act without a motive; but these motives, whatever they be, do not determine our acts. All men are firmly convinced of this truth, for everywhere there are laws prescribed to regulate their actions; and those who transgress them are held accountable for their acts. All men admit the difference between vice and virtue. But, were we not free agents, laws to regulate our conduct would be absurd, and vice or virtue would be mere names.

Now, since man's soul does not depend for its very act on its bodily organs, its life is not extinguished with that of the body. Besides, vice is not always punished here on earth, and virtue is often trampled under foot by the wicked; so that punishments and rewards must be meted out after death. There is, moreover, in man's breast an ardent and irresistible desire of happiness, which cannot be filled by possessing the finite, passing goods of this world; for the mind of man, capable of knowing and loving the infinite, cannot rest save in the full possession of the infinite. But the happiness we crave for must not only be complete, it must be endless too; and since God

Himself has put this yearning in the human soul, such a soul must live forever, and be made to find its true rest and happiness in the possession of God, which must be obtained by living, whilst here on earth, in accordance with His divine will.

24. These truths, which are more extensively developed in philosophy, must of necessity be supposed, before we can enter upon the evidences of religion. For, if there be no God, or if the soul of man be not an immaterial, immortal principle, accountable for its actions, to treat the question of religion would be folly; but, if there is a God, if man is capable of knowing Him, if we are accountable beings, then the duties of religion follow as a natural consequence. This is why infidels seek by every means to undermine these principles; they would fain persuade themselves and others that no restraints need be put on man's evil propensities, because, forsooth, there is none to whom he has an account to give for all his doings.

EVIDENCES OF RELIGION.

PART I.

ON THE NECESSITY AND EXISTENCE OF REVEALED RELIGION.

CHAPTER I.

ON THE NECESSITY OF WORSHIPPING GOD.

1. In what Religion consists.—2. What Worship is.—3. Necessity of Internal Worship.—4. Necessity of External Worship.—5. God does not need our Worship, but on our Part it is necessary.—6. Not Religion, but the Abuse of Religion, has caused many Evils.—7. -Religion does not unfit Man for the Duties of this Life.

1. As God, the Supreme Ruler of the universe, is our Creator and our last end,—that is to say, the only object in whose possession we can find our lasting happiness,—it follows that our whole being depends on Him, and that we are bound to regulate all our actions according to His divine will. The knowledge of our duties may be derived either from the consideration of the relations which exist between God and ourselves, or from the teaching of revealed truth. The knowledge

of these duties, and the practice thereof, constitute religion. Religion, therefore, does not consist, as some have imagined, in a mere sentimentalism, in a vague feeling of awe and reverence for the unknowable infinite; it supposes definite dogmas and duties toward God.

2. The giving to God that honor, reverence, veneration and service, which we owe Him as our Creator and our last end, is called worship. It may be performed either by internal or external acts, and hence our worship may be internal or external. Yet our external worship, in order to be worthy of God, must necessarily be the outward manifestation or expression of the inward feelings of our soul; otherwise, it would be mere mummery or hypocrisy.

3. That we owe to God both internal and external worship, is an obvious truth. Worship consists in acts of adoration, prayer, obedience to God's will, and love for Him. Now, the duty of performing these acts flows necessarily from the relations which exist between us and God. God is our Creator and our last end. Since He is our Creator, we are bound to acknowledge His infinite power and majesty, and His supreme dominion over us. We are therefore obliged to adore Him. We must acknowledge our entire dependence on Him; hence arises the duty of prayer, and of entire submission to His divine will. We are also bound to thank Him for all

the benefits we receive, whether temporal or spiritual, because to Him alone we owe them. As God is likewise our last end, we ought to direct all our acts to Him, we ought to prefer Him to all created beings; in other words, love Him above all creatures.

Moreover, God, in creating us, could have no other end in view than the manifestation of His external glory. Being infinitely perfect, He does not stand in need of anything. The end He has in view in His external acts, in order to be worthy of Him, must be none other than Himself. But man, endowed with intellect and free-will, can manifest God's external glory only by obtaining knowledge of Him through the contemplation of his works, and by directing all his acts to God's honor and praise; in a word, by worshipping Him.

4. We must also worship God by external acts. We are composed of soul and body, and our whole being depends on God. It is, therefore, our duty to acknowledge this entire dependence on God, not only by acts of the mind and will, but also by external acts of the body; the more so, as these outward acts are the spontaneous manifestation of the acts of the soul, which cannot be duly performed without them.

Besides this, man is naturally a social being, and therefore he must give to God a social worship; for, not only every individual, but society itself, the State as well as the family, must acknowledge this dependence on God, and worship Him. But this social worship must needs be an external worship, because men can unite in worship only by outward acts. Therefore, we owe to God an external worship.

5. The duty of religion and of worship can be gainsaid only by those who refuse to admit the existence of a personal God, the Creator and Supreme Ruler of the universe. For, to admit the existence of God, and to suppose man free from the duty of worshipping Him, implies contradiction To be sure, God does not need man's worship for, being infinitely perfect in Himself, He can derive no benefit from the honor we pay Him but He requires this worship, because our nature absolutely demands that we should acknowledge our dependence on Him, and He cannot dispense us from this duty: for, Almighty though He be, He cannot change the relation of dependency in which we stand toward Him.

6. The necessity of religion has been denied, because religion, it is said, has been the fruitful source of fanaticism and hypocrisy, and has kindled many bloody wars. But we must reflect that it is not the practice of true religion which has caused these evils; man, carried away by his passions, has often abused religion, using it

as a cloak to cover his evil deeds. It is evident, however, that the abuse of a thing does not make the thing bad in itself. True religion inculcates the principle of love to all mankind, and, if all men were faithfully to practise this duty, there would be no injustice upon earth.

7. Nor does religion unfit man for the duties of this life. On the contrary, it tends to restrain his passions, and affords him courage and strength to discharge his various obligations toward God and his fellow-men; it makes him a law-abiding citizen, a lover of right and justice, who does not shrink from any sacrifice, even that of his own life, at the call of duty. Religion does not condemn any honorable or lawful pursuit; it only forbids us so to attach our hearts to the things of this world as to lose sight of our eternal welfare.

CHAPTER II.

THE SUPERNATURAL.

1. Great Aversion of modern Unbelievers to the Supernatural.—2. Definition of the Natural and the Supernatural.—3. The natural State of Man.—4. The supernatural State.—5. Necessity of embracing revealed Religion, if given by God.

1. THE supernatural is the bugbear of our adversaries: they cannot hear its name without very serious alarm. Those who still believe in the existence of the supernatural are considered as men of dull understanding, incapable of perceiving the bright light of science. Their arguments in favor of the supernatural are deemed undeserving of the slightest attention, since, being ignorant of science, they cannot judge its claims. Mr. Buchner, in his "Man According to Science," indorses Mr. Page, who says: "Those who admit formulas or dogmas of faith, whether in philosophy or theology, cannot be lovers of truth; they cannot be impartial judges of the opinions of others. It is time to say to these men of faith that scepticism and infamy are on their side." And Mr. Buchner adds: "These golden words should be traced in brazen letters on the door of every church and school."

Mr. Renan (Preface to the *Life of Jesus*) says: "By the very fact that a man admits the supernatural, he loses all claim to science." It is extremely difficult to enter the lists with such self-sufficient and unreasoning minds. Were there no God, there could not, indeed, be any supernatural effect; but, the existence of God once admitted, it would be highly absurd to contend that the supernatural is impossible.

2. Although modern unbelievers are agreed upon rejecting the supernatural, they do not attach the same meaning to this word. Materialists call supernatural whatever transcends the domain of the senses; others apply this term to all the effects which would be in opposition to the laws of the physical world. It is evident that the first meaning is altogether wrong, because the acts of the mind, though beyond the domain of sense, are quite natural. And, though there exist effects which surpass the power of physical and human agency, as will be proved further on, many of these effects are produced by the natural powers of beings superior, indeed, to man, but still mere creatures. It might, therefore, be useful to give to the words *natural* and *supernatural* their precise meaning, so far forth as they relate to man.

The word *natural*, in opposition to *supernatural*, is used to signify the properties which constitute man's essence or nature, the faculties, powers, and tendencies which flow therefrom, and whatever is required in order that these faculties, powers, and tendencies be not frustrated of their proper object. The *supernatural*, on the contrary, is a perfection which belongs not to the nature of man, nor flows from it, nor is required by the exigencies of his nature, either as the term of his activity, or as the complement of his tendency. Whatever is natural is, supposing the act of creation, due to man—if not to every individual, at least to the human species in general; supernatural gifts are not due to man, but are freely bestowed by God. Supernatural perfections or gifts may either be wholly supernatural, *i. e.*, they may exceed the entire range of the nature upon which they are conferred, and then they are called supernatural as to their substance, *quoad substantiam;* or, while they do not exceed the order of nature, the manner in which they are bestowed may be beyond all the requirements of nature, and then they are called supernatural as to their manner, *quoad modum*. The revelation of a mystery whose existence could never be discovered by the native powers of human reason, belongs to the first class; the revelation of truths attainable by reason belongs to the second class. The supernatural does not destroy the natural, but supposes it, because it either perfects the natural tendencies, or elevates them to a higher order of perfection.

3. Let us now examine in what the natural and the supernatural state consist. God, the sovereign Lord and Master of all things, might have created man in the mere natural state, granting him only those means which are necessary for his attaining the end required by his nature, in order to his complete natural perfection. Man, being endowed with reason, is capable of knowing God and of loving Him. Man's understanding is, indeed, very limited; yet he may, from the consideration of the perfection he finds in creatures, rise to the contemplation of the principal attributes of his Creator. He may acquire the knowledge of the unity of God, His infinity, His omnipotence, His infinite wisdom, etc. But man cannot know God intuitively, *i. e.*, he cannot know His very essence as it is in itself; because, on the one hand, this knowledge exceeds the natural powers of all created intellects, and on the other, his soul being united to the body, he must acquire his knowledge by means of external perceptions: and so all his conceptions of the divine nature are formed by analogy with outward things. As we are intellectual beings, possessing a knowledge of the Infinite, no finite being is able to satisfy our cravings for happiness, which can be filled by God alone; for happiness is obtainable solely by a strict compliance with His will made known to us. God has imprinted on our souls the primary principles of the moral

law, so that no man having the use of his reason can ignore them. These principles may be obscured by man's passions, but they never can totally disappear. Hence all men, how degraded soever they may be, experience more or less the upbraiding of conscience, when they act in opposition to its dictates, and all nations agree in admitting these primary principles; they differ only as to their consequences or their practical application. Had God left us in the natural state, our duty would be to acquire, as best we might, that knowledge of our Creator which we can draw from the contemplation of His works, to honor and to worship Him, to love Him above all things, and to obey His divine will; and, by so doing, we should secure for ourselves the attainment of our eternal happiness. This happiness would consist in the *perfect* knowledge of God; but this knowledge, though immeasurably more perfect than that which we at present possess, would still be merely abstractive, since our mental faculties, of themselves, cannot reach a higher conception of the Infinite Being. This, however, would be sufficient for every natural craving of the soul after happiness. Our duties toward God, in this case, would be those which proceed of necessity from the relations existing essentially between God and man, in so far as we might know them.

4. But God, the Lord and Master Almighty,

THE SUPERNATURAL STATE. 47

may raise man *to a far higher destiny* than that to which his own nature can lay claim; in other words, God may raise man to a supernatural state. This supernatural state consists in our being destined to reach supreme happiness, *i. e.*, not in a mere abstractive knowledge of God, but in a close union with Him, seeing Him face to face as He is, and thus partaking of His own infinite bliss. Man in this state is no longer a mere servant of God, but is raised to the dignity of adoptive child of God, and as such is ultimately admitted to share the happiness of his Maker. This supernatural end could not be reached by mere natural means, for the means to an end must be in proportion with it. Hence, if God vouchsafes to raise man to the supernatural state, He also provides him with supernatural helps or graces. But, since neither the supernatural end to which man has been raised, nor the means to attain it, can be known save through a special revelation from God, such a revelation, in the present hypothesis, becomes of strict necessity. This revelation contains truths above the grasp of the human mind, and in consequence would be supernatural both as to its substance and manner, though it might comprise truths within the pale of our natural perception.*

---

* It is of the first importance to maintain the distinction between the natural and the supernatural state of man. A confusion of these two states has originated the errors both of Calvin and of Jansenius. They held that what we call the supernatural state is,

According to the teachings of Christianity, the natural state of man never existed; but God, on creating man, not only raised him to the supernatural state, and clothed him with all the supernatural graces necessary for an adopted child, and for the performance of all that is required to make his high destiny secure, but He also endowed him with the gifts of original justice. This entailed on man a freedom from concupiscence, or from those impulses which incline us betimes to evil in spite of ourselves, from illness, from every calamity, and from death

---

in fact, the natural one, and that God, in view of His wisdom, could not have created man in any other state. As man, by the disobedience of Adam, lost the gifts of sanctifying grace, which made him an adoptive child of God, as well as the gifts of original justice, they inferred the doctrine of the total depravity of man ; they asserted that any one who was by sin deprived of sanctifying grace could not but sin in all his acts; they also maintained that the freedom of the will was altogether destroyed in man by original sin. Even some Catholic doctors taught that the natural destiny of man was to find his happiness in the intuitive vision of God, but that the means to reach this end are supernatural, not natural. How in this theory the errors of Jansenius can be avoided, it is hard to perceive. The Ontologists, who assert that man, even in this life, has the intuitive knowledge of God, and that this direct—not reflex—intuition is the source of all our intellectual cognitions, do strive to find, by subtle distinctions, a means of maintaining the difference between the natural and the supernatural state of man, but in vain. If we naturally, by intuitive vision, know the essence of God, we must necessarily see Him as He is, and the difference between the natural and the supernatural disappears. A recent writer maintains that the incarnation of Christ is the necessary complement of the cosmos. If he speaks of the present order of Providence willed by God, he is perfectly right; but, if he means that God could not have decreed to create man without at the same time decreeing the incarnation of the second person of the Holy Trinity, in order to complete the creation, he is grievously mistaken, and he too confounds the supernatural with the natural order.

itself. All these gifts were forfeited through the disobedience of our first parents; and though, through the redemption of Christ, the right of adoptive sonship is restored by the sacrament of baptism, the gifts of original justice have not been regained.

But, even if God had left man in the natural state, He might have imparted to him the revelation of those truths which do not transcend the powers of his intelligence, so that the knowledge of those truths which are necessary for securing his final happiness should become both more easy and more certain. He might likewise have imposed upon him some duties besides those which are laid down for him by the natural law.

5. If God in His mercy vouchsafes to reveal a religion, and this revelation becomes known to us, we are bound to accept and profess it; for God, being our supreme Master and Lord, can impose upon us any duty He pleases. If, therefore, God wills that, to attain our last end, we should practise some other duties besides those contained in the natural law, we are bound to submit both our minds and wills to God's holy will; for God alone can connect our acts with the attainment of our last end. It is impossible to secure our salvation unless we make use of the means appointed by God for this purpose. Indifferentism in religion is, therefore, a crime; because we are obliged not only to worship God,

but to do so in the way He wills it. If God reveals a religion, and this revelation becomes known to us, He cannot remain indifferent as to whether we submit or not. It will not do to say: Provided we are honest, and fulfil our duties toward our fellow-men, God will be satisfied. We are bound to fulfil our duties toward God, as well as our duties toward our neighbor. He who neglects the former neglects the principal part of his obligations, and cannot be acceptable to God, nor secure his own eternal salvation.

CHAPTER III.

THE POSSIBILITY OF REVEALED RELIGION.

1. The Possibility of Revelation cannot be denied save by Atheists.—2. Proof of this Possibility.—3. Definition of Mysteries Natural and Supernatural.—4. Possibility of the Revelation of Supernatural Mysteries.—5. Mysteries are not altogether unintelligible.—6. The Difficulties raised against Mysteries are not insoluble.—7. Their Revelation is not useless.

1. THE possibility of revelation cannot be gainsaid, save by those who refuse to acknowledge the existence of a personal God. Atheists, denying God altogether, discard not only the supernatural order, but also every conception which transcends the domain of the senses. Pantheists seem at times to admit revelation, but this, in their opinion, is nothing more than the natural perception of the mind; they seek only to hide their errors under Christian expression, in order more safely to deceive the unwary.

2. That God can reveal truth to us, is a self-evident principle, for God must have the power to communicate truth to rational beings; and man is not only capable of instruction, but he stands in need of it. If we may be taught one by the other, how much more so may we be instructed by the Creator Himself! God, who

has given to man the power of imparting knowledge to others, must necessarily possess the same in an eminent degree, because this power, considered in itself, does not involve any imperfection whatsoever.

Moreover, God, who has endowed us with the faculty of reason, may, undoubtedly, enlarge the store of our knowledge by a direct communication of truth to our minds. It belongs to His supreme dominion over us to communicate to us His divine will, apart from the ordinary means bestowed upon us for acquiring knowledge. This cannot be denied without limiting the infinite power of the Creator.

This truth is, in fact, so plain, that it is admitted by the common consent of all nations; for all religions, which have ever been or are even now professed, are based upon a true or supposed intercourse of the Deity with man. There are, indeed, many fictitious revelations; but these would never have obtained any credence without the common belief of mankind in the existence of a true revelation; just as there would be no possibility of passing false coin, if there were no genuine coin in circulation.

'3. A mystery is a truth of which, if expressed by a proposition, we know that the predicate of this proposition is to be attributed to the subject, but without our perceiving the intrinsic reason of such agreement. There are mysteries

whose existence we know, or at least may
know, by the use of our reason, such as the fact
of our existence, of the union of body and soul,
and many others: these may be called natural
mysteries. Other mysteries there are, whose
existence would forever have remained unknown
to us, had not God revealed them: these are
supernatural mysteries. That there are such
mysteries is plain; for truth is coextensive with
being, since whatever is is *true*, inasmuch as it
is; hence, as being is infinite, truth is likewise
infinite. We must, therefore, admit truths which
surpass the limited power of our understanding;
to deny this were to make the finite the measure of the infinite.

4. God may, if He please, reveal supernatural
mysteries; for, on the one hand, God can reveal
truth, and, on the other, man can receive the knowledge of supernatural mysteries. Indeed, the only
difference between natural and supernatural mysteries is, that the former may be known to us by
our own reason, whereas the latter are admitted on
the authority of God, who, being Infinite Truth,
can neither deceive nor be deceived. Unlettered
men, relying on the authority of scientists, may
receive scientific truths which they do not understand, such as the fact of the earth revolving
around the sun, the distance of the sun from
the earth, etc. How much more, then, may we
admit truths manifested to us by God Himself!

5. It is unreasonable to say that we cannot hold as true any proposition of which we do not understand *how* the predicate agrees with the subject. It suffices for us to know that there is such an agreement, whatever be the source from which we derive this knowledge. As regards every revealed mystery, we have a sufficient knowledge of both subject and predicate; relying on God's infallible authority, we have the certainty that the predicate agrees with the subject; hence it is not true that a mystery is nothing else but words strung together, conveying no definite idea to the mind.

Infidels, who reject the mysteries revealed by God, are forced to admit many palpable contradictions. There is no need of speaking of the absurdities maintained by Atheists, Materialists, Pantheists and Positivists, though they pretend to the exclusive right to science. Even Rationalists, who admit the existence of a personal God, by rejecting revealed truth, are forced to deny His Providence; they must suppose that God is indifferent about His creatures, and cares nothing about their welfare.

6. There are many difficulties raised against mysteries, but these arise either from our not being able to understand how the predicate agrees with the subject: and such difficulties we are not bound to solve, because we admit mysteries on the infallible authority of God; or they spring

from the ignorance, real or assumed, of our adversaries, and are rectified by the true statement of our belief. Other difficulties are derived from philosophical principles, which are not evidently proven, but are either mere assumptions, or, at most, have only some slightly probable reasons in their favor. Such difficulties need not trouble us, for, if the revealed mysteries cannot be reconciled with these philosophical principles, we have simply to deny the latter. God's word being necessarily true, whatever is in opposition to it must necessarily be false. There can be no opposition between philosophical and theological truth, since both are derived from God. If the revealed mystery contained a real contradiction, or if it were opposed to any truth clearly established, we should be forced to repudiate it as not coming from God. Supernatural mysteries are *above* our reason, inasmuch as our reason is incapable not only of demonstrating them, but even of discovering their existence; but they are in no way *contrary* to reason.

7. The revelation of mysteries is not useless, for these revealed truths afford us the solution of many problems of the utmost importance, which have always perplexed the human mind unenlightened by faith, and which would have remained unsolved forever. These mysteries enlarge the horizon of our knowledge, since they unfold to us many truths appertaining to God,

and afford us a means of understanding better the infinite love and mercy of God for us. Some unbelievers have asserted that they would willingly admit the Christian religion, on account of the sublimity and purity of its moral teaching, if it were stripped of all its mysteries. But this is a mere pretence. It is not the necessity of believing the mysteries which prevents them from professing the Christian religion, but the moral obligations which Christianity imposes upon them. Could they be freed from these obligations, and follow the bent of their passions, they would have no objections against these mysteries, since they are ready to admit even the greatest absurdities, in order to find a pretext for refusing submission to the teachings of the Church. Were the moral duties of man to be inferred from the axioms of mathematics, they would refuse to admit them, just as readily as they reject the principles of Christianity.

CHAPTER IV.

MEANS OF KNOWING TRUE REVELATION.—MIRACLES.

1. Immediate and Mediate Revelation.—2. Definition of Miracles.—3. Possibility of Miracles.—4. The Constancy of the Order of Nature does not exclude the Possibility of Miracles.—5. Physical Certainty is not opposed to moral Certainty.—6. The Illiterate may be competent Witnesses to a miraculous Fact.—7. All the Laws of Nature need not be known, in order to judge whether a Fact is miraculous.—8. Miracles are a certain Proof of Revelation.—9. Necessity of a Criterion to distinguish true Miracles from false Ones.—10. The Criterion to be used for this Purpose.—11. Mesmerism.—12. Spiritism not opposed to Miracles.—13. Its Phenomena not new Inventions.—14. The Explanation given of these Phenomena is not unscientific.

1. GOD may speak to man either directly or through the instrumentality of others. If the former revelation takes place, God speaks to the mind so as to make it evident that the communication comes from Him. When God imparts truth to us through others, His messengers must be provided with such credentials as shall take away every shadow of doubt as to their mission; for, unless they be able to substantiate it by unmistakable proofs, it is our duty to disregard their testimony. Now, these credentials are either miracles or prophecies.

2. A miracle is a fact perceptible by the senses, and evidently in opposition to well-known laws of nature. Miracles are of two kinds. Some are quite beyond the power of created nature, which means that they require the intervention of the creative power of God; such would be the raising of a dead man to life, or the sudden restoration of a lost limb. Others, though not requiring for their production the creative power of God, are still above the power of material and human agency; for instance, a sudden restoration to health without remedies, when, according to the laws of nature, such a cure would be impossible. Miracles of this class may be performed by God, but they may also be the work of angels.*

3. The possibility of miracles can be gainsaid only by those who deny the existence of an almighty Creator and all-wise Ruler of the universe. For, since the laws of nature depend on the will of God, He has it in His power to suspend some of the effects which, according to the laws established by Himself, would otherwise be produced. But, even if these laws were the necessary consequence of the nature of material agents,—which we do not grant,—God could still prevent such laws from taking effect; in other words, He could perform miracles.

---

* Unbelievers do not admit the existence of angels, but this denial is of no account, the whole human race, by common accord, acknowledging their existence.

4. The principal argument brought against the possibility of miracles is, that the laws of nature are invariably determined, and admit of no change. But on what grounds do unbelievers assert this axiom? It is not self-evident, since the whole human race, with the exception of modern infidels, admits not only the possibility, but the actual existence, of miracles, and thus denies this assumption. It cannot be proved by reason, for reason shows us that the laws of nature depend on the will of God. It cannot be ascertained by experiment, because, on the one hand, experiments show only what actually exists, not what might take place; on the other hand, many miracles have really been performed. We grant, indeed, that the order of nature is constant, nay, we go farther: we assert that this principle,—" the order of nature is constant,"—is not an experimental principle, for all our experiments are based upon it; but both reason and experience prove most unmistakably that this constancy does not exclude the power of God to suspend, if He thinks fit, some effects of natural laws. Nor is the constancy of nature's order impaired by the performance of a miracle, since the laws established by God remain the same, and only in a particular instance is one of their effects suspended. When God preserved the three young men from the flames of the Babylonian furnace, the fire did not lose its property of consuming

combustible bodies; it was only prevented from *exercising* its power on these three youths. M. Renan asserts that science assumes the laws of nature to be absolutely unchangeable, and hence cannot but reject the possibility of miracles. But this is an assumption unwarranted either by facts or by reason. True science must admit that the order of nature is subject to the control of the Creator. If the world existed of itself, there would be no possibility of miracles, because there would be no cause capable of producing them. But to admit the existence of the world without the Creator is not only unscientific, but supremely absurd.

5. It is likewise objected that we have a physical certainty as to the constancy of the order of nature, whereas the existence of a miracle becomes known to us by moral certainty only, viz., by the testimony of those who say they witnessed it. Now, moral certainty is inferior to physical. Therefore, we are compelled to reject miracles, whatever may be the weight of testimony in their behalf. To this we answer: It is false that they at least who witnessed a miracle have no physical certainty of the fact. A miracle, being a fact perceptible by the senses, falls under observation like all other natural facts, and hence affords the same certainty. It is likewise false that moral certainty is inferior to physical, unless we mean by the former only a high degree of probability.

Certainty, whether physical or moral, excludes all doubt; hence the one cannot be opposed to the other. We are sure that the order of nature is constant, that all bodies are subject to the law of gravity, that fire consumes combustibles, etc.; but we likewise know that these effects of nature's laws will surely not take place if God, in His infinite wisdom, decrees to suspend them. If, therefore, competent witnesses testify that a miracle has been wrought, if their testimony be accompanied by all those circumstances which exclude any suspicion of their being deceivers or dupes, then may we conclude, without fear, that in this particular case it has pleased God to suspend the operation of one or more laws of nature. If the testimony of competent witnesses cannot be relied upon, natural science becomes an impossibility: for natural science is based on the observation of facts which can be verified only by a few scientific men: the rest of mankind must accept these facts as testified to by those who observed them.

6. But, it may be urged, those who attest the existence of miracles are not scientific men; they are persons without learning, ignorant of natural science, who, from their liking for the marvellous, cannot safely be trusted. In the first place, it is false that only unlettered men have given their testimony to miracles. They are frequently attested, even in our own days, by men well versed

in physical science. Moreover, the illiterate, having their five senses as well as the learned, can grasp external facts as well as any member of a scientific academy, and, therefore, their testimony, if otherwise trustworthy, is not to be rejected; the more so as their testimony has no reference to the supernatural nature of the fact, but only to its existence inasmuch as this is perceivable by the senses. No fact is to be considered a miracle so long as a reasonable doubt exists as to whether or not it may be accounted for by a natural cause. But when a clearly proven fact is found to be in opposition to the known laws of nature, then it must be the effect of an agency either supernatural or at least preternatural. Some infidels have had the impudent flippancy to ask that, when a miracle is to take place, notice should be given beforehand to some scientific academy, that it might appoint a committee to be present, and to report thereon. God performs miracles for the good of mankind when and where He pleases, but not to satisfy the idle curiosity of men blinded by self-conceit. Miracles take place even in our own days; and if unbelievers were sincere, they would have occasion, more than once, to examine some of them. But they do not wish to do so. If they hear of any miracle, immediately, without a shadow of inquiry into the foundation of the report, they deny the fact; or, if this be too well established, they, without much ado, assign for its existence some natural cause yet undiscovered, or they seek a shallow refuge in the power of imagination, in nervous derangement, and the like, without giving a moment's examination as to whether the fact be explainable on grounds such as these. They fear to meet a miracle face to face, lest their cherished prejudices should receive a fatal shock.

7. In order to decide whether a fact be miraculous or not, it is by no means necessary to have a thorough knowledge of all the laws of nature; it is sufficient to know that the fact in question is opposed to some universally admitted law of nature.

When God performs a miracle, He does not change His mind; for, being all-wise, He from all eternity determines when and where He will make an exception to the general rule.

8. Now, since miracles are possible, and since, when they are genuine, God is either personally, or by means of His angels, their author, it follows, as a necessary consequence, that any revealed religion confirmed by miracles has God's sanction, and we are bound to embrace it; for God, being truth itself, can sanction no falsehood.

9. There is no difficulty as regards miracles of the first order, for these, being beyond the power of created agencies, can come from none but God. But when we are dealing with mira-

cles of the second order, there arises a question which calls for solution. It is the general belief of mankind (and our holy religion confirms this belief) that there exist evil spirits who, possessing a thorough knowledge of the properties of natural agents, with the power of applying them at will, may produce effects contrary to the known order of nature, which effects may appear to us true miracles. These spirits endeavor by every means to deceive mankind. They might, therefore, abuse their power, to perform miracles of the second order in confirmation of a falsehood. They may, in a certain manner, mimic those of the first order, so as to produce, in appearance, the same outward effects. When Aaron stood up before Pharao, he cast his rod on the ground, and by the creative power of God it was changed into a serpent. The magicians of the Egyptian king, by enchantments and secret devices (*Exod.* vii), did the same; their rods seemed to become serpents too, not indeed by an honest transformation of a lifeless wand into a living creature, but by a sudden substitution of real serpents, due to the activity of the spirits at work. Therefore, were we not possessed of a criterion whereby to distinguish true miracles from false ones, the former could not be used as proof positive of a revealed religion.

10. The criterion to distinguish between true miracles and a deception of the evil spirits is, to consider, first, the doctrine which is confirmed by

an effect contrary to the known laws of nature. This doctrine should not be immediately evident; otherwise a miracle to confirm it were unnecessary. It must not be in opposition to any truth known with certainty, whether by reason or by faith; nor must it involve any contradiction. Secondly, we must examine the effect itself which is produced, the manner and the end of its occurrence, and every other concomitant circumstance. If aught be found unworthy of God, or not in strict harmony with His divine attributes, we cannot ascribe the effect to His immediate action, nor can we suppose the fact to have taken place with His positive approbation. Thus, if he, by whose agency a *non-natural* effect is produced, act in a spirit of vainglory, for ostentation, for the sake of temporal gain; if he claim to possess the power of producing these effects at will, or if they be directed to the satisfaction of idle curiosity; if they tend to unbridle men's passions, to lower the standard of morality; or, if the doctrine confirmed by such facts be at variance with some known truth, there can be no doubt that it is not God who speaks to us. If, on the other hand, the doctrine confirmed by a *non-natural* effect is not opposed to any truth, if all its attendant circumstances are in accordance with God's divine attributes, we are bound to acknowledge that the doctrine so proclaimed bears the sanction of God Himself. Were we not bound to admit such doctrine, then would it follow, as a necessary consequence, that communication between God and man would be impossible. For the mere proposing of some doctrine is not sufficient to enforce the adhesion of our intellect without evident proof. The combining of some mere natural effect with this enunciation cannot suffice for its confirmation, since there is no connection whatever between the fact and the doctrine proposed. Therefore, by *non-natural* effects alone can God show us with certainty that the messenger speaking in His name is, in truth, empowered by Him, and has a claim on our belief.

Furthermore, if a doctrine confirmed by miracles such as we have described were not the voice of God, we should necessarily be led into error, and this error would be attributable to God Himself. For, on the one hand, man feels the need of intercommunication with God, as he is well aware that reason cannot of itself give him the solution of many a highly important problem bearing upon his final destiny. On the other hand, mankind has always been fully persuaded that a miracle is the voice of God; and here our adversaries agree with us, for the only reason why they so persistently deny the possibility of miracles, is their repugnance to admit a revealed religion: they know well that the granting of the former implies, of necessity, the admission of the latter. So that, if we could be deceived when a doctrine is confirmed by a miracle under the circumstances above stated, our error would become unavoidable. God's providence, therefore, will never allow the evil spirit to perform a *non-natural* effect, when those who are witnesses are unable to detect the fraud.

11. Some unbelievers acknowledge the facts called miracles, but they pretend to explain them by means of Mesmerism or animal magnetism. This force, they say, produces its wonderful effects through natural agencies yet unknown, but which, let us hope, may soon come to light through the rapid progress of natural sciences.

The strange effects produced by the so-called mesmeric fluid or magnetism, have been denied by many, or have been considered as the result of mere jugglery. But not a few trustworthy authors, well versed in physical and medical science, have testified to the reality of the mesmeric phenomena. In the year 1831, on the 21st and 28th of June, a report was read before the members of the French Academy of Sciences by eleven physicians, commissioned by this academy to study these phenomena, and to report upon them. They mention the power which the magnetizer acquires over those who allow themselves to be put under his influence,—a power so great that he can produce the magnetic sleep at will, even when the person to be acted upon is not present. They also testify to the facts of clairvoyance. From the writings of other physicians, as Deleuze, Bertrand, Billiot, and others (Conf. De Mirville, *Des Esprits*), we are informed that magnetized persons, though entirely ignorant of medicine, are able to state the exact bodily disposition of sick persons living at a great distance, provided they be put in communication with them by holding some object belonging to them; they indicate the seat of the disorder, its nature and progress, its complications; they propose simple and efficacious remedies, using not unfrequently technical terms which were certainly unknown to them before. The magnetizer may ask the magnetized person about persons and things at a great distance, and their answers are, generally speaking, found perfectly correct. They are able to read letters with their eyes shut, or to point out objects entirely removed from their sight. They manifest the thoughts of others, reveal family secrets, answer questions put in languages of which they know nothing; yet, when awakened from their trance, they, as a general rule, have no recollection of what they have said, nor of the scenes they have described.

To deny facts attested by so many witnesses of every nation, belonging to different religious denominations, or professing no religion whatever, is quite impossible. Many of these witnesses, before entering upon the investigation of such phenomena, were entirely opposed to admitting them, and, being well versed in physical sciences, took every possible precaution against fraud and deception. Yet the attempt to ascribe these effects to natural agencies has proved a failure. A kind of artificial somnambulism may no doubt be produced by natural means; and, as in natural somnambulism, there occur certain phenomena of lucidity or clairvoyance, some of the strange effects produced by mesmerism may likewise be attributed to natural causes. But it would be unreasonable to account by natural agency for the power of the magnetizer over persons not actually present to him. And no natural causes are sufficient to explain how magnetized persons can behold the internal disposition of the bodies of persons living at a distance of hundreds of miles; how they can possess medical knowledge, without ever having learnt anything in that line, or how they can understand languages they have never studied. Were we even to grant the entirely groundless supposition, that the magnetic fluid, passing from the magnetizer to the magnetized person, conveys to the latter the thoughts and the impressions of the former, it would still remain true that this fluid could not convey thoughts and knowledge not possessed by the magnetizer, which often takes place in these phenomena.

12. The same holds good for the phenomena of Spiritism, or the turning, talking, and writing of tables or other things. That deception has often been practised, is undeniable, but all the facts of spiritism cannot be denied; for oftentimes they are attested by many unimpeachable witnesses, who, being incredulous, took every possible precaution against deception. To attribute every well-ascertained phenomenon of table-talking and writing to natural causes, is impossible. The magnetic fluid, involuntary muscular action, and the like, cannot account for the facts which imply an intelligence distinct from both operator and medium. An intelligent cause with free will is clearly at work, since not unfrequently the desired effect is not obtained, though all the means considered necessary for its production have been employed.

Now, what kind of intelligence is the cause of all these phenomena? Spiritists affirm that it is the souls of departed persons communicating with the living. This is inadmissible; for neither the souls of the blessed nor those of the damned are under the control of human agency, nor does God allow the practice of evoking the dead. (*Deut.* xviii, 2.) Nor can we rely upon the word of the spirits supposed to be present, since spiritists confess that many of them are lying spirits. God, therefore, cannot be looked upon as the author of these phenomena, nor as sanctioning them. It is the evil spirit who is the author of the phenomena indicating intelligent agency, and he makes use of all this to deceive mankind. Moreover, if to these facts we apply the criterion established above, we clearly perceive that to God they cannot be ascribed. And why? Because they are performed for the sake of gain; they tend only to feed a morbid curiosity; they often have an openly immoral tendency; and, finally, they are the means of establishing false and impious doctrines. Hence, the whole practice of mesmerism and spiritism is to be branded as impious and detestable.

13. Nor are such impieties of new invention; they were known to the ancients. Pagans had their oracles whom they consulted; they applied to their priests and priestesses, who acted as mediums; from them they sought relief in illness and adversity. Even at the present day this is a custom among idolatrous nations. Spirit-writing is extensively practised in China, while Africans and Hindoos are great adepts in table-turning. All these strange effects of mesmerism and spiritism, supposing, as they do, an intelligent cause, belong to the order classified as witchcraft; but the *modus operandi* is not the same. Formerly, these unseen agencies kept their operations secret; now they have withdrawn the veil, and appear in public and in private, at the concert-hall as well as in many a fashionable drawing-room.

14. Our adversaries, if they so please, may object that this intelligent cause spoken of here, not being within the compass of physical causes, is out of court, since it would be solving the problem unscientifically to seek refuge in such an expedient. Science, they proclaim, has nothing to do either with disembodied spirits or with demons interfering with natural laws. To this we answer: The facts being such as they are, they must be dealt with according to their nature; it is unscientific to seek out causes in the material order, when effects call for intelligent causes distinct from, and superior to, human agency. There is no doubt that our adversaries shrink from acknowledging this spirit-power, because it upsets all their materialistic doctrines, and they fear lest the admission of preternatural agents should compel them to recognize the existence of a supernatural order.

CHAPTER V.

ON PROPHECIES.

1. Definition of Prophecy.—2. Possibility of Prophecy, and its validity as a proof of revealed Truth.—3. Pagan Oracles are no valid Objection against Prophecy.

1. ANOTHER proof of the truth of revelation is prophecy.

By prophecy we understand the foretelling with certainty some future event, which could not in any manner have been foreseen in its natural causes. Thus, to foretell an eclipse would be no prophecy, because it is foreseen in its causes. Statesmen may oftentimes foresee coming events, owing to their acquaintance with the dispositions, resources, etc., of those on whom the issue principally depends; they may shrewdly guess what turn things are likely to take; but they foresee the event in its causes, and their forecast lacks that certainty which prophecy requires.

2. The possibility of prophecy cannot be denied, unless we deny the existence of an all-wise, infinitely perfect Being. God's act of knowledge being one, unchangeable, eternal act, embraces at one glance the whole extent of time past,

present, and future. With regard to Him, there is no future. Besides, God can reveal truth to man. Therefore, prophecy is possible.

Prophecy is an argument of unquestionable worth in demonstrating the truth of a revealed religion: for the future is God's alone. All finite intellects deal simply with the present; the past they may remember, the future is to them a sealed book. If, therefore, a doctrine is confirmed by a true prophecy, it bears the sanction of God Himself.

3. Perhaps it will be urged that Pagans had their oracles, whom not only the vulgar and the illiterate, but even the learned and the powerful, were wont to consult. Now, oracles must not unfrequently have been found correct in their statements, otherwise they would neither have acquired nor preserved the confidence of antiquity. But Christians declare that these utterances were the sayings of the evil one; therefore, it is said, we must conclude that the evil spirit too enjoys the privilege of predicting future events.

In answering this objection, while we must grant that numberless deceptions were in fact practised by the priests of heathenism, still the reasons are grave for asserting that many a time it was, in truth, the evil spirit who uttered these oracles; yet it by no means follows that he possesses any sure knowledge of the future. The answers given by him had reference either to the past or to the present, both of which are within the scope of his vision. Were he consulted about the future, and were the event to take place at no distant period and by the instrumentality of persons then living, the issue could easily be calculated, even more easily than statesmen do the result of political steps. And thus could the spirit of lies foretell, in a general manner, some future event, though at the risk of seeing his prophecies more than once turn out false, by the change of will inherent to free agents whatever be their disposition at present, and owing to the fact that God may at any moment interfere with the course of events which would otherwise have come true. But as to determining circumstances of time, or place, or action, this power the evil spirit has never possessed, no more than the power of foretelling what future ages have in store.

CHAPTER VI.

NECESSITY OF REVELATION.

1. Distinction between physical and moral Necessity.—2. The moral Necessity of Revelation proved from the fact that all Nations deprived of Revelation fell into Idolatry.—3. Paganism was Demon-worship.—4. Paganism a School of Vice.—5. The same Effects manifested where revealed Religion is discarded.—6. The Perfectibility of Man insufficient to do away with Revelation.—7. Man did not progress from total Ignorance to higher Knowledge.—8. Idol-worship not the primitive Religion of Mankind.—9. Pagan Philosophers never reached a sufficient Knowledge of Truth.—10. Even had they attained its full Knowledge, still Revelation is necessary.—11. An external Rule necessary to keep down Man's Passions.—12. Without Revelation Sinners not sure of Pardon.—13. Revelation necessary for social Worship.—14. Would Revelation have been necessary, had Man been created in a purely natural State.—15. The primitive Revelation lost through Man's Fault.

1. It is not our purpose, in the present chapter, to speak of the necessity of a revelation containing supernatural mysteries; we wish simply to inquire whether, taking man as he is, those truths belonging to God and our final destiny, which are not beyond the grasp of reason, would necessarily call for a revelation, in order that they might be practically apprehended by the human mind.

We must distinguish between physical and moral necessity. The former implies a total want of capability in man to perform certain acts; the latter supposes that the act might indeed be performed, but that, owing to the many difficulties to be overcome, such an act will never be performed. Thus we know that any grave magistrate has indeed the physical power of parading in broad daylight through the most fashionable thoroughfares in night-shirt and slippers, and still, allowing to this person the full use of reason, such a thing will never take place. Now the necessity we are going to deal with, in our inquiry about revelation, is a moral, not a physical one.

2. To prove the moral necessity of a revelation as to the principal attributes of God, the various relations in which we stand toward Him, the nature and destiny of our souls, the means of reaching our last end, it is enough to cast a glance at the human race, from its earliest ages to our own times. We find, indeed, all nations, save the Jews, in the lowest stages of idolatry. The Chaldeans, the Persians, the Phenicians, worshipped the heavenly bodies, besides a host of other gods and goddesses. The Egyptians, one of the most civilized nations of antiquity, from whom the Greeks received their arts and sciences, paid divine honors to every kind of animal: to the bull Apis, to the crocodile, and even to

cats and dogs. The mythology of the Greeks and Romans is known. Everywhere, all over the world, idols of wood, stone, and metal, were honored with divine worship.

Some modern writers have attempted to excuse Pagans, by saying that the worship paid to idols was only relative; that they acknowledged one supreme God, under the name of Jupiter, Bel, Odin, etc., and that the other divinities received inferior homage. Now, this theory was started by certain sects, in order to censure with more success the veneration for the saints which ranks so high in the Church of God; but, ingenious though it be, it is wanting in truth. Holy Writ is there to inform us that Pagans really adored their idols, and gave them divine honors. Some of their philosophers no doubt laughed in private at the popular superstitions they sanctioned in public. When Christianity had spread the light of truth, a few Neo-Platonicians, who blushed at the absurdity of idol-worship, tried to give it a less ridiculous shape; but their explanations came too late, and the people rejected them, and either turned to Christianity, or held on to their idols. Horace shows very plainly what was the opinion of the people with regard to their idols:

> Olim truncus eram ficulnus, inutile lignum,
> Cum faber, incertus scamnum faceretne Priapum,
> Maluit esse Deum. Deus inde ego.

PAGANISM WAS DEMON-WORSHIP.

See likewise the Book of Wisdom, chaps. xviii and xiv.

Fetich worship is still practised in our own days by African tribes. Idols are worshipped over the entire East, and in Polynesia.

3. It may be well to remark that Pagans, while they adored their idols, would never have fallen so low as to worship statues or animals, had they not possessed a conviction, based on repeated experience, that there was an unseen agency behind these outward objects; and these unseen spirits they adored in and with their idols. Even the most degraded savage who worships his fetich, would never pay any honor to it, if he were not confident that this charm is the means or medium used by some spirit to commune with him, and to vouchsafe him his assistance. Pagan worship is in reality demonolatry, and hence Holy Writ tells us that the gods of the Gentiles are devils. (*Ps.* xcv, 5.) In 1 Cor. x, 20, we read: "But the things which the heathens sacrifice, they sacrifice to devils and not to God."

Idolatry without the intervention of the evil spirits is a riddle without solution; with them the answer is easy. Originally man worshipped the true God; he also revered the angels as His ministers; but either pantheistic views led men to divinise material agents, or the desire of entering at will into communication with the spirit world exposed them to the danger of falling into the snares of the Evil One, who thus succeeded in persuading them that he and his fellows were the rulers of the world; and from this point the transition to idol-worship was easy: for, as the evil spirits made use of sensible objects to manifest their presence, these objects soon became, as it were, identified with them, and shared in the worship given them.* The earliest form of idolatry seems to have been Sabaism, or the worship of the sun and the other heavenly bodies; for every nation of antiquity believed these bodies to be ruled and presided over by spirits. Pagans did not consider the sun and the planets as mere symbols of the divinity, but as the visible manifestation of the gods themselves, and thus identified them with these bodies. The evil spirit, the better to deceive mankind, left most of their primitive traditions untouched, and this is why the old religions of Pagans afford us the sublimest truths in company with the most glaring absurdities; this, too, accounts for the similarity we often find between the rites of Paganism and the religion of the Jews. To pretend that the first religion of mankind was the vilest fetichism, and this without supposing a spirit behind the fetich, is simple nonsense.

4. Not only did Pagans worship idols, but,

---

* St. Augustine, *De Civitate Dei*, lib. viii, capp. 23, 24. Testimonium Hermetis Ægyptii.

blinded by their own passions, they attributed to them all the vices and passions which agitate the human breast. Their poets celebrated the adulteries of Jupiter and of the other gods; vices were deified, altars raised to them, and some of the divinities were supposed to take these vices under their special protection. Thus Mercury was the god of thieves, Venus the goddess of lust, Mars the god of war as well as of brutal violence. Many of the temples were nothing better than public places of shameless prostitution; human victims were but too often sacrificed in honor of the idols, so that the Pagan religion was nothing less than a public school of general demoralization. We have but to read Pagan authors, to know the baneful influence which idol-worship exercised over national morality. Had some nations only, deprived of the light of revelation, fallen into these deplorable excesses, our argument would be of little worth; but all nations, without any exception, fell more or less into the same state of degradation. And it is a remarkable fact that the grossest idolatry was practised precisely by the most civilized nations among the Pagans. The idol-worship of the Germans and the Gauls was less stupid than that of the Greeks, Romans, and Egyptians.

5. Even in our own days the same ignorance and immorality prevail among all the nations

which until now have refused divine revelation. Nay, wherever infidelity and irreligion begin to overspread a country, the result is invariably an ignorance most profound of religious and moral truth. We need but read the works of modern unbelievers, to convince ourselves of this fact. God and the spirituality of the soul are denied: the foundation of all moral truths destroyed; and, what is worse, the denial of these truths is considered enlightenment, and they who thus bring down man to the level of the brute, style themselves the only friends of science. Beyond a doubt, Paganism, in its worst form, would once more revive in Europe, were it not that the teachings of the Catholic Church still have a hold even upon those who have rebelled against them. Was not Paganism openly practised in Paris, at least for a short time, during the French Revolution of the last century, when, on the high altar of Notre Dame, a shameless woman, personating the Goddess of Reason, was enthroned, to receive incense and homage?

6. Let rationalists boast, as much as they please, of the great powers of reason; of man's perfectibility, which enables him to enlarge the field of science every day. Here are facts irrefutable, manifesting themselves from the very origin of historic times down to the present day; facts which demonstrate most clearly that, great as may be the power of invention with which the

human mind is endowed as regards the material order, our minds and our wills are powerless, if left to themselves, when there is question of the moral order. Man is indeed perfectible; this perfectibility constitutes the line of demarcation between him and the brute; yet this perfectibility does not imply that man, unaided by instruction, does acquire the knowledge of all those moral truths necessary for his leading a life in harmony with his intellectual and moral nature. Children, too, are perfectible; but abandon a child to itself, or supply only its material wants, and you will see it grow up in almost total ignorance; and, though it may have some perception of right and wrong, still its moral faculties will lie dormant, and will not be called into action, unless it come in contact with persons in whom these faculties are already developed. Thus it is with all mankind. Man, left to himself, might, indeed, acquire the knowledge of those things which belong to the natural order; but, to perfect his moral being, he stands in need of guidance and direction from a higher power.

7. Infidel writers, who deny the existence of a revelation, suppose that the human race began improving from the depth of ignorance, and is gradually raising itself by its own native powers to an ever-increasing degree of perfection; hence, they infer, no other instruction is required than what is derived from the book of nature open

to all. They grant that Christianity has been an instrument of civilization; but they maintain that, even had Christianity not appeared, humanity would still have progressed, since, at the coming of Christ, there was a general tendency toward Monotheism.

In answering the last part of this objection, we begin by conceding that at that time there was manifested, among a certain class of people, a great spirit of contempt for idol-worship; but this arose from a spirit of scepticism produced by the Epicurean philosophy, not from a tendency to Monotheism. The strenuous opposition kept up during three hundred years against Christianity, shows how far the whole Roman people was from renouncing its attachment to Polytheism. The objection itself is based on the false principle refuted in moral philosophy, that the original state of man was the savage state. All reliable historical records testify that the human race was civilized from the beginning; that Monotheism was its primitive religion; that Paganism, and the savage state, were steps backward. History, moreover, teaches us that no savage tribe has been able to rise from its degraded state to a higher one, without coming in contact with other nations already civilized. Pagan philosophers did not exercise a beneficial influence on the people; nay, by their sophistry and scepticism, they sapped the foundation of those moral principles which the people had derived from traditional teachings. The philosophers who taught purer doctrines could do but little. Socrates had few disciples, and was condemned to death as an atheist and a corrupter of youth. Plato had few followers.

8. If we trace back the history of the human race, and look up its primitive traditions known in antiquity, we find that the nearer we get to the cradle of our race, the purer do religious traditions become. On every side we meet with unmistakable vestiges of Monotheism: the primitive traditions agree in their main features with those preserved in the Mosaic record. The Vedas, the sacred books of the Hindoos, written in the Sanscrit language, inculcate the pure doctrines of Monotheism; they contain hymns and prayers which any Christian might recite without hesitation. It is only in the subsequent writings of the Hindoos that we discover traces of a Pantheism which was a rapid step toward the worship of idols. The Zend-Avesta, attributed to Zoroaster, also admits the unity of God, the Creator of the universe; in its most authentic parts there is no mention made of the two principles, the one good, the other bad, possessing equal power, and opposed to each other: this dualism is of later origin. The Egyptians, also, had their sacred writings, the Books of Hermes, which have been lost. From fragments of them, preserved in ancient writers, and from the testimony of both pagan and

Christian authors who had perused them, it seems evident that, however much they may have been falsified or interpolated, the primitive belief in Monotheism may still be clearly traced in them. Nay, some inscriptions, and certain papyri, found in sepulchres, according to the Viscount E. de Rougé (*Conférence sur la Religion des Egyptiens*, Paris, 1869), contain the doctrine of one, sole, unique God, who has made everything, and who alone has not been made. The Greeks, known to us by our classical authors, seem to be impregnated with idolatry from the very start; yet even they can be shown to have had, in remoter times, conceptions of the Deity far higher than those contained in the absurd mythologies prevalent during the classical ages. This may be deduced from the few remnants of the Orphic poems preserved in some ancient authors. Pythagoras, who did not derive his doctrine from mere speculation, but who had carefully consulted the old traditions, taught the unity of God. Many ancient traditions, in accordance with those of the Mosaic record, are found here and there in poets, both Latin and Greek. That the Chinese were originally worshippers of one God, may be gathered from the ancient book, Y-King, which existed before Confucius and Lao-Tseu, and has been attributed to Fo-hi; for mention is there made of a supreme deity, originator of the visible world, and whose name is Ly and Tao, Law and Reason. (Conf. *Gentilism*, by the Rev. A. Thébaud, S. J., New York, 1876.) Now the main feature in the history of all these nations is that, in proportion to their progress in material civilization, was the depth of their fall into the extravagancies of idol-worship.

9. Though some Pagan philosophers wrote beautiful treatises on many moral subjects, it is, nevertheless, beyond doubt that no one was equal to the task of drawing up a complete code of morality; the few truths discernible in their writings are buried under a heap of hideous errors. Socrates, with all his moral lessons, knew how to give to lewd women practical advice for the ensnaring of paramours. (Xenoph., *De Dictis et Factis Mirab.*, lib. iv, cap. 11.) Epictectus allowed free scope to sexual intercourse. (*En Enchir.*, cap. 48.) " The divine Plato," as Cicero styles him, proclaimed the doctrine of free love in his model republic; and Aulus Gellius (*Noctes Atticæ*, lib. xiv) speaks of the most shameful amatory verses composed by the same great teacher. What did they know, these philosophers, about the end of man? Varro, according to the testimony of St Augustine (*Civit. Dei*, lib. xix, cap. 1), enumerates two hundred and eighty-eight different views about the sovereign good, or the final end of man. What their ideas were upon the nature of God may be gathered from Cicero, in his work, *De Natura' Deorum*.

The whole skill of these pagan philosophers, like that of our modern infidels, was in their efforts at overthrowing the vapory constructions of others, at spreading scepticism and unbelief, at destroying the convictions of the masses; but as to building up a new fabric of doctrine, they proved themselves utterly incompetent. Christian philosophy, in the light of revealed religion, can nowadays draw up a complete treatise on moral philosophy, independently of the arguments taken from revelation, because the teachings of revelation have educated and strengthened our minds; but they who reject divine authority can never produce a moral code free from the admixture of many a fatal error.

10. But let us suppose that some philosophers gifted with superior genius have, by dint of study, succeeded at last in discovering all the truths necessary to compose, without admixture of falsehood, a code of morality and religion, would this assumed success be sufficient to make a divine revelation superfluous? By no means, since these sages could not be teachers fit for the people. Truth can be imparted by two ways only, demonstration or authority. The teacher must either elucidate his proposition, and advance the arguments in support of his assertions, or else his disciples must be called upon to submit their intellects to his authority, and to accept his teachings as truth, though the grounds on which

they rest are unseen. Now it is self-evident that neither of these methods of instruction can suffice for the masses. All men cannot grasp moral and religious truth by means of demonstration, since, to apprehend the proofs brought forward to establish the existence of a personal God, His divine attributes, the nature of the soul, and the whole system of moral doctrine, it is absolutely necessary to be familiar with logic and metaphysics, a study exacting long and careful training of the mind. Teachers of philosophy know well that those susceptible of such a training are few. What, then, shall become of the large majority of mankind who have neither aptitude, nor time, nor opportunity, for such abstruse studies? How could they, who must toil from morn to eve for their daily bread, afford time and energies for the mental efforts required by pursuits so arduous? Such a style of instruction is, consequently, out of the question. As to authoritative teaching, unless we suppose the fact of a divine revelation, nothing more absurd can be conceived. Men must be taken as they are. Whilst a few philosophers might try to inculcate sound doctrines on the people, many others would be teaching false ones. How, then, are the people to find out who among the claimants of truth is the rightful heir, that they may safely trust him? Each of these philosophers would use every effort to persuade his hearers that he alone is able to lead them to true wisdom. How could they discriminate the true from the false doctrines? Judging from man's dispositions, there is every reason to suppose that the false teachers would have the best chance of collecting the largest band of followers, for doctrines friendly to evil passions are more readily embraced than those which oppose them. Therefore, teachers of truth can be made known to us only on the hypothesis that God himself gave them credentials, constituting a claim upon the adhesion of all men. Now this is nothing else but a true revelation.

11. Besides, considering the present condition of man, a mere knowledge of truth is not sufficient for him, if he have no other guide than his reason. Duty often clashes with man's passions and self-interest. In such a case it would be only too easy for him to be blinded by his self-love, and the mind, obscured by doubts, would soon lose sight of the reasons making plain the line of duty. Therefore, men stand in need of an external rule, sanctioned by God Himself.

12. Moreover, man is liable to break God's law, and thus to sever the link binding him to his last end. Now man of himself can do nothing to regain God's friendship, since God is not obliged to accept any of our acts as atonement for offences against Him. Hence, without revelation, man would neither know if there were hope of forgiveness, nor by what means such hope might be real-

ized; but, if there be no hope of pardon, despair ensues, and, as a natural consequence, free scope is left to every evil passion.

13. Lastly, it is not man alone, but society too, that must worship God, and without revelation social worship is an impossibility; for such worship must be public, attended by all the members of society. It must, therefore, be a worship determined by God Himself, or imposed by the authority of the state. Now the authority of the state, whether wielded by monarch or people, has no right to lay down its manner of worship, because, owing to its inherent fallibility, it is incompetent to teach religious truth; and yet this power of teaching would in this case be required, since public worship must be the outward expression of inward belief, or it becomes mere mummery.

We must therefore conclude that, in the present order of Providence, a revelation of truths not exceeding the limits of our minds is a moral necessity, at least for the great bulk of mankind; for, though each individual might, by the use of reason, come to the knowledge of these truths, the difficulties in the way are so great that, in point of fact, a scarce perceptible fraction of the human race, if any at all, could have passed through them without direct help from God. Indeed, in the designs of God, no other means than revelation itself would make this knowledge a moral necessity for mankind in general. (Franzelin, *Appendix de Habitudine Rationis ad Fidem*, pag. 558. Edit. Rom., 1870.)

14. But it may be asked, Would the necessity for a revelation be the same, had man been created in the purely natural order? On the one hand, it is plain that in such a case the condition of men, as regards the requirements of their nature, would not have been different from the present one; the same difficulties would have had to be overcome, hence the same moral impotency would have prevailed. On the other hand, we must admit that God, in his providence, would have furnished them with means proportionate to their last end, and with remedies against that powerlessness to attain truth which afflicts our race at present. For God, who hates none of the things which He has made (*Wisd.* xi, 25), who, being all-wise, cannot will an end without adequate means, would sincerely have wished the salvation of man, and thus have prepared what would be sufficient to make its attainment a moral possibility. He might have given a revelation, if it so pleased Him, but, being Almighty, He might have used other means. He might have endowed man with a clearer perception of the truths necessary to salvation, and, through the natural objects perceived by him, have inspired into his mind and heart thoughts and feelings which would render morally possible

the observance of the natural law. (Franzelin, *Ibid.*, page 556.)

15. It may be objected, since revelation is so necessary, why were we left so long without it? Christianity appeared after men had existed for more than four thousand years. The Jewish religion was instituted about two thousand years before Christ, and, being a national religion, cannot be considered a revelation to the whole human race. To this we reply, that a revelation was in truth given to mankind from the very first, as we shall prove in the next chapter. This primitive revelation was partly lost and partly obscured, through man's own fault, so that ignorance of truth is attributable, not to the want of a revelation, but to those on whom it had been bestowed.

CHAPTER VII.

ON THE EXISTENCE OF REVELATION.

1. The Existence of Revelation proved from its Necessity.—2. From the common Consent of Mankind.—3. From the national Traditions of Antiquity.—4. From the Rite of Sacrifice.—5. How this Rite originated.

1. SINCE the human race stands so much in need of a divine revelation to teach it the way to salvation, we cannot for a moment harbor the thought that God, infinite in His goodness, has left man without this all-important gift. For though, strictly speaking, it is certain, as we have said, that man, by the right use of reason, might discover truth, the impediments in the way are of such a nature that man, by the use of reason, would never have reached this knowledge unaided. Similarly, although God was not obliged to institute a means of pardon after man had, by wilful sin, offended Him, yet, considering God's mercy, we cannot suppose that He would have left us without a means of reconciliation. We are therefore entitled to conclude that a revelation has been made.

2. This fact is also supported by the belief,

constant and universal, of the human family in a revelation. All nations have admitted the existence of special communications from the Deity to man; every religious system supposes such intercommunications, and is grounded upon them. Now a belief so constant and general cannot be the result of mere accident, but must, of necessity, have its origin in truth.

3. If we consult the national traditions of antiquity, we find that, as far as they are positive and definite, they agree in substance with those of the Mosaic record. They all admit a state of bliss, a golden age, when man was enjoying familiar intercourse with the gods; they say that this happy condition was lost through man's wickedness; they agree upon the awful catastrophe of a Deluge as a punishment for man's crimes. All this points to a primitive revelation.

4. But the most convincing proof of the existence of a primitive revelation is the common belief in the necessity of sacrifice, in order to appease the wrath of the Deity offended by sin. No nation of antiquity has been found whose worship was without sacrifice, and, though forms varied, the object was everywhere the same, viz.: to honor the Deity, to return thanks for benefits received, to beg for new ones, and, above all, to obtain remission for sin. But what can be the source of this common practice among nations living far apart and without intercourse? The

fact of human reason is not a sufficient explanation; for, though we might assume that men could think it proper to offer to God, as a tribute to His supreme dominion, some of the gifts bestowed upon them, it is impossible that reason should have given birth to the idea that the destruction of anything in honor of God, and above all the shedding of blood, could be a means of appeasing His anger, and atoning for sin. Between these two terms there exists no analogy. Can we, of ourselves, conceive that the shedding of an animal's blood may wash out the stain of guilt? Nor can it be plausibly maintained that it was an arbitrary practice, sanctioned and handed down by tradition; for, had it possessed no other authority, it would soon have been set aside and forgotten. The general use of sacrifices is, therefore, a most convincing proof of a primitive revelation.

5. Indeed this universal belief becomes intelligible, only when viewed in the light of the primitive revelation recorded in Genesis. After the fall of our first parents, God promised them a Redeemer who, by His own death, was to free them and their posterity from the consequences of their disobedience. Hence the oblations of gifts, and especially of victims, became types of the sacrifice to be offered up by the promised Redeemer, as they were also an outward manifestation of the belief in His coming. This, to-

gether with a sincere repentance and a firm purpose of amendment, was the condition required by God for the grant of pardon. Count de Maistre (*Soirées de St. Pétersbourg, Eclaircissements sur le Sacrifice*) justly remarks that no nation ever had a doubt as to the expiatory virtue of blood shed in sacrifice. History on this point does not furnish a single exception. This theory rested on the doctrine of reversibility. Mankind believed, as it has always believed, and as it ever will believe, that the innocent could satisfy for the guilty. That these sacrifices were regarded as types is likewise shown, as the same author remarks, by the fact that carnivorous animals, or those which are entirely estranged from man, such as wild beasts, serpents, fishes, birds of prey, etc., were never offered up. The animals chosen were always those that were most esteemed for their usefulness, for their mildness and innocence, and that stood in closer relation with man by their instincts and habits. The offering of human victims, more or less common among Pagan nations, was simply a perversion of the same doctrine.

CHAPTER VIII.

ON MAHOMETANISM.

1. There is no Need of passing in Review all religious Beliefs.—2. Idolatry evidently absurd.—3. Mahomet's Want of Credentials, and his Contradictions.—4. The Koran full of Fables; Immorality of the false Prophet.—5. Ignorance of Mahomet.—6. Recommends only external Observances.—7. Baneful Effects of Islamism.—8. Its rapid Spreading no Proof in its Favor.

1. TRUTH being necessarily one, it is clear that, if any one of the host of creeds professed by men be proved true, to investigate the others is no longer a necessity; being opposed to the divinely revealed truth, their falsehood is apparent at first sight. It would suffice, therefore, to establish at once the truth of Christianity, without bestowing a thought on Mahometanism and Judaism. Still it may not be amiss to cast a passing glance on the religion of the famous Arabian impostor.

As to the Jews, they come within the scope of our work, because their belief is the basis of our own.

2. It were needless to note the many forms of idolatry which either have existed, or do still

exist in our own days. For the existence of One, Almighty, All-wise Ruler of the universe, on whom men depend, and to whom they are accountable, is a truth of which no one can be invincibly ignorant. Hence, idolatry is an inexcusable crime.

3. With regard to Mahometanism, that its founder was an impostor is a fact easy to demonstrate. In the first place, he claimed a divine mission to put down idolatry, and to restore the ancient religion of Abraham and the prophets. He was to perfect the law of Christ, which he said was divinely revealed; but never did he, by any miracle, substantiate the authority of his pretended commission from God. He declares himself that he had not been sent to work wonders (*Koran*, chaps. 13 and 17), since Moses and Jesus had done enough in that way, and yet men had not believed. He affirmed that visions of the Angel Gabriel had been granted him, but these rest on his word alone. His trip to heaven, detailed in the Koran, is an extravagant rhapsody. Besides, while admitting that Jesus Christ is a divine messenger, he opposes his doctrines, and thus exhibits himself in his true light, that of imposture.

4. The Koran, which contains his pretended revelations, is a tissue of fables, taken from the Talmud, from apocryphal gospels, and from certain traditions current among the Arabs; it teems

with absurdities, and palpable errors in history, geography, and chronology. It gives us, nevertheless, a sufficient insight into the immorality of Mahomet. He even went so far as to take other men's wives; and, though he had forbidden this in his Koran, he pretended to have obtained a special dispensation from God, and for this purpose he drew up the thirty-third and thirty-sixth chapters of his book. The Koran itself shows Mahomet to be a revengeful, ambitious, and violent man. He proposes the doctrine of absolute predestination, destroying free-will and the very foundation of religion.

5. He shows his gross ignorance of the dogma of the Trinity. To prove that there cannot be three persons in God, he says: God can have no son, because He has no wife. The description he gives of the last judgment, the bridge on which the souls must pass, and which is as keen as a razor, is childish. His paradise, which is made up of mere sensual delights, is one that a man sunk in the sins of lust could alone have imagined.

6. In the Koran many virtues are recommended, but the whole tenor of its prescriptions shows that much more stress is laid on certain external observances than on virtue itself. The author declares that the crime of idolatry or infidelity is the only one which can deprive any of his followers of the joys of Paradise; and they firmly believe that a pilgrimage to Mecca is of itself

qnte sufficient to efface every kind of sin and crime.

7. We have only to look at the countries under the sway of this monstrous system, to discover at a glance its destructive effects. It has changed the fairest lands into sterile wastes. Tyranny is everywhere supreme. Ignorance is fostered, and this has been, in fact, one of the main causes why the Mahometan populations have been kept faithful to their creed. Being allowed no inquiry, they are prevented from examining into the motives of credibility on which their belief rests.

8. The rapid progress of Islamism has been set forth by its adepts as a sign of its truth, but to no purpose. No nation was ever brought, by persuasion, to the profession of the Mahometan religion. Conversion was wrought by the sword. The motive of credibility urged by the missionary of Mahomet was: believe or be exterminated. In the beginning the false prophet was opposed to violence (*Koran*, chap. ii), but, when he grew powerful, he changed his language. Fight, he tells his followers, fight against the infidel, till every false religion is exterminated—do not spare them; and when you have weakened them by carnage, reduce them to slavery, and overwhelm them with taxes. (Chap. viii, 12, 39; chap. ix, 30; chap. xlvii, 4.) After he had succeeded in uniting the Arab tribes by treachery and violence, he waged war against the surrounding

nations, who, being enervated by vice, and divided among themselves, became an easy prey to the conqueror. No choice was left them but acquiescence or death, or, at best, slavery: what wonder, then, that many preferred the former alternative! Besides this, Mahometanism, far from being a religion to curb the passions of men, has, on the contrary, but few restrictions for its followers.

CHAPTER IX.

ON THE JEWISH RELIGION.

The Genuineness of the Pentateuch.

1. Genuineness of the Pentateuch proved from the Jewish Tradition.—2. The Pentateuch existed before the Schism of the Ten Tribes.—3. It is anterior to the Time of the Judges.—4. Its Author contemporaneous with the Exodus.—5. His Legislation bears the Impress of the Desert.—6 He is perfectly acquainted with Egypt.—7. The Objection against the Genuineness of the Pentateuch has no Weight.—8. Solution of Objections. Facts not in Accordance with the Existence of the Mosaic Law.—9. The Author did not live after the Conquest of Palestine.

1. THE dogmas and precepts of the Jewish religion are contained in the Pentateuch, or Five Books of Moses: if, therefore, it can be proved that the Pentateuch is both genuine and authentic, it follows that the Jewish religion is divinely revealed, because it is confirmed by the most splendid and stupendous miracles, which could be performed only by God Himself, or with His positive approbation. Now the Five Books of Moses are both genuine and authentic. Therefore the Jewish religion is a revealed one.

The Pentateuch is genuine. A book is said to be genuine when it is the work of the author whose name it bears. This may be known, if we have a constant and uninterrupted tradition asserting the authority of the book, such tradition going back to the very time when it was written. If this tradition was handed down, not by some individuals, but by an entire people, whose civil, political, and religious institutions are all based on it, the proof becomes so convincing that a doubt as to the authorship would be tantamount to denying the possibility of establishing the genuineness of any book whatsoever. Now such is the case as regards the Pentateuch. The whole Jewish nation, from the very first, has ever considered these five books as the law written by Moses, and on them have rested their civil, political, and religious institutions.

At the time of Christ the Pentateuch existed in its present form, and was believed to be from Moses; and since that period no substantial change could have been introduced, because it was preserved with the utmost care both by Jews and Christians. It existed two hundred and eighty years before Christ, because about that time the Greek or Septuagint version was made; and this version is in all points concordant with the Hebrew text. It could not have been composed by Esdras, after the Babylonian captivity, since we possess the Samaritan version, which agrees with the Hebrew text now extant. In the Book of Kings (4 *Kings*, xvii), we read that the new settlers who were established in the country of the ten tribes, were greatly annoyed by lions, which killed many of them; and this plague was ascribed to the fact that the strangers knew not the ordinances of the God of the land. Whereupon the Assyrian king gave order that one of the captive priests should go and dwell among them, and teach them the law of the God of the land. This was done; the priest brought with him the law, dwelt in Bethel, and taught the people how to worship the Lord. This law was no other than the law of Moses, for since that time the new settlers, together with the Israelites who were left behind, acknowledged the Pentateuch, as we see from the version held in veneration by them, though they did not much conform to its precepts. The ten tribes must, therefore, have possessed the law of Moses at the time of their separation from the tribes of Juda and Benjamin; for, as there always was a great opposition between the two sections of the Jewish nation, had the ten tribes not admitted the Pentateuch as the law of Moses at the time of their separation under Jeroboam, they would never have accepted it afterward, because this law was in direct opposition to some of the practices introduced by the kings of the ten tribes, and also because they rejected all the canonical books written subsequently to their separation.

2. It might be objected that, as we learn from

Nehemias (xiii, 28), and the Jewish historian, Josephus (*Antiq.* xi, 7), after the Babylonian captivity, the satrap Sanaballat compelled the Samaritans to accept as their high-priest his son-in-law, Manasseh, who was a relative of the Jewish high-priest. Manasseh may, therefore, have brought with him the Pentateuch as accepted by the Jews, and have imposed it on the Samaritans. But this objection is easily settled. The Samaritan text is written in the ancient Hebrew letters, which, after the Babylonian captivity, were replaced by those now in use. Had the Samaritans received the Pentateuch from Manasseh, it would have been written either in the modern form, or else in their own characters, but not in the ancient characters of the Jews, since these were no longer in use. Moreover, had Manasseh succeeded in forcing the Pentateuch on the Samaritans, they would not have maintained such a determined opposition against all the other canonical writings of the Jews; and yet, in point of fact, for them Moses was the only prophet. Had these books been imposed upon them, they would have rejected them as soon as they were freed from the compulsion they were under; the enmity between the two nations was too strong and too deeply rooted to allow of Jewish law becoming permanent among the Samaritans. The foregoing answer applies equally well to the objection

ANTIQUITY OF THE PENTATEUCH. 107

raised by some infidel writers, that at the time of King Josias (621 B. C.) the Books of Moses had been lost, and were then composed by priests from the current traditions.*

3. The Samaritan version also proves conclusively that the Pentateuch must have been in existence long before the time of Solomon: otherwise the ten tribes would not have accepted it as the law of Moses, nor continued to make it the fundamental code of their civil, political, and religious constitution. Most eagerly would they have rejected it, could they have proved that Moses was not its author, because it condemned both their schism and their idolatry. Had it been invented but lately, the fraud would easily have been detected, since all the Levites, priests, and magistrates, were bound to have a knowledge of this law, which was the institute regulating all the affairs of the nation whether civil or religious. At the time of the Judges and of Josue, it was likewise in existence, because it is often mentioned in the historic record of those times, and because

---

*The fact related (2 *Paral.* xxxiv, 14) shows that the book found at the time of Josias was the very copy written by Moses and preserved in the ark of the covenant; the reading of the threats contained in Deuteronomy against the transgressors of the law, from the very text of Moses, produced wonderful effects both on the king and on the people. It is absurd to suppose that all the copies of the law could have been lost, since all the priests and magistrates, and the king himself, had to possess this law, in order to administer justice and observe the rites of worship. Nay, the king was obliged to make for himself a copy of the law from the standard copy kept in the temple. (*Deut.* xvii, 18.)

the entire legislation and all the national customs were an expression of what is laid down in these five books. The tradition, therefore, goes back as far as Moses himself.

4. If we now consider the intrinsic motives of evidence, we must come to the same conclusion.

There is mentioned in the Pentateuch no fact posterior to Moses. The last verses of Deuteronomy, which relate the death of Moses, could not, indeed, have been written by him; but they form, as it were, part of the following book. The annals of the Jews were not at first divided into chapters and verses, as they are at present: this was done much later; and then the story of the death of Moses was added to the Pentateuch. There is an allusion made to the institution of kings and to a captivity, but these are mentioned *prophetically*, not *historically*, as clearly appears from the context.

The writer must have been contemporary with the events of Exodus, for he speaks in entire ignorance of what happened after the crossing of the Jordan; he contemplates future arrangements which were never realized, such as the boundaries of the land to be possessed by the children of Israel (*Deut.* i, 7), boundaries which were never reached, not even under kings David and Solomon; he speaks of the facts he relates as an eyewitness, giving an account of passing events.

5. Besides, the legislation of the Pentateuch

bears the impress of the desert. This appears from the tabernacle, its furniture and appurtenances. The condition of the tribe of Levi must have been defined before the conquest of Canaan, else they would have claimed a share in the conquered lands. The arrangements for the carrying of the tabernacle and its furniture by the Levites could apply only to a wandering people. The law of sacrifice (*Lev.* i and vii) supposes the desert and the camp. A later compiler would have endeavored to make these laws square with the circumstances that followed the conquest.

6. Another remarkable fact is that the writer of the Pentateuch is intimately acquainted with the land of Egypt, its laws and customs; his every statement has been found in perfect agreement with monuments of ancient Egypt. He also writes for those who knew Egypt well, but were as yet little acquainted with Canaan. He takes his illustrations and comparisons from Egypt, nor does he stop to explain the Egyptian words which occur more than once in his work.

It cannot be said that at the time of Moses the art of writing was unknown; monuments still existing, some of which are anterior to him, prove contrariwise, and the Jewish leader was well versed in the arts and sciences of the Egyptian priesthood.

7. Unbelievers have raised many objections against the genuineness of the Pentateuch, be-

cause on it rests not only the Jewish, but also the Christian, religion. These objections are of little weight. Should there be some few which, owing to our insufficient apprehension of certain expressions and statements employed in the Pentateuch, we could not at present solve to the satisfaction of all, this would not invalidate the testimony of the whole Jewish nation from the days of Moses down to our own.

8. Some critics have pointed out facts which took place at the time of the judges or the earlier kings, and which, say they, are not in accordance with the law of Moses; whence they infer that this law could not have existed then. Now the writers of both Judges and Kings constantly refer to the law of Moses; they show that the Jewish nation was governed according to it; they state that the many calamities which befell the Jews were in consequence of transgressions against this law. And, moreover, it is plain that the neglect or the setting aside of a law can by no means argue its non-existence.

9. The author of Genesis says (xii, 6), "The Canaanite was at that time in the land;" hence it is inferred that, when this was written, they were no longer in possession of it. But the Hebrew word translated by *at that time* means also *actually; i e.*, that the Canaanites already occupied the land at the time of Abraham.

It is urged, again, that Genesis must have been

written at the time of the kings; for (*Gen.* xxxvi, 31) we read: "And the kings that ruled in the land of Edom, before the children of Israel had a king, were these." Now, it is said, the kings mentioned here are only eight, and from Esau to Saul we have seven hundred years; therefore each of these kings must have been on the throne about ninety years, which is undoubtedly by far too long a time for an average reign. True; but if we take the period from Esau to Moses, we have only two hundred and eighty-eight years, and this gives an average of thirty-six years for each Edomite monarch. Besides, King Adad, mentioned in Genesis, can by no means be the same as the one who was contemporaneous with Solomon, for Adad is the fourth on the list of kings mentioned in Genesis. In a word, Moses, relating the history of Esau, who, as it was foretold to Rebecca, was to serve his younger brother, Jacob, states in Genesis the line of kings who ruled over Edom, whilst the Israelites were just beginning their national existence, giving the people to understand that, notwithstanding these circumstances, the prophecy made at the birth of the twins would be fulfilled, and that, when there should be kings in Israel, as Moses knew from Jacob's prophecy would be the case, "the elder [people] was to serve the younger." And this prediction came true at the time when "the children of Israel had a king."

Again, the author of the Pentateuch uses the word *seaward* for *westward;* but for one who lived in Egypt, *seaward* would express the north or the east; hence, we are told, the writer must have lived in Palestine. To this we answer that, whilst the Jews were in the desert of Arabia, the Red Sea was westward of them Besides this, the word *seaward* was used for *westward* in the land of Canaan, whose language the children of Israel spoke when they went into Egypt.

In Deuteronomy i, 1, we read: "These are the words which Moses spoke to all Israel beyond the Jordan;" therefore, it is said, the writer must have lived in Palestine. But the Hebrew expression translated by *beyond* is promiscuously used for either side, signifying both *Cis-* and *Transjordanic* territory, irrespective of the position of the writer. (*Num.* xxxii, 19; *Deut.* iii, 20 and 25; *Jos.* ix, 1; *Judges* vii, 25; 1 *Kings* xxxi, 7, etc.)

Moses speaks of the city of Dan, which was called Lesem, and which received the name of Dan only after the conquest. To this we may reply, as some have done, that this name, as better known to the Jews, was subsequently substituted for Lesem; but it is more probable that the city had two names, Dan and Lesem: in fact, these two names signify the same thing; and this may have been the reason which prompted the

Danites to take possession of this city, though it was not included within the limits assigned to their tribe, but to that of Nephthali.

The same holds good of Hebron. At the time of Moses it was called Cariath-Arbe, but this name came from Arbe, one of the Anakim, who had taken it whilst the Jews were in Egypt. At the time of the patriarchs it was called Hebron, and under this name it was dear to the Jews, because it was the place where Sarah, Abraham, Isaac, Rebecca, Lia and Jacob were buried. After the conquest the Jews restored its old name.

Many other objections of the same kind have been urged by various infidel writers, but they are of small account in face of the constant and uninterrupted tradition of the Jewish nation.

CHAPTER X.

AUTHENTICITY OF THE PENTATEUCH.

1. Its Authenticity rejected by Infidels, on Account of the Miracles contained in it.—2. The Pentateuch underwent no Change.—3. That Moses is a trustworthy Author is proved from his Style.—4. He could not be an Impostor.—5. The Miracles related by him are intimately connected with the History of the Jews.—6. The Jews were convinced of their Reality.—7. The Jews could not have been deceived by Moses.—8. They considered themselves bound by the Law of Moses, even after his Death.—9. The Worship of the Jews a standing Memorial of those Miracles.—10. The Sabbatic Year a constant Miracle.—11. Mention made of Mosaic Miracles by Pagan Authors.

1. THE genuineness of the Pentateuch having been established, it remains to show that this work is authentic, which means that we may safely accept all the facts therein related. As to the purely historical facts, unbelievers have no difficulty in admitting them; what they reject is the miracles mentioned by Moses, which, if true, must proclaim his divine mission. Could these wonders be proved mere fables, like the mythical legends of other nations, our inquiry into religious truth were at an end. The importance of this point has not escaped the notice of infidel writers; for, to upset the divine character of the Penta-

teuch is to sap the very foundation, not of Judaism only, but of Christianity, so that infidelity or irreligion would be the necessary consequence.

The main argument put forth by our opponents is the *a priori* supposition that miracles are impossible. Whenever, in Holy Scripture, they come across a fact of this nature, they set it down as an addition to the original text, or they give it a mythical signification, or look upon it as hyperbole, or again they seek its explanation in natural causes. The assumed impossibility of miracles has already been disposed of; nor can those miracles related by Moses be explained by the help either of myths or laws of nature. That they have not been added to the text by later writers is likewise plain.

2. The miraculous events narrated by Moses could not have been added, because, on the one hand, they are intimately connected with the whole series of events, so that, if they were left out, the history of the Jews would become unintelligible. On the other hand, such changes would have been utterly impossible, for the law of Moses was not a book hidden in the recesses of the temple, accessible only to a few privileged individuals: it was known to all Levites, priests and magistrates. Additions, therefore, could not have been made to it without supposing that the whole nation would have agreed to such interpolations, and that they were introduced simul-

taneously into all the copies in circulation. Had any such change been attempted, some opposition would have been raised, the more so on account of the great veneration in which the law of Moses was always held. In fact not a single law can be pointed out which had been changed or abrogated from the time of the conquest of Canaan to that of the kings before the captivity; after the return from the Babylonian bondage it was the chief care of Nehemias and Esdras to reconstruct the Jewish nation in strict accordance with the Mosaic law. It is certain no change took place after the separation of the ten tribes: never would they have sanctioned modifications made by their enemies, and they looked upon the two remaining tribes as enemies after the schism. Any change introduced before that time would have been of too recent a date to escape notice, and the ten tribes would never have accepted the authority of the Pentateuch which condemned both their schism and their idolatry. If, therefore, the ten tribes did acknowledge the authority of the Pentateuch, this acknowledgment can be due only to their firm conviction that it contained the unaltered writings of Moses. Now the kings of Samaria, though interested in its rejection, did not dare to proscribe it, lest they should shock the feelings of the people, and give them a pretext for returning to their allegiance to the house of David.

3. Moreover, Moses is a trustworthy witness of the miracles he relates. He has all the characteristics that distinguish a reliable author from a narrator of fiction. His style is most simple, without rhetorical ornaments. He uses no oratorical precautions against difficulties; he states plain facts in the plainest possible manner; it is only when exhorting the people that his words take a higher flight. The characters of all those who figure in the events recorded are in perfect keeping with their actions. What he says of the customs and manners of the nations he describes, fully agrees with the accounts found in Hesiod, Herodotus, Diodorus of Sicily, and others; many of his descriptions and allusions have been confirmed by Egyptian monuments lately deciphered.

4. An impostor, always cunning, pretends to special communications with God, of which he can give no proof; he flatters men in power, so long as he himself is not powerful enough to dispense with their protection; he puts on the mantle of piety, but seeks only his own profit and advancement. None of these characteristics belong to Moses. In conduct he is ever simple; he flatters neither princes nor people, but upbraids them severely whenever they do wrong. All his actions, from the time he is appointed the leader of his nation, are stamped with the seal of genuine piety and true devotedness to the welfare of his people. He seeks neither his own advan-

tage nor that of his family. He confers the priesthood on his brother, not on his own children, who are ranked only among the Levites, nor are they favored in any special manner either during his lifetime or after his death. The priests and Levites were to receive no share of the lands to be conquered from the Canaanites; some cities were assigned to them, but for their daily sustenance they must rely on the voluntary offerings of the people, whereas in Egypt the priesthood were, in fact, together with the crown, sole owners of the land. The successor he appointed to take his place as leader of the nation belonged to another tribe. No impostor would have dared to write as Moses did. He would not have recorded the people's ingratitude, their stubbornness, their rebellions, and their idolatry. He would not have stated, without some attempt at excuse, the crimes of the fathers of his nation, such as the incest of Ruben, that of Juda with Thamar, the selling of Joseph into slavery. Thus Josephus, in his *Antiquities of the Jews*, says nothing of the incest of Juda, nor of the golden calf, nor of the dissolute conduct of the Jews with the daughters of Madian. The authors of the Talmud have endeavored to find many excuses to lessen the guilt of the fathers of their nation. Moses does not spare himself nor his own family; he states the faults of his brother Aaron, and of his sister Mary; he mentions his own want of confidence when the Jews murmured on account of having no water, and the punishment inflicted on himself by God of not entering the promised land. He mentions, indeed, the great favors he had received from God, but these were visible to the whole nation; and he always refers everything to the divine glory.

5. But now, as to the miracles, are they to be believed? If there were implied any absurdity in any of them; if they were aimless or unworthy of God, we should be justified in rejecting them. But the very contrary is the case. Every miracle is intimately connected with the narrative, and without them the history of the Exodus becomes inexplicable. Unless the ten plagues had afflicted the Egyptians, how could the Jews have succeeded in leaving the country? What road could they have taken save through the Red Sea? How could they have lived in the desert for forty years without agriculture, unless they had been miraculously fed with the manna? Yet the fact of their leaving Egypt, of their dwelling in the desert, is attested not only by Moses, but also by pagan authors.

6. Considering that the whole Jewish nation gave credence to Moses, the marvels mentioned in his book must, of necessity, be facts. Moses could never have succeeded in deceiving the people. He did not perform his miracles in presence of a devoted few: they were public,

and seen by all. Could an impostor have made the people believe that they had been spared from the ten plagues; that they had passed the Red Sea, whilst the whole army of Pharaoh was swallowed up in its waters; that they had been miraculously fed with manna from heaven every day for forty years; that they had been protected and guided by a cloud during the day, and a column of fire during the night? No false prophet could be found bold enough to tax to such an extent the credulity of a nation. It is true that infidels have vainly attempted to account for these facts by natural causes; but their supernatural character must remain beyond dispute.*

7. That the whole Jewish nation were convinced of the miracles wrought by Moses is plain from the fact that they submitted to his guidance and his laws, though these laws were at variance with their natural inclinations. Often did the people show their unwillingness to submit to the law imposed upon them; not only did they give

---

* Some writers asserted that the ten plagues had nothing supernatural about them, but were merely the unusual effects of an overflow of the Nile. If this had been the case, why did the Egyptians so ardently wish for the departure of the Jews? Why did Pharaoh allow the Jews to leave the country against his own will? Why were the Jews exempted from these scourges?

As to the passage of the Red Sea, some said that the Jews took advantage of the tide, which left a large tract of the sea-bed dry; they compare it to the passage of part of Alexander's troops over an arm of the sea at Pamphylia. But at the place where the Jews crossed, the bed of the sea never became dry by any ebb; the time when the tide was out could not have sufficed for the crossing of over a million of people on foot, with their droves of cattle and a

vent to their displeasure in murmurings, but they repeatedly rose in rebellion against him, and yet they always returned to their allegiance, though he usually stood alone. When the Jews had sacrificed to the golden calf, the tribe of Levi sided with Moses; but how could one tribe, neither the most numerous nor practised in the use of arms, have mastered the remaining eleven? Even the tribe of Levi was not always faithful: some of its most influential members, Core, Dathan and Abiron, together with two hundred and fifty principal men of the synagogue, rose up against Moses. He could not have withstood such rebellious attempts, unless God had miraculously intervened, and it is on this intervention that Moses relies. "By this you shall know," said he to the people at the time of Core's rebellion, "that the Lord hath sent me to do all things that you see. . . . If these men die the common death of men, and if they be visited with a plague, . . . the Lord did not send me; but

---

quantity of household goods. The Egyptians, well acquainted with the laws of the tide on their own coast, would not have been so foolish as to enter the sea immediately after the passage of the Jews, but would have waited till the tide was out again, when they could have crossed in safety.

The manna is said to be a fruit of certain shrubs growing in the Arabian desert, which even now is called manna by the Arabs. That there are such shrubs in the Arabian desert is not denied; but how could a few plants, found here and there, be the sole food of more than a million of people? This shrub bears fruit only during a short part of the year; how, then, could the people find the manna ready for their use every day, except on the Sabbath? Attempts to explain away these facts by natural means are absolutely futile.

if . . . the earth . . . swallow them down, . . . you shall know that they have blasphemed the Lord." (*Num.* xvi, 28-30.)

8. Not only did the Jews acknowledge themselves bound to submit to the law of Moses during his lifetime, but even after his death they recognized the same necessity. Frequently they proved unfaithful to the precepts of the lawgiver. Now, had Moses deceived them by affecting to establish his authority upon miracles which their fathers had never seen, they would not have failed to urge this as a sufficient reason for their conduct. Yet this they never did; they invariably acknowledged their wrong, and returned to their duty, so that the whole nation must have felt assured of the right Moses had to impose this law upon them; for man never submits his will to irksome decrees, when he has power to resist, unless he is fully convinced of the authority by which such commands are made. Therefore the Jews must have had a firm belief that the miracles constantly appealed to by Moses were real ones. And Josue, his successor, takes the chiefs of the nation to witness of the miraculous facts related by Moses, and urges them as the most powerful motives for keeping the people in their fidelity to the Lord. (*Jos.* xxiv.)

9. The whole ceremonial of worship instituted by Moses is a standing memorial of the miracles which took place at the exodus and in the desert.

The ark of the covenant contains a golden vessel filled with the manna, the rod of Aaron, and the tables of the law; around the altar are seen the plates made of the censers of those who, with Core, wanted to usurp the priesthood. In the sanctuary is kept the brazen serpent which Moses had erected in the desert to cure those who, for their rebellious spirit, had been bitten by serpents. The Pasch is celebrated every year, in grateful remembrance of the deliverance from the bondage of Egypt. The feast of Pentecost reminds the people of the law given on Mount Sinai; that of the tabernacles, of the sojourn in the desert. The offering of the first-born was to testify their gratitude for having been preserved from the plague which carried off all the first-born of Egypt.

10. Furthermore, the Jews had a constant miracle before their eyes as a test of the Mosaic record. Moses (*Exod.* xxiii; *Lev.* xxv, 3-22) had commanded, on the part of God, that every seventh year the land should lie fallow: " But if you say, What shall we eat the seventh year, if we sow not, nor gather our fruits? I will give you my blessing the sixth year, and it shall yield the fruits of three years; and the eighth year you shall sow, and shall eat of the old fruits until the ninth year." This law was observed; it was in vigor after the captivity (1 *Mach.* ii, 48); and Josephus (*Antiq.* lib. xiv, 10) informs us that

the Jews obtained of the Romans exemption from paying tribute every seventh year, and also (*Ibid.*, lib. xi, 8) that, when Alexander the Great was at Jerusalem, the high-priest Jeddoa asked him to exempt the Jews from paying tribute in the Sabbatic year, which favor was granted. Tacitus (*Hist.*, lib. v, 1) attests the same fact, though, not knowing the cause of this observance, he attributes it to laziness. Now, could this law have been observed during so many centuries, if the promise made by Moses had not been fulfilled? It was no natural event to have, every sixth year of the seven, such an abundant harvest: this is certainly not the case at present. It is true that under some kings this law was violated; but this was also one of the principal reasons why the land lay desolate during the seventy years of the Babylonian captivity (2 *Paral.* xxxvi, 21), as Moses had foretold if they broke the law. (*Lev.* xxvi, 34.) Hence, after the return of the Jews from captivity, they took the solemn engagement of observing faithfully the Sabbatic year. (*Neh.* x, 31.)

11. It has been objected that such extraordinary facts ought to have been mentioned by other historians. But we must remember that Moses is the oldest of all historians. The first profane histories were written many centuries later; nor had the writers of these last much interest in what concerned the Jews. The Egyptian monu-

ments hitherto deciphered do not mention the marvels of the Pentateuch, because the Egyptians, no doubt, did not care much about perpetuating their own disgrace. But these miraculous events were not unknown to other nations. Achior, one of the captains of the children of Ammon, speaking to Holofernes, relates all the principal miracles recorded by Moses: the ten plagues, the passage through the Red Sea, the manna with which the Jews were fed in the desert. (*Jud.* v, 6-25). Eusebius (*Præp. Evang.*, lib. ix, cap. 8) cites the pagan author, Numinius, a Pythagorean philosopher, who states that Jannes and Mambres, by common consent of the Egyptians, were chosen to oppose, by the magical arts in which they excelled, the wonders of Moses. Artapan, quoted by Eusebius (*Ibid.*, lib. ix, cap. 27), observes that the priests of Memphis did not admit the miraculous passage of Moses through the Red Sea, but that those of Heliopolis, on the contrary, did not deny it. According to Herodotus (lib. ii, cap. 3), the latter were considered the most versed in the lore of antiquity. Justinus relates that Moses, flying from Egypt, took with him the gods of that country, and that the Egyptians, who pursued him, were compelled by a great storm to return home. Tacitus (lib. v, cap. 3) states that under the reign of King Bocchoris the Jews, led by Moses, left Egypt, and that the event took place on account of severe contagious diseases.

CHAPTER XI.

PRINCIPAL EVENTS RELATED IN GENESIS.

1. Moses a competent Witness of the Events related in Genesis.—2. The Words *Elohim* and *Jehovah* do not point to two different Authors.—3. The six Days of Creation do not furnish a valid Objection against Genesis.—4. Objections taken from ancient Chronologies and geological Facts.—5. Age of the human Race according to Genesis.—6. Chaldean Chronology.—7. Egyptian Chronology.—8. Egyptian Monuments no Argument for the great Antiquity of the human Race.—9. Chinese Chronology.—10. Prehistoric Times.—11. Quaternary Formations of comparatively recent Date.—12. Stone Ages no Proof of the high Antiquity of Man.—13. Fossil Remains of Man found together with extinct Species of Animals.—14. Peat Formations and Lake Dwellings.—15. The State of Civilization of ancient Nations no Proof of the Antiquity of the human Race.—16. Traditions regarding the Deluge.—17. Unity of the human Race.—18. Tower of Babel.

1. MOSES having clearly shown that he was a messenger sent from God for our instruction, it is evident that he is to be believed, not only as to the facts of which he was an eye-witness, but also as to the events related in Genesis. These he might have learnt partly by revelation, partly from monuments and the oral tradition of his own nation, as well as of the Egyptians and the Chaldeans. The principal events mentioned in Genesis, such as the epoch of the creation of man,

his fall, the flood, the building of the Tower of Babel, the confusion of tongues, and the dispersion of the human race over the earth, were facts too remarkable to be easily forgotten. There are, besides, only a few links of tradition between Moses and Adam. Levi, the great-grandfather of Moses, had lived thirty-three years with Isaac, whose father, Abraham, must have known Arphaxad, the son of Sem; and Noe's father, Lamech, was already born when Adam died.

As infidel writers have strained every nerve to attack the authenticity of Genesis, we are bound to say a word or two on the score of their principal objections.

2. Some contend that more than one author is perceivable in the compilation of Genesis, since, in some places, God is called *Elohim*, in others *Jehovah*. Were we to admit that Moses found some documents of whose authenticity he was perfectly certain, and which he incorporated into his work, this admission would imperil neither the authorship of Moses nor his veracity. But the objection is worthless, because the two words are used in relating one and the same event. Thus, in the narration of the sacrifice of Isaac (*Gen.* xxii, 1-19), the Hebrew text has Elohim in the first ten verses, and Jehovah in the nine others. In the account of the Deluge, the word Elohim is used throughout the sixth chapter, save in verse eighth; in the seventh chapter the word

Jehovah is used in the first, fifth and ninth verses, and both appear in the sixteenth verse. It is absurd to suppose that these passages were composed by two different authors.

3. Geological facts are brought to bear against the record of Moses. The world, it is said, has existed much longer than the time assigned by the Jewish writer, as various coal deposits and the fossil remains of species long extinct declare. To this we reply : Moses does not give the age of the world, but that of mankind alone. There are two ways of explaining the difficulty. We may admit a long lapse of time from the creation of the heavens and the earth to the first of the six days ; during this period every change indicated by the study of geology may have occurred, and after some great convulsion, which covered the earth with water, and caused thick vapors to hang over it, a new epoch opened in which the work of the six days was accomplished as described by Moses. Or we may hold that each of the six days means a length of time other than twenty-four hours. The word *day* is often used in Holy Writ to express an indeterminate period of time. (*Gen.* ii, 4 ; *Amos* viii, 11, 12 ; *Jer.* l, 30 ; *Ezech.* xxix, 21 ; etc.) The expression, " There was evening and morning, one day." (*Gen.* i, 5), does not, of necessity, imply a day of twenty-four hours, for from eve to morn we have only a night ; it seems much more probable that it is

meant to signify that the creations spoken of proceeded gradually to their full growth, as the day grows out of the night. The seventh day, on which God rested from work, does not mean a space of time comprised within twenty-four hours, but the whole period of time which begins with the creation of man, and lasts even now. Hence there is nothing which compels us to take the six days for natural days.

We must, moreover, bear in mind that it was not the intention of Moses to compose a work on cosmogony or geology; he simply meant to impress on the minds of his people that all those things which the surrounding nations adored as gods, were only creatures of the Most High.

Infidels accuse the Church of changing her lines by assigning a meaning of indefinite periods to the expression *day*, of the first chapter of Genesis. But the Church has never defined in what precise meaning this word, as found in Genesis, is to be taken. St. Augustine, wellnigh fifteen centuries ago, gave to this word an allegorical meaning, and his interpretation has never been censured. Catholic writers were always at liberty to assign to this word that signification which they looked upon as more closely in accordance with the sacred text. So long, therefore, as the lately discovered fossil remains did not afford any motive for attributing to the term *day* a meaning at variance with the usual one, Catholics commonly accepted it in this obvious way; for it is in conformity with a general rule wisely followed, that Scriptural words ought to be taken in their literal sense, unless there be valid grounds for another interpretation. It is enough for us that the word *day*, in the first chapter of Genesis, may have the signification of *period*, without any violence to the sacred text, and that the Church is far from forbidding such an explanation.

4. But our adversaries reply: The human race dates from a far remoter period than that marked by Moses in Genesis, for his chronology is in contradiction with that of all other ancient nations, such as the Chaldeans, the Egyptians, and the Chinese. And, moreover, the fossil remains of man, the stone implements used by him, and which are found in the quaternary strata of the globe, indicate that man must have existed long before the time at which Moses places the birth of the human race.

5. To see our way out of these difficulties, we must, first of all, investigate the age of man as recorded in the Bible. We have three principal versions of the Pentateuch: the original Hebrew, the Samaritan, and the Greek version called the Septuagint. These three versions agree perfectly in the main; but when we compare the series of patriarchs who lived before and after the Deluge, and their respective ages, we find that

the versions differ. According to the Septuagint, from Adam to the Deluge two thousand two hundred and forty-two years are generally reckoned; according to the Hebrew text, we have one thousand six hundred and fifty-six years, and the Samaritan gives only one thousand three hundred and seven years. As to the time which elapsed from the Deluge to Abraham, the divergence between the Greek and Hebrew texts is greater still, the former assigning more than one thousand years, the latter, according to different computations, from two hundred and ninety-two to three hundred and fifty-two years. The Samaritan, on the other hand, in this point agrees pretty much with the Septuagint. Which of these readings is to be preferred? We have no means of settling the question. In some of the versions an error must have crept in through the carelessness of copyists, but in which of them we cannot determine. As this alteration affects no doctrine, either of faith or of morals, the authority of Holy Writ is not lessened on this account. The Church has, indeed, sanctioned by her authorization the Latin version made by St. Jerome from the Hebrew text; yet, in doing this, she has only declared that the Latin version, called the Vulgate, is to be followed, and that it is authentic in regard to all things concerning faith and morals. But, at the same time, the Septuagint has always enjoyed a high authority in the

Church, because the quotations from the Old Testament, made by the inspired writers in the New, are taken from that text. Pope Gregory XIII had the Septuagint revised, and ordered it to be received by all, and to be used for the better understanding of the Latin text and the writings of the fathers. The Latin version, used in the Church during the first four centuries, was made from the Septuagint. If, moreover, we consult the primitive traditions of Christianity, we find a universal belief that from Adam to Christ five thousand five hundred years had elapsed. This is atttested by St. Cyprian, Lactantius, Julian the African, and others. We are not, therefore, bound to hold as an article of faith the chronology founded on the Vulgate; and hence, if it could be proved that some ancient monuments, either Egyptian or Assyrian, point to a somewhat more remote antiquity than that assigned in the Hebrew text, this fact would in no wise be contrary to Holy Writ. However, the monuments as yet discovered do not require us to accept the longer period of the Septuagint.

6. The authority of Berosus, Manetho, and others, is brought in to disprove the Mosaic chronology. But how can the obscure and fabulous accounts of these writers be confronted with the clear and coherent statements of Genesis? Moses, besides being the oldest historian, was versed in the sciences of Egypt, since he was educated at

the court of Pharaoh; he had access to all the documents of Egypt, and made himself master of them; he was, moreover, familiar with the traditions of his own nation and with those of the Chaldeans, among whom his ancestors had lived. So that, had Moses come across any authentic documents placing the age of mankind at a remoter period, he would not have dared to put forward the facts contained in his work; for no impostor would be so awkward as to furnish his opponents with statements that expose his fraud at a glance.

But Berosus is not really in opposition to the Mosaic chronology. The first ten kings, to whose reign he assigns so long a period, bear a close resemblance to the ten patriarchs who lived before the Deluge, not indeed as to their names, but in regard to the meaning of those names. Now, in the fragments of Berosus, we find that these kings lived one hundred and twenty saros, and a saros was supposed to contain six neros of six hundred years each; thus giving the sum total of four hundred and thirty-two thousand years. Dr. Sepp, of Munich (*Life of our Lord Jesus Christ*, vol. ii, p. 417), has proved that, according to Pliny, the saros contained two hundred and twenty-two synodical months, or eighteen and six-tenth years; so that one hundred and twenty saros would give two thousand two hundred and thirty-two years. Suidas affirms that the hundred and twenty saros were equal to two thousand two hundred and twenty-two sacerdotal or cyclical years, which amount to one thousand six hundred and fifty-six solar years. Both explanations make the period shorter than what is allowed, not only by the Septuagint, but even by the Hebrew text. Pliny, indeed, asserts that the astronomical observations of the Chaldeans, at his time, dated as far back as seven hundred and twenty thousand years. Diodorus of Sicily allows them four hundred and seventy-two thousand years; but Ptolemy, who with the greatest care collected all the astronomical observations he could lay hold of, states that no reliable observations could be found prior to the time of Nabonassar, who was contemporaneous with the Jewish king, Ezechias.* If the Chaldeans possessed a certain amount of astronomical knowledge, we must bear in mind that they did not owe it all to their own observation, but also to the tradition perpetuated among them after the Deluge. Of late, Assyrian libraries of works written on tablets or cylinders of burnt clay have been dug up from the ruins of ancient cities; but the historical notices (which greatly confirm in many respects

---

* There is a letter said to have been written by Callisthenes, a follower of Alexander the Great, to Aristotle, in which he gives him a long catalogue of observations made at Babylon, and dating as far back as one thousand nine hundred and seven years B. C. Admitting the authenticity of this letter, the date is still subsequent to the Deluge. There is nothing astonishing in the fact that the Babylonians should, at an early period, have observed the stars, for astronomy was intimately connected with religion by all the ancient nations.

the statements of the Bible), the dates of which can be determined, are not more remote than the ninth century B. C.: some are believed to date 1300 B. C., and one is supposed to date 1800 B. C.; but even this supposition would make the writer of it contemporary only with Josue.

7. As to the Egyptian chronology, the main support of the attacks against Moses is the authority of Manetho, who, by the side of the Jewish historian, may be looked upon as almost a recent writer. In the Pentateuch we possess a full list of patriarchs; its statements are clear and precise. Manetho, on the contrary, has interwoven his catalogue with fabulous accounts. The Mosaic records we possess entire; of Manetho we have only some fragments, and these, in three different shapes, are by no means in accordance with one another. Moses had consulted the original documents; he understood full well the hierography and the native tongue of Egypt. Manetho had to rely on the Egyptian priests, after many of the primitive documents had been destroyed by Cambyses, and what escaped the flames had been carried off to Persia. After the departure of Cambyses, the priests must have made efforts to reconstruct their annals, partly from monuments, but partly from memory, to which fancy leht its help; and as several attempted the same task, many considerable discrepancies were found in these reproductions. They took

for solar years the periods which, in the ancient monuments, were only sacred years, consisting first of one month, and afterward of four. (*Diodorus Siculus*, lib. i, cap. 26.) They likewise introduced into the line of kings some governors of provinces, or independent sovereigns of certain parts of Egypt. The catalogues of Diodorus of Sicily and of Eratosthenes, written under the dictation of the priests of Memphis and of Thebes, ought also to possess some weight in the matter; yet they do not bear much resemblance to those of Manetho. The reigns of the gods or demigods, to which Manetho assigns such incredible periods of time, are palpably those of the patriarchs previous to the Deluge, since he himself states that his own history of Egypt was compiled from inscriptions made on columns by the first Mercury before the flood. This Mercury is the famous Toth, who bears a striking resemblance to the biblical Seth.* Menes, according to Manetho, is the first real human king, and he can be no other than the Noe of Holy Writ. Herodotus tells us how traditions of Egypt bear that, at the time of Menes, the whole of Egypt was submerged save Thebes. The whole history of Menes and Thebes (which signifies *ark*), in Herodotus and Diodorus of Sicily, is but a re-

---

* The Chinese and the Indian chronologies have their reigns of the gods, whose sway lasted very long ; but these, too, point to the biblical patriarchs, and, like them, are ten in number.

miniscence of the history of Noe and of the ark. We find there the ship, the dove, the altar, the sacrifice, meat as food, the vine, which the Thebans said they were the first to cultivate.*

8. None of the Egyptian monuments go beyond the time of the Deluge. It is true that several Egyptologists assign to the first dynasty the year 5750 B. C., but they have no sure data on which to base their calculation. Lipsius places the first dynasty of Menes at 3892 B. C., and the fourth at 2280 B. C.; which calculation may be reconciled with the Mosaic record. Besides, the epoch assigned to the fourth dynasty is confirmed by the great pyramid, known to have been constructed by Cheops of the fourth dynasty. Mr. George Smith, of the British Museum, and other scientific men, have shown that this pyramid was not destined to serve as a sepulchre, but rather to perpetuate the knowledge of certain mathematical and astronomical truths, expressed by the various dimensions of the pyramid, and by their relations to one another. In fact we may deduce from them the ratio of the diameter of the circle and its circumference, the distance of the earth from the sun, the exact length of the year, the weight of the earth, the cycle of the precession of the equinoxes, etc. The outer opening of the smaller corridor, exactly in the line of the meridian, points to a spot in the

---
* Abbé Moigno, "*La Foi et la Science,*" p. 182.

heavens which, two thousand one hundred and eighty years B. C., taking into account the precession of the equinoxes, was occupied by the star *a* of the Dragon; but at the same time there passed over the meridian, above the pole, one of the constellation of the Pleiades. That the architect had this constellation in view, appears from some ornaments which adorn the larger corridor; and, strange to say, tradition has likewise always connected this pyramid with that very group of stars. The Pleiades had, at that time, the same right ascension as the vernal equinox, and could thus be used as a fresh starting-point for the chronology of the human race. Ancient nations seem to have preserved the recollection of the Pleiades opening the spring, for Virgil sings: *Candidus auratis aperit cum cornibus annum Taurus*, though at his time this star, which is one of the Pleiades, no longer coincided with spring, the beginning of what was then the new year. (*Civiltà Cattolica*, Ser. ix, vol. vii, p. 458 et seqq.) Mr. Haliburton has proved that in the East many tribes, even now, take the Pleiades as the opening of the new year, but principally the savages of Australia, who carefully observe the passage of this cluster of stars over the meridian at midnight. What could have determined these ignorant savages to choose a group of stars which in their latitude does not rise more than $50°$ above the horizon, and which, owing to atmospheric peculiarities, is never very brilliant, if not the tradition these tribes brought with them, pointing, as it does, to the same era as the pyramid of Cheops,—an era not far distant from the flood and the dispersion of mankind? (Abbé Moigno, *La Foi et la Science*, p. 164.)

9. As regards China, Confucius, who lived 550 B. C., could find no reliable data for the events recorded in Chinese history beyond two hundred years prior to himself; so that this chronology cannot stand in presence of the Mosaic one.

10. Before answering the objections drawn from geological facts, we must remark that, in order to vindicate the authority of Moses, it is sufficient for us merely to show that none of these facts necessarily require that length of time imagined by infidels, and that they may all have happened within the time assigned by him. But our adversaries, in order to impugn the statements of the Pentateuch, must prove by arguments most convincing, that their views about the antiquity of man are not only probable, but necessarily true, that these geological facts are not susceptible of any other explanation than theirs; for all our arguments to show the veracity of the statements of Moses are based on solid and indisputable facts totally separate from geology: they cannot, therefore, be overthrown by mere surmises. Unbelievers constantly speak of prehistoric times. If they mean a time which is anterior to Adam,

we positively affirm that such prehistoric age of mankind never has existed. But we readily admit that there may be found vestiges of events which happened before the known historic times of several nations: for the early history of many nations is, for the most part, unknown.

11. Let us now review the facts which are brought to bear against the authority of Moses. Remains of man have been found in the quaternary strata of the globe in many places, and these strata, they say, must be far more ancient than the time marked by Genesis, even if we take the more prolonged statement of the Septuagint. But, when we come to analyze the grounds on which these geological arguments are based, we find in them no species of agreement. Geologists are generally eager to contradict the affirmations of others, and to prove them untenable. Some candidly confess that we know very little about these quaternary formations. How, then, are we, on such uncertain grounds, to base arguments against Mosaic authority? The quaternary deposits were formed, beyond a doubt, when the water-courses were of far greater extent than at present. Now, we gather from history that, shortly before the foundation of Rome by Romulus, the Tiber had not yet ceased to be in the condition requisite for quaternary formations. Ancient writers attest that, when at its height, the Tiber still overflowed a great part of the valley,

and united with the various lakes and marshes there. The old appellative of the Tiber was not *flavus*, from the sands which it carries with it, but *albula*, owing to its whiteness and its clearness, due to the melting of snow on the mountains. In the old pagan rituals of Rome, it is mentioned that the Tiber was also called *Serra* and *Rumon*, on account of its erosive powers and the swiftness of its currents. The place where Æneas built his new city of Troy in Latium was, as has been ascertained, at the quaternary outlet of the Tiber. Even after the foundation of Rome, the condition of the river was other than it was afterward, or than it is at present. Its overflow was more frequent; the climate of the surrounding country was different, for historians mention heavy falls of snow, which sometimes remained on the ground forty days. In the fifth century of Rome the Tiber froze twice. These facts tend to show that at that period the condition of the climate was as yet not so far removed from the time when the Tiber still retained its quaternary state. (*Etudes Religieuses*, Paris, Oct., 1874, p. 547 et seqq.) If, then, the quaternary formation of the Tiber's valley falls within the historic period, why should other rivers point to a higher antiquity?

12. The stone weapons and instruments found in various places have given rise to the supposed paleolithic and neolithic periods of prehistoric

times; those dug up at Amiens and Abbeville were given as instances of the former; those found at Moustier, of the latter, because polished and more carefully made. But such a distinction is quite arbitrary: at Amiens many specimens were found of the same shape and finish as those of Moustier. Stone weapons cannot, by any means, furnish a ground for asserting the great antiquity of man; they have been used in all ages; some savage tribes make use of them even at present; they have coexisted with metal weapons and instruments. The Jews, at times, used stone knives in their rite of circumcision; the Eygptians always for embalming the dead. Nay, sharp stones were often employed in quarrying. In 1868 a stone quarry was found at Wady Magharah, on Mount Sinai, in which stone instruments were used for quarrying. Close to it were the remains of a village, near which there had been a lake, whence the workmen obtained their food. Here we possess all we need to build up a prehistoric station; and yet this quarry, as appears from inscriptions, was worked only one thousand seven hundred years B. C. (and perhaps even later), when the surrounding nations were conversant with the use of metals. At Marathon, where Miltiades defeated the Persians, many stone arrowheads were found, together with brass weapons, in the tumuli erected by the Athenians over their dead. Nor does the absence of any vestige of iron or of brass conclusively show that stone instruments only were employed at the period to which they belong, for metals are oftentimes entirely destroyed by length of time, while flint-stone is unimpaired.

13. As to the fossil remains of man found in various places, they do not afford any solid ground for establishing the antiquity of the human race. It does not require any very great period of time to reduce bones to a fossil state, nor is there any safe criterion for determining the relative age of fossils. Even great geologists have been imposed upon, so as to take for ancient fossils bones which had been only a few centuries in the ground. The famous Moulin-Quignon jawbone, which was believed, by M. Boucher de Perthes and other geologists, French as well as English, to be a genuine old fossil of prehistoric times, bears witness to the fact. (*Revue des Deux Mondes*, July, 1873.)*

The depth at which genuine fossils or instruments have been found cannot be taken as evidence of their great antiquity, for the remains of a city supposed to be Troy are actually from twenty to thirty metres below the ground. (*Civiltà*

---

* Some workmen having dug up human bones from a spot used as a graveyard for those who had died of the plague in the fourteenth century, buried them in some other place ; after these bones had remained in the ground for some months, they took care that M. Boucher de Perthes should be present at their discovery, in order to obtain the reward he had promised for the finding of fossils.

Cattolica 25th Nov., 1873, p. 556.) Nor is the conformation of skulls of any weight in the matter, since all those hitherto found do not differ from those of races or individuals of historic times; and we know that, even at present, some tribes purposely deform their skulls in youth. The cavemen, who are supposed to be one of the most ancient races, are a mere creation of sciolist fancy. In the earliest ages some people dwelt in caves; but this has taken place in all ages, and instances may be found in our own days. Yet, we are gravely told, these cave-dwellers were coeval with the cave-bear, the mastodon, and other long-extinct species; their fossils, it is argued, cannot always have been washed into the caves used as places of burial, for more than once we find on these bones evident marks of scraping; at times they are split, as if with a view to extracting the marrow. In the Brixham cave, in Devonshire, a perfect sample of a stone-knife was found alongside of the hind leg of a cave-bear, not a bone of which had been displaced. Even should we grant all this, our adversaries have first to tell us the exact time at which these extinct species of animals disappeared from the globe. Many post-pleiocene animals continued to exist when other species appeared; and there is not a single fact which can be adduced to substantiate the assertion that they disappeared before the time of the Mosaic record. Some of these species have died out within the memory of man. The *bos primigenius* existed at the time of Julius Cæsar. Among the Indians of North America there are traditions about an animal bearing a close resemblance to the mastodon, entire skeletons of which are not unfrequently found. They speak of a great elk or buffalo, which, besides enormous horns, had an arm protruding from the head, with a hand at its extremity (proboscis). The South American Indians have a tradition about a giant bear, called the naked bear.

14. Sir Charles Lyell, considering the thick beds of peat which cover some spots where human relics are found, as also the so-called lake-dwellings recently discovered all over Switzerland, inferred the great antiquity of man. But these peat formations afford him no solid proof. At Amiens there is a peat formation from twenty to thirty feet in thickness; and yet this cannot be so very ancient, because at a considerable depth relics of Roman art have been found. We have no criterion whereby to estimate the age of peat formations, since moisture has the property of greatly accelerating such deposits, and the conditions of climate of many places have considerably changed during historic times. The existence of lake-dwellings does not necessarily point to the great antiquity of those who constructed them, for we find such dwellings mentioned in history. Sir Charles Lyell supposes that all geological

changes must have taken place gradually and uniformly,—a groundless supposition, as many geological facts point to sudden and abrupt changes. Besides, the very changes called gradual often take far less time than our adversaries are willing to allow. The coast of Scotland has been raised from twenty-five to twenty-seven feet since the Christian era; some ancient Roman harbors are now above high-water mark. In Glasgow canoes were dug up at a considerable depth, as also objects of art. Were it not known that at the time of the Roman occupation that spot was under water, Sir Charles Lyell might have urged this fact in proof of man's great antiquity. The peat deposits on the coast of Denmark, in which human remains were found, show successive periods of vegetation: the Scotch fir, the birch, and the oak follow each other in succession; yet even this is far from establishing the point in question. It happens very often in North America that, a forest having been destroyed by fire, a new growth of trees appears, not unfrequently of a different kind, and in less than a century we have a new forest on the ruins of the old.

In Egypt relics of pottery and bricks were dug out from the alluvial deposits of the Nile at a depth of from ten to seventeen metres. Sir Charles Lyell, calculating the annual increase of the alluvion, as it stands at present, allows thirty thousand years for these deposits. But Sir Charles Lyell, to justify his calculation, should prove that in former times the deposit was not greater than at present. According to Herodotus, nine hundred years were sufficient to produce a difference of level amounting to seven or eight cubits, or about twelve feet. The Nile delta itself does not seem to be more than five or six thousand years old. (Moigno, *La Foi et la Science*, p. 183.) Moreover, we must bear in mind that heavy objects, which have fallen on ground periodically softened by inundations, tend continually to sink deeper at every additional softening.

15. Some writers have attempted to deduce the great antiquity of man from the high state of civilization among the Egyptians and other nations at the very dawn of history. They say it must have taken countless ages to reach such a degree of perfection by gradual development. This line of reasoning would be conclusive, did we admit, with the Darwinians, that man is nothing more than an improved ape, and that his original state was savagery. These absurd suppositions have both been refuted already. (Introduction § 4; Part i, chap. vi, § 8.)

16. Concerning the Deluge, infidels sometimes ask where all the water came from to cover even the highest mountains, and what became of it after the flood. Now, as we do not pretend to explain the Deluge on natural principles, we can

scarcely be called upon to answer such inquiries. Still geologists tell us that at one time the whole earth must have been covered with water; that there was an ice-period, when a great part of the globe was covered with immense glaciers, several thousand feet deep, as appears from the striæ and abrasions observed on mountains. There was, consequently, water enough for a deluge.

That the globe was visited with this calamity is a tradition found among many nations. The Chinese tradition (*Chou-King*, ch. x, translated by Father Gaubil) speaks of a great inundation which covered the hills on all sides, and rose above the mountain-tops. In the fifth chapter, the author, speaking of the same subject, alludes to the permission then given to use the flesh of animals as food.

In the Indian book, *Bhagavata Pourâna*, translated by Sir W. Jones, we read that Vishnu appeared to Satyavrata to inform him that in seven days the world would be plunged into an ocean of death, but that he would send him a large ship, in which he should put medicinal plants, and various kinds of grain; and that, accompanied by the saints, and surrounded by a couple of every species of animals, he should enter the ship, in order to save himself from the waters of the Deluge.

Alexander Polyhistor (ex *Beroso* apud *Syncelle*) gives a passage from Berosus mentioning the

Chaldean tradition about the Deluge. Chronus, or Saturn, is supposed to have appeared to Xisuthrus in a dream, and to have warned him that, on the 15th day of the month Dæsius, the human race was to be destroyed by a flood. He therefore commanded him to build a vessel, and to enter it with his friends and relatives, after having stored in it the necessary provisions, together with birds and quadrupeds. Xisuthrus did as he was commanded. The Deluge took place; and, after it had abated, Xisuthrus let loose some birds, which, finding neither food nor place of rest, returned to the vessel. Some days after, he let them out again, and they returned with mud on their feet; but, when he let them go a third time, he saw them no more, from which he understood that the earth was beginning to dry. (See *Ancient History of the East*, by Lenormant and Chevallier, vol. i, bk. iv, ch. 6, sec. 5.)

Abydenus mentions the very same tradition. (See Eusebius, *Præpar. Evangelica*, lib. ix, cap. 12.)

The Greeks and Romans had some knowledge of the tradition, as we see from the fable of Deucalion.

The Mexicans, in the extreme West, held the same tradition; it was represented in their hieroglyphic pictures. The Brazilians related that a stranger bore a deadly hatred to their nation, and caused them all to perish in a most terrible inundation, but one brother and sister were saved and re-peopled the earth.

17. Moses states that the whole human race sprang from one couple: and here again the traditions of mankind coincide with his assertion. Great stress has been laid on the variety of races: the European, the African, the Asiatic, etc., but this, nowadays, has not even a shadow of difficulty, for Mr Darwin, though unsuccessful in proving that new species may be evolved, has abundantly established the fact that great varieties may originate in the same species, which, once introduced, may become permanent, and be transmitted by generation.

There is no need of showing how America may have been peopled from the common stock. Navigation was known from the earliest ages, and ships could easily be driven by storms from one hemisphere to the other. In December, 1731, a boat laden with wine, with a crew of six men, entered the port of St. Joseph, situated twelve leagues from the mouth of the Orinoco: this boat had been driven thither by a storm from the Island of Teneriffe. (Gumilla, *History of the Oronoko*, vol. ii, cap. 31.) Besides this the tradition of a great continent stretching from near the coast of Africa to that of America, called *Atlantis* by Plato and other ancient writers, confirmed by traditions current among some American tribes, supposes some intercourse between the inhabitants of the two hemispheres. That this tradition rests on something more solid than mere fiction may be gathered from the fact that the so-called Sargasso Sea, which caused so much uneasiness to Christopher Columbus and his crew, extended much farther than at present, and was studded with sunken rocks, of which no vestiges remain. This is attested by several ancient writers, and points, beyond doubt, to a gradual sinking of the bottom of the ocean in those parts.

As to the confusion of tongues, we must remark that the statement of Moses affords the only explanation of the great variety in the languages spoken throughout the globe. The different languages have a common origin, as is clear from analogies existing between them; yet mere changes of dialect, the introduction of new words, etc., could not account for the many radical differences noticeable in these various tongues.

18. The traditions of the Tower of Babel were not forgotten by the nations remaining near the cradle of the human race. Abydenus (Eusebius, *Præp. Evang.*, lib. ix, cap. 14) says: There are some who affirm that the first men born of earth, being proud of their strength and their great size, wished to become superior to the gods; they therefore undertook to raise a tower of very great height on the spot where Babylon is now built. This tower was reaching up to the

heavens, when the winds came to the assistance of the gods, and overthrew this enormous mass on the builders. The ruins of this tower were used in the construction of Babylon; and mankind, which up to that time had only one and the same speech, began to speak in different tongues. Eupolemus (Eusebius, *Præp. Evang.*, lib. ix, cap. 17) also states that the city of Babylon, and the tower so much talked of by all historians, was built by those who escaped from the Deluge (they were giants); this tower having been destroyed by the power of God, the giants were scattered and dispersed over the earth. It is true that the original works cited by Eusebius are no longer extant, and that he is a Christian writer who lived at the time of Constantine the Great; but these authorities do not, on this account, deserve less credit; for, when Eusebius wrote, the works cited by him were still in existence, and could then be easily compared with his quotations. As Eusebius wrote his book principally for pagan philosophers, who were conversant with the works from which he quoted, he could not expose himself to the danger of quoting imaginary texts, and thus incur the ridicule of his adversaries.

But late discoveries, made by digging among the ruins of ancient Chaldean cities, have confirmed this tradition. Colonel Rawlinson found tablets at Borsippa, marked with cuneiform characters, which were translated by M. Jules

Oppert, member of the Asiatic Society of Paris. Nabuchodonosor speaks of the restoration of a temple built on the foundations of a former one, which had been destroyed long before. In this translation we read: "As to the second, which is this edifice, the temple of the seven lights of the world, . . . and which the first king has begun (there intervene forty-two human lives between that time and the present), without finishing the top. . . . There they had expressed their thoughts in *confusion*. An earthquake and thunder shook the building, which crumbled to pieces and formed hills." (*Annales de la Philosophie Chrétienne*, Nov., 1856, p. 346.)

CHAPTER XII.

THE JEWISH RELIGION, AS TO ITS CEREMONIAL, WAS TO BE PERFECTED BY A NEW REVELATION.

1. The Jewish Religion, in its Ceremonial, typical of the Messiah.—2. Promise of a Messiah.—3. The Messiah believed in by the Jews.—4. Expected by the Generality of Mankind.—5. The Messiah was to give a new Law.—6. To establish a new Sacrifice and a new Priesthood.—7. The Religion established by the Messiah a Perfection of the Mosaic One.

1. As Moses confirmed his mission by many miracles, it is clear that the religion proclaimed by him was divinely established. Yet the Jewish religion, as regards its ceremonial, was not to last forever. The Jews were set apart to keep alive on earth the knowledge and worship of the true God, to hand down from one generation to another the prophecies, concerning the Redeemer or Messiah, made from the beginning of the world, and renewed from time to time by the acknowledged prophets of the nation. This Messiah was to destroy the works of Satan, and free mankind from the guilt of sin into which it had fallen by the disobedience of our first parents. The whole ceremonial law, the sacrifices, the external worship offered to Jehovah, were typical of the

coming Messiah. It was, therefore, necessary that, when the prophecies concerning the Messiah were fulfilled, the typical ceremony should cease, and that He should proclaim a new law, and establish a new worship embodying and expressing the belief in the new order of things inaugurated by God.

2. That a Messiah was promised to the human race appears from Genesis (iii, 15): "I will put enmities between thee (the serpent) and the woman, and thy seed and her seed," etc. The Jews always understood this text to refer to the Redeemer of mankind. In Gen. (xii, 3), God promises to Abraham that in him (in one of his descendants) all the nations of the earth should be blessed. The blessing spoken of here is not a superabundance of temporal goods, because this was possessed by many independently of Abraham, but the true blessing of God, consisting in the reinstatement of man in His friendship. Jacob (*Gen.* xlix), on his deathbed, prophesied that the sceptre should not be taken from Juda, nor a lawgiver from among his children, until the coming of Him who is to be sent, and who will be the expectation of the nations. In Deuteronomy (xviii, 18), God tells the Jews that He will send them another prophet like unto Moses, who will give them another law. The same promise was repeated by all the prophets of the people of Israel.

3. The belief in a Messiah to come was common among the Jews at all times; even nowadays they expect Him. But at the time of Christ they did not wish to understand that the principal office of the Redeemer was to restore God's kingdom on earth, and to destroy the power of our spiritual enemies, as had been the belief of their forefathers, and as had been foretold by the prophets. Smarting under the Roman yoke, and misled by the misinterpretation of the prophecies that refer to the second coming of the Redeemer, they expected that the hoped-for Saviour would restore the nation to its ancient splendor. This they would no doubt have obtained, had they, as a nation, acknowledged Christ for the Messiah, and sought first the kingdom of heaven; but, rejecting him, they lost both their national existence and their privilege of God's chosen people.

4. The general expectation of the Messiah, which pervaded the whole nation, is also mentioned by pagan historians, as well as by Flavius Josephus (*De Bello Jud.*, lib. vi, 5) who says: "The principal reason which determined the Jews to wage war against Rome, was an oracle from Holy Writ announcing that at that time a man would rise up in their country who was to rule over the whole world." Tacitus (*Hist.*, lib. v, cap. 13) says: "Most of the Jews were convinced that in the ancient books of their priests it was foretold that in those times the East would prevail, and

the masters of the world would come from Judæa." Suetonius (*Vita Vespas.*, n. 4) says: "Through the whole East was spread the ancient and constant opinion that the fates had decreed that in those times the rulers of the world should come from Judæa." Even pagan nations shared this general expectation of a coming Saviour. The Chinese emperor, Ming-ti, in those times sent messengers into the West to inquire about the saint spoken of by Confucius; but these, unfortunately, were misled, and introduced Buddhism into China. (Abbé Huc, *Christianity in China*, t. I.) As to the dream which led Ming-ti to seek spiritual enlightenment in the West, see *Foe-Koue-Ki, ou Relation des Royaumes Bouddhiques, traduit par Abel Rémusat*, chap. vii, note 7.

The same tradition we find among the Romans, as may be seen from the Fourth Eclogue of Virgil. Hence either all those who aspired to the empire applied these oracles to themselves, or their partisans did it for them. The sibyls had foretold a new era, a Saviour. The Emperor Constantine, at the Council of Nice, cited the acrostic of the Erythræan sibyl, the initial letters of which formed in Greek these words: "Jesus Christ, the Son of God, Saviour." Cicero had seen these verses; for, though in his book, *De Divinatione* (lib. ii, cap. 54), he denies their prophetic value, he hints very clearly that they speak of a new king, a Saviour, and a new religion; hence he wishes that the sibylline books should not be read at all without the permission of the senate, and that interpreters should find therein anything else than a king, whom neither the gods nor the people would tolerate in Rome.* These sibylline oracles, though carefully secreted by the senate, had, however, become known. Christian writers of the first ages often appeal to them. Lactantius himself, who had been a Capitoline priest, and, as such, had had opportunity to consult these books, kept at Rome, fearlessly appeals to them as to arguments which Pagans could not gainsay. (*De Ira Dei*, cap. xxii; *Divinar. Instit.*, lib. i, cap. 6.) It has been said that these oracles were fabricated by Christians; but, had this been the case, how could Pagans have accepted them as genuine, so that not only Lactantius, but other fathers of the Church, could cite them to Pagans as cogent arguments against them? That these books may have contained interpolations, we do not pretend to deny; we simply maintain that, in their general drift, they were genuine.

5. That the Messiah was to establish a new law, and abrogate the ceremonial of the Jewish worship, is clear not only on the ground that, when the Messiah came, all the ceremonies typical of His coming had no longer any reason to be; but also

---

* St. Augustine cites the acrostic of the Erythræan sibyl (*De civitate Dei*, lib. xviii, cap. 23), though he sets no great value on these oracles (lib. xviii, cap. 47).

from the prophecies which foretold His advent. The Jewish religion was a national one. Other nations were not held to adopt its ceremonial; before the coming of Christ they could be saved by the observance of the natural law inscribed in their hearts, with the belief in the Redeemer to come. But the promised Saviour was to gather all nations into one fold, and thus His religion was to be no longer national, but catholic or universal. The ceremonial instituted by Moses could not, therefore, be adapted to the new order of things to be brought about by the Redeemer. This gathering of the Gentiles into the Church of God is one of the principal characters of the Saviour, foretold by the prophets. It is promised to Abraham, Isaac and Jacob, that in their seed, viz., in and through the Messiah, all nations should be blessed. Jacob foretells that all nations shall be brought to the obedience of Him who is to be sent. In the second Psalm we read that the promised Saviour was to impose a law on the Gentiles, that He would proclaim it in Sión, that He would obtain the nations for His inheritance, and that His kingdom would extend to the limits of the earth; that kings and princes would conspire against His power in vain. In Isaias (ii, 2) we find that all the nations of the earth will come to Christ; that they will exhort each other: " Come and let us go up to the mountain of the Lord, and to the house of the God of Jacob, and

He will teach us His ways, and we will walk in His paths: for the law shall come forth from Sion, and the word of the Lord from Jerusalem." Isaias (xlix, 5, 6) said of the Messiah: "Behold, I "—it is God who speaks—" have given thee to be the light of the Gentiles, that thou mayest be my salvation, even to the farthest part of the earth." (See likewise *ibid.*, v, 23, and *Isa.* lv, 4, 5.)

This kingdom of the Messiah, which is no temporal one, shall abide forever. (*Ps.* ii; lxxxviii, 30–39.)

God also promised that the law given by the Saviour should be different from the Mosaic law. (*Jer.* xxxi, 31–33; *Isa.* lix, 19–21; *Ezech.* xxxix, 28, 29; xxxvi, xxxvii.)

6. The sacrifices of the Mosaic law were to cease. (*Dan.* ix, 26.) A new sacrifice was to be offered, not only in the temple of Jerusalem, but in every place from the rising to the setting sun. (*Malach.* i, 10, 11.) Christ is a priest, not according to Aaron, but according to Melchisedech. (*Ps.* cix.) Isaias (lxvi, 18 et seqq.) tells us that God will congregate all nations and all tongues; that He will send some of the Jews who are saved to the Gentiles, to the sea, to Africa and Lydia, to Italy and Greece, and to the distant islands, to those who have not heard of the Lord, nor seen His glory. In the twenty-first verse it is stated that God will take from the Gentiles priests and Levites. The priesthood of Aaron

must therefore cease; for, according to the law of Moses, one of its essential characters was its exclusiveness: it was reserved " to Aaron and to his seed after him." (*Ex.* xxviii, 43.) But a new covenant, a new sacrifice, a new priesthood, constitute a new religion, and consequently show that the ceremonial of the Mosaic law was at an end.

7. The abrogation of the Mosaic law did not imply the revelation of an entirely new religion, for its dogmatical part was not changed. What God reveals is essentially true, and truth cannot clash with truth. But the law given to the Jews was completed by the law of Christ; He added new truths to those already revealed, and instituted fresh channels of grace for the sanctification of man.

CHAPTER XIII.

THE MESSIAH PROMISED TO THE JEWS IS ALREADY COME.

1. The Advent of the Messiah proved from the Prophecy of Jacob.—2. Of Daniel.—3. Authenticity of Daniel's Prophecy.—4. Proof from the Prophecies of Aggeus and Malachias.

1. WE know that the Messiah promised to the Jews is already come, because the time marked by the prophets is long since gone by. Jacob (*Gen.* xlix) foretold: " The sceptre shall not be taken away from Juda, nor a ruler from his thigh, till He come that is to be sent, and He shall be the expectation of nations." Some centuries after the coming of Jesus Christ, the Jews, perceiving that the prophecy of Jacob stood in their way, tried hard to devise means for explaining it away. Some wished to apply it to persons anterior to Christ; others, again, said that the Hebrew word *shebet*, translated by *sceptre*, means the rod of affliction; others asserted that the word *ad-ki*, rendered *until*, signifies *never—because*, and read the prophecy thus: " The sceptre shall *never* depart from Juda, *because* the Messiah is to come." Some even invented

the fable of a Jewish kingdom still in existence, though unknown to the rest of mankind. But all these interpretations came too late; they are contradicted by the one which the whole Jewish nation accepted, both before Christ and for some time after him; for the Greek of the Septuagint agrees with our Latin version. Onkelos, a Jewish rabbi, who lived about the time of Jesus Christ, gave a Chaldaic paraphrase of the Hebrew text, interpreting it thus: "The ruler shall not be taken from Juda, nor the scribe from the sons of his sons, till the time when the Messiah comes, and Him shall the nations obey." The *Targum of Jerusalem*, a work written by Jews after Christ, translates as follows: "There shall not be wanting kings of the house of Juda, nor learned doctors of the law of the sons of his sons, till the time when the King, the Messiah, comes, to whom the kingdom belongs, and to Him at last all the kings of the earth shall be subject. How beautiful is the King who is to rise from the house of Juda!" Jonathan, another famous Jewish rabbi, gives the same interpretation. Besides, the Jew Aquila (A. D. 90–130), who endeavored to translate the Hebrew text *ad litteram* into Greek, renders the passage thus: "The sceptre of Juda shall not fail, nor the learned in the law who issue from his loins, till He comes to whom it is given, and to Him it shall be."

The sceptre of which the prophecy speaks cannot mean the regal power, since Juda obtained it only many centuries afterward; and it was done away with during the Babylonian captivity. Still, for five hundred years after this time, no Messiah of the Jews appeared. The prophecy must, therefore, speak either simply of political independence, or at least of the existence of the nation under its own laws, though subject to another. Now, the Holy Land became a Roman province shortly before Christ, and after His death the Jews were dispersed over the entire earth, so that they ceased to have any national existence at all. This state of things has been going on for the last eighteen centuries; therefore, the promised Messiah has appeared ages ago,

2. Daniel (ix) prophesied that, from the time of the decree of the Persian king allowing the restoration of the temple and the rebuilding of the walls of Jerusalem to the leader, Christ, there should intervene seventy weeks, not of days but of years. That in this prophecy there is question of the Messiah, is evident from the character and office ascribed to Him: for it is through Him that "transgression may be finished, sin may have an end, iniquity may be abolished, everlasting justice may be brought, vision and prophecy may be fulfilled, and the Saint of saints may be anointed." It is likewise prophesied that, sixty-two weeks after the rebuilding of the temple, Christ was to

be slain by His people, who were to deny Him; and in punishment thereof the sacrifice should cease, the temple should be destroyed, never to be rebuilt.

Now, although there may be some difficulty in determining the precise epoch from which to begin the seventy weeks, because the chronology of these times is somewhat obscure, still we know with certainty the period beyond which they could not extend, viz.: the destruction of the second temple of Jerusalem. This was destroyed more than eighteen hundred years ago. Therefore the time for the coming of the Messiah is long since past.

The Jews, moreover, were firmly convinced, at the time of Christ, that the seventy weeks of Daniel were drawing to a close, since at that precise time they eagerly looked for the promised Redeemer. For this reason the Jewish authorities sent to St. John, to ask him if he was the Messiah; hence, also, various impostors, who pretended to be the Expected One, succeeded for a time in finding many adherents among the people. Had the Jewish priests known that the time for the coming of the Messiah had not yet arrived, they would have silenced the apostles of Christ by simply telling the people so; still they never urged this argument. This shows, also, that the interpretation modern Jews give of the seventy weeks, which they pretend to be weeks not of years but of centuries, is absurd; besides, there is in Holy Writ no warrant for such interpretation; whereas the weeks of seven years are expressly mentioned in the twenty-fifth chapter of Leviticus.

3. A word now on the prophet himself. Daniel, having foretold the four great empires, the various vicissitudes which were to befall the Jewish nation, but, above all, having been so explicit about the time of the birth and death of the Messiah, is very unpopular with rationalistic critics. Some consider a myth whatever bears the impress of the supernatural; thus Daniel could have no existence, in spite of every historical document in his favor. Others, while admitting his existence, contend that he never wrote the prophecies attributed to him; they would like to make out these prophecies to be the work of some Christians. But this cannot be, since even the Jews acknowledge their truth. Hence others pretend that they were compiled at the time of Antiochus. Even this is a vain device, because the prophecy is contained both in the Hebrew and in the Septuagint, and the canon of the Jews was closed at the time of Esdras, about 400 B. C. Flavius Josephus, the Jewish historian, in his *Antiquities* (lib. xi, cap. 8), states that Alexander the Great not only spared the city of Jerusalem, but even conferred some privileges on the nation, because the High-Priest

Jeddoa had shown him the prophecy of Daniel, which foretold the overthrow of the Persian empire by the Greeks. This fact is, of course, also rejected by these modern critics, because it is their way to deny all things not suiting their preconceived theories. Yet the historical fact of Jerusalem having been spared, though Alexander had the intention of treating it in the same manner as he did Tyre, requires to be explained; and no other reason could be found than the one stated by Josephus, who certainly knew the history of his own nation far better than our contemporaries.

Moreover, the Jews would never have ranked the Book of Daniel among the writings of the other prophets, had they not been fully convinced of its authenticity, because their national pride would have been too deeply wounded by the prediction of their utter dispersion among the nations, the destruction of the temple, and the ceasing of the sacrifice. No impostor would have dared to predict so dire a calamity.

It has been objected that some words of Greek origin are found in Daniel, and hence it is inferred that the book must have been written at a period when Judæa was under Greek dominion. But the Greeks had already had much intercourse with the Persians at the time of Daniel; and thus it is not at all to be wondered at if a few of their expressions were adopted by him in his writings.

It is also urged that Daniel could not have written the prophecies, because the castle of Susa never belonged to the Babylonian kingdom. Yet even now, at that very spot, the tomb of Daniel is venerated, as it has been from time immemorial, by Christians and Mahometans alike. But, after all, what do Rationalists gain by saying that the prophecy of Daniel was composed two hundred years B. C.? It still remains a prophecy fulfilled in every point. The prophecy was, some critics contend, a spontaneous presentiment that had sprung up in the whole Jewish people; and so, to deprive Daniel of the gift of prophecy, they do not hesitate to bestow it on the whole nation. The Jews felt, no doubt, the spontaneous presentiment of their own destruction, two hundred years B. C., while, at the same time, as history shows, they expected that the coming Messiah was not only to restore their ancient splendor, but also to raise them above all other nations.

4. The Messiah was to come whilst the second temple of Jerusalem was still standing. For the Prophet Aggeus (ii, 10) foretells to the Jews that the second temple, though inferior in magnificence to the first, shall be more glorious, on account of the Messiah, who shall honor it by His presence. Malachias (iii, 1) likewise predicts that the Lord whom they seek, and the angel of the covenant, will come to this temple. Now, we repeat, it is eighteen hundred years since the destruction of the second temple.

CHAPTER XIV.

JESUS CHRIST IS THE MESSIAH PROMISED TO THE JEWS.

1. Christ alone realized what was foretold by the Prophets.—2. All the Prophecies are fulfilled in Him.—3. Dispersion of the Jews after His Death.

1. THOUGH many claimed, from time to time, to be the promised Messiah, and found some adherents, yet none save Jesus Christ realized everything foretold of him by the prophets. He alone, as facts prove, founded a religion spread over the entire earth; He, by means of His disciples, overthrew Paganism, and proclaimed the knowledge and the worship of the true God. He came, too, at a time when the Jews had lost their political independence, and shortly afterward they ceased to exist as a nation, and were dispersed through every land. At His time the seventy weeks foretold by Daniel were over; He visited the second temple of Jerusalem which, forty years after His death, was totally destroyed, and has never since been rebuilt, even in spite of the efforts of Julian the Apostate, who, though he tried his best to falsify Christ's predictions, was forced to desist from his enterprise.

2. Besides, all the prophecies relating to the Messiah were fulfilled in Jesus Christ: we shall mention only the most striking ones.

The Messiah was to be of the house of David (*Ps.* cix): Jesus was born of Mary, of the house of David.

He was to be born in the city of Bethlehem (*Mich.* v, 2): this was the birthplace of Mary's Son.*

He was to perform many miracles (*Isa.* xxxv, 4-6): these Christ did perform, as is related in the Gospels the authenticity of which we shall prove further on.

He was to die for our sins. (*Dan.* ix, 26; *Isa.* liii; *Ps.* xxi.) That there is question in this Psalm of the Messiah, we see from what is attributed to the one who is spoken of: " He shall declare the name of God to His brethren, He shall praise God in the midst of the church, and by His death many shall remember and be converted; all the nations of the earth and all the kindreds of the Gentiles shall adore in the sight of God."

---

* M. Renan pretends that Jesus Christ was not born at Bethlehem, because St. Matthew, who devotes a whole chapter to showing that this was His birthplace, states elsewhere that He was from Nazareth: really, a most conclusive argument! But he also objects: St. Luke states that the enrolling commanded by Augustus was made by Cyrinus, whereas from Josephus we know that Cyrinus was Governor of Syria only ten years after Archelaus; hence he concludes the story of Bethlehem and the Magi to be pure inventions subsequently added on. This is not a new objection. Various answers are given to it. Some say that the Greek text of St. Luke is to be translated thus: "This enrolment was made *before* Cyrinus was Governor of Syria." Others read: " Was first completed *when* " etc. Others

In the same Psalm the kind of death the Messiah was to suffer is foretold: His hands and His feet are to be pierced, *i. e.*, He is to be crucified, not according to the manner of the Jews, for they did not take off the clothes of those whom they attached to the cross, whereas it is here prophesied that those who were to crucify Him would divide His garments. Now all these circumstances were verified at the death of Jesus Christ.

3. The Jews, in punishment of their rejecting the Messiah, were to be dispersed among the nations of the earth. (*Dan.* ix, 26; *Isa.* viii, 14, 15; *Osee* iii, 4; *Jer.* xxx, 11; *Ezech.* xxxvii, 21, 22.) This took place shortly after the death of Christ, nor have they ever returned to their country as a nation. Yet, at the time when they were dispersed, they were not guilty of idolatry, but were most zealous in maintaining the law of Moses, at least outwardly.

---

answer that, though Cyrinus was titular governor only after Archelaus, he might have held the governorship *pro tem.* at the time mentioned by St. Luke. Be this as it may, St. Luke was too well informed of the events he relates for us to suppose him liable to so egregious a blunder. His work was read by many as well versed as himself in the history of their own times, and yet no exception was taken to it. Had this fact been invented, as our adversaries suppose, the mistake would have been corrected when perceived; but the fact itself of the mention of Cyrinus remaining intact shows that St. Luke's account is correct. This passage was not impugned by the first enemies of Christianity, though their facilities for proving such chronological misstatements were obviously far superior to those which critics of our day can boast of.

CHAPTER XV.

THE GENUINENESS AND AUTHENTICITY OF THE GOSPELS.

1. Genuineness of the Gospels proved by the testimony of the Writers of the first Centuries of the Church.—2. They could not have been Forgeries.—3. They were acknowledged by the Heretics of the earliest Ages.—4. The Jews admitted their Genuineness.—5. So did Pagan Writers.—6. The Gospels have undergone no Change.—7. Authenticity of the Gospels.—8. Christ's Miracles admitted by the Talmud.—9. Also by Pagan Writers.—10. Testimony of Josephus.—11. Genealogy of St. Matthew.—12. Assertions of modern Critics of the Rationalistic School.

1. THE history of Jesus Christ, His life, His doctrines, the miracles He wrought to confirm His divine mission, and to prove that He was the Messiah promised to the Jews and expected by them, are contained in the Four Gospels: St. Matthew's, St. Mark's, St. Luke's and St. John's. It is, therefore, necessary to establish both the genuineness and authenticity of these four books.

They are genuine, because they were always held to be the work of those whose name they bear, not only by Catholics, but also by heretics, Jews and Pagans. This tradition can be clearly traced in all the writings of every ancient ecclesiastical author. St. Justin the Martyr, in his first Apology (Nos. 66 and 67), states that at his time the Four Gospels were read publicly in the churches throughout the entire Christian world. Tertullian (*Contra Marcion.*, lib. iv, capp. 2, 4, 5; *De Præscript.* cap. 36) and Origen testify to the same fact. St. Irenæus, the disciple of St. Polycarp, who was himself instructed by the Apostle St. John, sums up the tradition of his time in the following words: "What concerns our salvation we have learnt solely from those through whom the Gospel has reached even unto us. They first preached it, and then gave it to us in writing, to be a foundation and a column of our faith. Thus Matthew, among the Hebrews, published a Gospel in their own tongue, whilst Peter and Paul preached the gospel at Rome, and founded the Church. After their departure, Mark, disciple and interpreter of Peter, left us in writing what Peter had preached; and Luke, the disciple of Paul, has written what the latter proclaimed. Afterward John, the disciple of the Lord, gave his own Gospel whilst living at Ephesus in Asia. . . . Lastly, the Gospels are so well established that the heretics themselves bear testimony to them, and each one endeavors to ground his own false doctrine on them. . . . There are neither more nor less than than the Four Gospels mentioned above. (*Contra Hæreses*, lib. iii, capp. 1 et 2.)

2. The authors of the first century do not mention the Four Gospels explicitly, but we find in their writings quotations evidently taken from the first three (as St. John's Gospel was written toward the end of that century). They do not always cite the texts *verbatim*, they give the sense rather than the words; but they follow the same method in quoting the Old Testament. Now, if the Four Gospels were read publicly in the churches in the second century, and acknowledged to be the work of the authors whose name they bear, they must necessarily be genuine. Had there been any forgery, this must have taken place either during the lifetime of the apostles, or shortly after their death, when many who had known them were still alive, for St. John did not die till the beginning of the second century. But, in either case, forgery was impossible, as the apostles or their disciples would have protested against the fraud, and thus the Gospels would never have been received as genuine by all the churches. This is confirmed by the fact that several apocryphal gospels were in circulation, which for a time were adopted as genuine by some individuals and even by some churches, but the imposition was soon detected and exposed, protests arose, and so their general acceptance was prevented; whereas, with regard to the Four Gospels, no such protests were ever made.

3. The earlier heretics, such as the Ebionites, the Valentinians, the Encratites, and others, admitted the Gospels; but either they endeavored to interpret them in their own fashion, or they rejected some parts of them. At their time the fraud, if any, was too recent not to be detected; and, as Catholics used the Gospels to refute these heretics, the latter would not have failed to deny their genuineness, had it been possible to do so. The Gnostics pretended that the evangelists had written for the people only, not for philosophers, who had received a higher and sublimer doctrine. The Ebionites asserted that the sacred writers, with the exception of St. Matthew, had favored the Gentiles too much. They thereby acknowledged the Gospels as written by the authors whose name they bear.

4. The Jews, though it was their interest to look upon the Gospels as fictitious, never thought of impugning their genuineness. In their Talmud, they attribute the miracles related in the Gospels either to witchcraft or to the unlawful use of the name of Jehovah.

5. Celsus, Porphyrius, Hierocles, and Julian the Apostate, pagan writers, most deadly enemies of Christianity, never dreamt of denying the genuineness of the Gospels. Celsus attributed Christ's miracles to magical arts; Porphyrius is satisfied with finding contradictions in the Gospels; Hierocles only tried to set off against

the miracles of Christ the pretended prodigies performed by Apollonius of Tyana. Though the genuineness of the Gospels was never questioned by the enemies of the Church in the first ages, when the supposed forgery, being so recent, could easily have been detected, modern critics, after eighteen hundred years, have undertaken to show that the Gospels were written, not by the evangelists, but by some Christian writers in the second and third centuries, when the notion that Christ was the promised Messiah and God had already taken deep root in the minds of His disciples. They have even found (in their imagination) a primitive gospel in the Aramean tongue, which is said to be the main stock on which subsequent writers grafted their own inventions and embellishments, though none of the Christians of the first ages ever had any inkling of the existence of such a work. But this is a special privilege of the modern critical school. If documents are wanting, they draw them from the innermost recesses of their self-consciousness.

6. That the Gospels have come down to us without substantial change, is proved from the agreement of the most ancient versions, such as the Syriac and the Italic; also from their agreement with the quotations made by the earliest Christian writers. Besides, it would have been impossible to tamper with the Gospels: because, first, they were considered as the word of God,

a most sacred deposit, containing the title-deeds of the Church, and the main part of the divine revelation intrusted to her; secondly, because the leading principle of the Church, that in matters of faith no change whatever is to be tolerated, prevented the introduction of any substantial change in the sacred writings. Then again, the Gospels were not hidden in some obscure library, known only to a few; but copies of them were successively written, which the different churches were eager to obtain for public reading during divine service; and with their spread the difficulty of introducing the slightest change increased. Now, as, according to St. Justin's testimony, the Gospels were read publicly in every church in the second century, it is evident that no substantial change could have gone unremarked.

To this we must add the great veneration in which the Gospels were held. Bishop Spiridin, as Sozomene remarks, openly rebuked a fellow bishop, who, in quoting a text, substituted another word having the same meaning as the original, but which appeared more elegant. St. Jerome could with difficulty be prevailed upon by Pope Damasus to revise the Latin version of the Bible, for fear of being looked upon by the people as a corrupter of the sacred text, should they find some alterations. (*Præfat. ad Evang. ad Dam.*) And this fear of St. Jerome's was certainly not groundless, as we learn from a letter of St. Augustine to the same (*Epist.* 71, *ad Hieron.* Edit. 1679): "A bishop of our province," writes the saint, "having begun to read your translation of the Bible in his church, came to a passage of the prophet Jonas, which you have translated differently from what was known to the memory and ears of every one, and sung during many generations. Thereupon a great tumult arose among the people, caused principally by the Greeks, who cried out that the text was falsified. The bishop saw himself obliged to appeal to the testimony of some Jews; these, either through ignorance or malice, stated that the Hebrew text was the same as the Greek and the old Latin version. The bishop, not to remain without a flock, after this great danger, was obliged to correct the passage as if it were a fault."

7. The Gospels are authentic. When they were written, many were still alive who had witnessed the facts therein related. The evangelists would never have dared to deceive the people in recording events of the highest importance, that were well known and had been witnessed by many. Nor had the sacred writers any motive whatever for imposture, as we shall prove in the next chapter. Moreover, many Jews embraced Christianity, and thereby bound themselves to a law which not only did not offer to them the slightest worldly advantage, but actually

exposed them to persecution, loss of property, and even loss of life. Now, as the motive that impelled them to do so was plainly their conviction that the facts related in the Gospels were true, and as they could easily have discovered any imposture in this matter, we should have to reject all human testimony before denying the truth of these facts.

8. Infidels do not deny Gospel facts, so long as they are not miraculous; their sole objection lies against the supernatural ones. But these miracles were not denied by the Jews, the worst enemies of the Christian name. For, in the Talmud, both of Jerusalem and Babylon, they pretend that Christ found the name of Jehovah engraved on a stone, and with this talisman worked all his wonders.

9. Pagans themselves admitted the truth of these miracles, but in general they attributed them, as we said before, to witchcraft. Tertullian and Eusebius * relate how the Emperor Tiberius was so much struck with the report sent in by Pontius Pilate, that he proposed to the senate to place Christ among the gods of the empire; but this the senate declined. Lampridius (*Alexand. Severi Vita*, pp. 123 et 129, Edit. 1620) states that the Emperor Hadrian had the same desire of ranking Christ among the gods, but the pagan priests thwarted his design.

---
* "*Historia Ecclesiæ,*" lib. ii, cap. 2.

10. The testimony of Josephus (*Antiq. of the Jews*, lib. xviii, cap. 4) has been rejected by many critics, because he mentions the miracles of Christ, His death and resurrection; but such rejection is groundless. Josephus, in his history, could not omit mentioning Christ, because the events our Lord was connected with were too important to be ignored; he also speaks of St. John the Baptist and of James the Less. The passage is coherent with the whole context. Eusebius read this passage in ancient manuscripts, and cites it against the Jews (*Demonst. Evang.*, lib. iii, cap. 5; *Historia Eccles.*, lib. i, cap. 11); and it is still to be found in many copies. It was wanting in some manuscripts; but, as the work was a Jewish history, it must often have been transcribed for that people, and some of these Jewish copyists must have left out the passage relating to Jesus Christ. The Vatican library contains a manuscript copy, perhaps the most ancient; the text may be seen there, but effaced, most probably by a Jewish hand.

11. It has been urged against us that the genealogy of St. Matthew does not agree with that of St. Luke. There is, no doubt, an apparent contradiction; still, as it was known to the first Christians, who, being able to point it out, did not find in it the slightest ground of doubt, we may with certainty affirm that there is not any real contradiction between these two accounts.

Various ways have been proposed to reconcile this seeming discrepancy. Perhaps the best is to say that St. Matthew gave the genealogy of St. Joseph, while that of St. Luke is the genealogy of the Blessed Virgin Mary.

There are some few other difficulties of the same kind; but, as they could not have escaped the first Christians, a great number of whom were not unlettered, and as no opposition was made by them, nor even the slightest attempt to correct these apparent contradictions, we are forced to admit the truth of the Gospels, and to confess that these difficulties arise solely from our ignorance of the customs and manners of the Jews at the time when the sacred record was written. Besides, there is not one of these difficulties that has not been fully explained by ecclesiastical writers both ancient and modern.

12. Some infidel writers were bold enough to assert that the apostles were mere impostors, who wrote and preached what they knew to be false. This supposition has been pronounced untenable, even by many in their own camp; the whole conduct of the apostles shows their sincerity and firm conviction of the truths they proclaimed. Hence recourse is had to the convenient makeshift of hallucination. This is indeed a new and startling theory. A dozen of ignorant maniacs set about reforming the whole world, and are eminently successful. Though deprived

of all human assistance, they succeed in establishing a Church, the most stupendous of institutions, which, for nearly nineteen centuries, has withstood all imaginable attacks from without and from within. And these maniacs compiled a body of doctrine and a code of morals which has been admired and followed by the greatest minds among men. Such a theory, forsooth, can be none other than a foolish dream!

Another class of writers look upon the facts related in the Gospels as substantially true, but they endeavor to explain away on natural grounds everything miraculous. Thus, the star which guided the Magi was a lantern; the walking on the sea, a mere swimming feat; the multiplication of the loaves and fishes, a judicious distribution of the food which was at hand; the apparition of angels, men covered with white sheets; the Resurrection, an awakening from a trance; the Ascension, a clever disappearance during a fog. These are the deep thoughts of the naturalistic school. The mythical school, on the contrary, asserts that none of the miracles related in the Gospels ever took place; yet the writers are not to be looked upon as liars, for they used these miraculous events as mere myths, or symbols, with which to convey some truth to the mind. Strauss even goes so far as to consider Christ himself as a mere myth. Between these two schools a most relentless war is waged. The former assert that it is absurd to deny all facts without sufficient ground. The latter laugh at the miserable attempts made to explain miracles by natural means. We must, say they, either admit the whole fact together with its supernaturalness, or deny it altogether. Thus it is that our adversaries end by refuting each other. Indeed, the very blows they aim at the truth of the Gospels are a clear proof that nothing reasonable can be urged against the evangelists.

CHAPTER XVI.

THE RESURRECTION OF CHRIST ATTESTS HIS DIVINE MISSION.

1. Christ foretold His Death and Resurrection.—2 His Death was real.—3. Christ rose from the Dead.—How His Enemies account for this Fact.—4. The Apostles were not deceived.—5. Did not deceive.—6. Could not deceive, even had they wished.—7. Testimony of the Apostles confirmed by the Behavior of the Jewish Authorities.—8. They confirmed their Testimony with their Blood.—9. Why the Jews refused to believe.—10. Apparent Contradiction between St. Mark and St. John.—11. Spread of the Gospel throughout the whole World.

1. CHRIST foretold both His death and resurrection, giving this resurrection as a sign of His divine mission. (*Matt.* xii, 39, 40; xvi, 1–4.) This prediction was known to His enemies: the priests and the Pharisees asked Pilate to have the sepulchre guarded, for fear His disciples should steal away the body, and give out that He had risen from the dead. (*Matt.* xxvii, 62–66.)

2. Some unbelievers pretend that Christ was not dead, but simply in a trance, and thus they expect to get rid of the testimony of the apostles, who affirmed that He rose from the dead. But Christ did really die. This is attested by the

evangelists, and their testimony cannot be gainsaid. The sufferings Christ endured during His passion were sufficient to cause death. Had Christ not been dead, the spear-thrust in His sacred side would of itself have been fatal. Pilate did not allow the body of Christ to be taken down from the cross without having first ascertained His death. The priests and the Pharisees who placed guards around the sepulchre would not have omitted to ascertain whether Christ's body was in the tomb, and whether life was really extinct. Had there been the least spark of life in Christ after His taking down from the cross, the manner of His burial, His body being embalmed in spices, would have extinguished it. The Jews, to account for the disappearance of Christ's body from the sepulchre, never had recourse to the supposition that Christ had revived from a trance, for they were sure of His death.

3. Christ rose from the dead. It is a well established fact that, on the morning of the third day after His death, His body had disappeared from the tomb, in spite of the precautions taken by the Jews to guard it. To account for this fact, the Jewish authorities spread the report that His disciples had stolen the body whilst the soldiers, put to guard it, were asleep. The disciples, on the contrary, affirmed that Christ rose from the dead, that they had seen Him and conversed with Him for forty days; and St.

Matthew openly charges the Jewish authorities with having bribed the soldiers who had witnessed Christ's resurrection. In view of these two accounts, we are compelled to infer that, since the Jewish magistrates had no better reason to allege, they well knew the truth of Christ's resurrection, but did not wish the people to become aware of it. How, indeed, could the disciples have mustered up courage enough to carry out the supposed theft? They were afraid to show themselves in public; how, then, would they have dared to meet the Roman soldiers? And, even had they been so bold as to attempt it, they could never have succeeded. The soldiers knew too well the importance of the post intrusted to them; they could not have been so forgetful of their duty as to have all deliberately fallen asleep together. But, granting this to be the case, the disciples could not have rolled from the mouth of the sepulchre the huge stone which closed it, without awakening the soldiers who, if they slept, were lying close by; and, if they were really asleep, and did not awake whilst the body was being carried off, how could they testify that the disciples had come to steal it? The soldiers, moreover, were not punished, as they should have been, for such a serious dereliction of duty: on the contrary, they received a great sum of money to spread the report that the body had been stolen.

4. The account given by the apostles, on the other hand, is entirely trustworthy ; for they were neither deceived themselves, nor could they have deceived others, even if they had wished. They were not deceived themselves: because Christ was seen, not by one person alone, or by a few individuals, or a few times only, but again and again He appeared, now to some, now to all the apostles united together; they ate with Him, they conversed with Him, they could touch Him, they could behold the marks of His wounds in His feet, and hands, and side ; they saw Him work miracles. At last He was seen by five hundred persons at once. The disciples were not over-credulous: they refused to give credit to those who first reported having seen Him, and believed only when they themselves had been witnesses of the fact. To suppose a hallucination in such a case is utterly absurd.

5. They did not deceive others, because they had no motive whatever for doing so. They could not have been led thereto by any temporal motive: being aware of the hatred of the Jewish nation, principally of the priests and magistrates, against Christ, they knew that, by spreading the report of Christ's resurrection, they would draw upon themselves the fury of their enemies, who had both the power and the will to make them rue their attempt at deception. They could not imagine that, by preaching a counterfeit resurrection,

they would do something agreeable to God, and promote their eternal welfare: for they well knew that, if Christ did not rise from the dead, He was an impostor; and they were not ignorant of the heavy punishment threatened in the law of Moses against those who dared to spread false doctrines among the people. The apostles, therefore, could have no motive whatever to deceive, but every motive, both human and divine, deterred them from doing so.

6. Granting, however, that they wished to deceive, never could they have entertained even the slightest hope of success, for they asserted a fact which could most easily have been verified: they were in the power of the Jewish authorities, who had at hand every means to detect the fraud, and whose duty and interest prompted them to punish it most severely. Moreover, the apostles preached a doctrine distasteful both to Jews and Gentiles,—a doctrine opposed to their opinions, prejudices, customs and habits; they inculcated precepts difficult to practise; they flattered none of the passions of the human breast; and at the same time they could not promise to their followers even the slightest temporal advantage: they could hold out to them nothing but contempt, loss of property and social standing, persecution, nay, even the most cruel death, which awaited the followers of Christ. Nor could those who embraced the doctrine proclaimed by the apostles

entertain the hope of soon seeing these persecutions followed by temporal prosperity; because they had been expressly told the contrary. Now, it is a fact that the apostles succeeded in converting multitudes from every class of society; and this, in spite of the persecutions to which all those who embraced their doctrine were exposed. It is, therefore, necessary to confess that the proofs which the apostles proposed must have been undeniable, since, as experience shows us every day, no one allows himself to be subjected to obligations disagreeable and painful to nature, unless he hopes to derive therefrom great temporal advantages, or unless he sees that those who impose the duty have a full and indisputable right to do so. But the principal proof brought forward by the apostles was the resurrection of Christ. (1 *Cor.* xv, 14, and *Acts, passim.*) Therefore this fact must have been beyond the possibility of doubt, or the existence of Christianity baffles explanation: it becomes an effect without a cause. Fanaticism may indeed induce some to brave death, in order to uphold a falsehood; but it is absurd to suppose that this could have actuated so many millions of Christians of every rank, age and condition, and under such cruel torments, during such a length of time. Fanatics are far from being meek and humble: love for their enemies is not their characteristic virtue; yet this was, without exception, the leading trait of every Christian martyr.

7. Nay, the very behavior of the Jewish magistrates confirms the testimony of the apostles. It was both the duty and the interest of the authorities to investigate juridically the alleged fact of Christ's resurrection, and to convict the apostles of fraud and impiety. They had the power to institute an inquiry into the matter. If the testimony of the apostles was false, they were guilty of a great crime, and, according to the law of Moses, deserved death. Yet no such investigation took place. The apostles were, indeed, brought before the tribunal, but not tried; they were merely threatened with punishment if they should persist in announcing the name of Christ; again they are cited before the judges, they are condemned to be scourged, but still no trial is instituted. The only reason for the neglect of this duty, to the fulfilment of which the Jewish authorities were urged by religion as well as by self-interest, pride and hatred, was their dread of a public trial, lest the fact which they knew to be true should become still more widely known, and be juridically established. They preferred to hush up the matter.

8. The apostles, moreover, confirmed their assertion by many miracles, which were not denied, because witnessed by too many persons, but which were attributed to witchcraft. All of them, without a single exception, sealed their testimony with their blood. True, St. John did

not die a martyr; but he underwent the torments of martyrdom when he was thrown into a caldron of boiling oil.

9. But it may be asked why the Jews, seeing so many miracles, and having the certainty of Christ's resurrection, did not receive Him as their Messiah. The reason is, that Christ's doctrine was in opposition to their passions and their much-cherished prejudices. They did not feel inclined to follow a law which attacked their pride and self-love. Besides, they hoped for a Messiah who should be a temporal ruler, and free them from the hated yoke of the Romans. They cared little for the spiritual kingdom Christ sought to establish on earth, and hence tried to attribute all His miracles, and those of His disciples, to diabolical illusions and witchcraft.

10. It is urged that there is a contradiction between the accounts of St. Mark and St. John, as regards the time of Christ's crucifixion; for one states that it took place at the third hour, and the other at the sixth. But we must remark that at that time there was among the Jews a twofold way of counting time. The day was divided into four parts, each containing three hours; these parts were also called hours: hence the third hour began at noon. The day was also divided into twelve hours, beginning at six o'clock in the morning, so that, according to this computation, the sixth hour was noon. Now St.

Mark made use of the former method, and St. John of the latter.

Christ, it is said, foretold that He would remain in the tomb three days and three nights; whereas, according to the Gospel narrative, He remained only one whole night—from Friday to Saturday—in the sepulchre. To this we reply that, according to the Jewish custom, a part of a day or night was considered, in ordinary language, as a whole day or night. (Conf. Lightfoot, *Horæ Hebraicæ*, Lipsiæ, 1684, ad cap. xii, 40, *Matt.*)

There are some apparent contradictions in the Gospel accounts as to the time of the resurrection, and the various apparitions; but these seeming differences vanish before a careful comparative scrutiny of the sacred writers. They have long since been cleared up by the ancient Fathers of the Church. (See Hesychius of Jerusalem, in his sermon on Christ's resurrection, which is generally found among the works of St. Gregory Nyssen, to whom this sermon was formerly attributed.)

11. Lastly, we may add that the existence of the Christian religion, in spite of every possible obstacle to its establishment at its rise and to its continuance ever after, is a fact which, unless we admit the truth of the miracles of Christ and of His apostles in confirmation of their teaching baffles explanation, and would, of itself, be the most astounding miracle of them all. St. Augus-

tine has beautifully developed this thought in his work, *De Civitate Dei* (lib. xxii, cap. 3). How, in truth, could a few ignorant men, devoid of all human aid, succeed in converting not only the Roman world, but many other nations, to a doctrine so much at variance with human pride and self-love; and this in spite of the most cruel and relentless persecutions, which began at the very birth of Christianity, and lasted for about three hundred years? Even under the more humane Roman emperors, the persecuting laws were never repealed; and we read of many martyrs who suffered during their reign. Some enemies of Christianity have pretended that the number of martyrs was greatly exaggerated by Christian writers; however, we have not only their testimony, but also that of pagan authors, such as Tacitus (*Annal.*, lib. xv), who says that under Nero a vast multitude (*multitudo ingens*) of Christians were put to death. The policy inaugurated by this emperor was, with but few exceptions, continued more or less by his successors, principally by Domitian, Trajan, Severus, Decius, Valerius and Aurelian; but the last persecution, under Diocletian, Maximian, and Galerius, was so terrible that Eusebius of Cæsarea, who lived in those times, could say that the multitude of those who suffered for Christ could not be counted. (*Hist. Eccles.*, lib. viii, cap. 4.) The slaughter was so great that the persecutors, flattering themselves that they had blotted out the very name of Christian, struck a medal with the inscription, "*Nomine Christiano Deleto;*" and all in vain. When Constantine, shortly afterward, became Roman Emperor, the world was Catholic, and the words of Tertullian (*Apologia*, sec. 50), " The blood of martyrs is the seed of Christians," were then, as always, verified. The tortures inflicted on Christians are incredible. Nero had them covered with pitch, to serve as lamps in his gardens. They were put into red-hot brazen bulls, so that their cries might imitate the bellowing of the animal; they were burnt by slow fires, placed on gridirons to be roasted to death, stretched on the rack, torn to pieces with iron combs, exposed to wild beasts, beaten to death with clubs or scourges; nay, the governors of provinces vied with one another in inventing new and unheard-of torments, to win the favor of the emperors. Many thousands were always condemned to the mines and quarries, and there left to a lingering death. Not only men of robust health were subjected to these torments, but persons of every age, sex, condition and rank, from the slave to the senator, and persons of imperial lineage. Yet they suffered with resignation, and even with joy.

It has been urged that the converts to Christianity were only slaves, or persons belonging to the lowest strata of society, who were enticed by the doctrines of liberty and equality preached by Christian teachers. But, on the one hand, these teachers were far from preaching rebellion: they inculcated the duty of obedience to masters and to the constituted authorities, in all things not opposed to the law of God; the liberty they held out was the liberty of the children of God: freedom from sin, and the conquest of self. On the other hand, it is an egregious historical mistake to fancy that only slaves and the lower orders professed Christianity. Pliny the Younger, toward the end of the first century, writes to Trajan (lib. x, cap. 97): "It seems to me to be worthy of consideration, on account of the great number exposed to danger (of being put to death for their faith); for many of every age, every rank (*omnis ordinis*), of both sexes, are and will be liable to danger."

Tertullian, in his *Apology* (cap. 37), says: "We are but of yesterday, and we have filled every place among you—cities, islands, fortresses, towns, market-places, the very camp, tribes, companies, palace, senate, forum: we have left nothing to you but the temples of your gods."

Among the Christians of the first ages were many men of eminent learning. It is enough to name St. Polycarp, St. Ignatius of Antioch, St. Irenæus, St. Justinus, Clement of Alexandria, Ammonius, and Athenagoras. The Christian school at Alexandria was from the first renowned for its learning, and was frequented even by many pagan scholars. (*Hieronym. in Præfat. ad Catal. de Script. Ecclesiasticis.*) Among the earlier martyrs, we have members of the imperial family, persons of consular dignity, senators, magistrates, officers of the highest rank in the army, philosophers, and many wealthy citizens.

The infidel Gibbon, in his *Decline and Fall of the Roman Empire*, has attempted to account by natural means for the fact of the rapid spread of the Gospel. First, he says, the easy intercommunication established by the Romans through the whole empire facilitated the spread of the new religion. This is very true; but it did not make the doctrine of Christ more acceptable to the people, nor take away the great opposition which the preachers of Christianity met with from the opinions and passions of men. If the easy communications enabled missionaries to penetrate everywhere, the persecuting edicts of the Roman emperors could also speed with extraordinary rapidity through the whole empire, and reach even the most retired nooks where Christians would be seeking shelter.

Many, says Gibbon, were inclined to mysticism, and despised the extravagances of idol worship. This tendency might dispose a few chosen spirits to embrace the truth, but many others were led by it into the absurdities of Neoplatonism. The great majority of pagan philosophers were the most deadly enemies of Christianity. The contempt for Paganism manifested by many of them did not originate in a love for truth, but in a spirit of scepticism and unbelief; the Christian religion was hateful to them, and, with all their contempt for Paganism, they upheld the national religion through political motives. As to the people, they were animated with a bitter hatred against Christians, which was purposely fostered by many calumnies spread by the more educated classes of society, in order to keep men from accepting the doctrine of Christ.

Gibbon also pretends that the many wars waged by the Romans against barbarous nations greatly helped to spread the knowledge of Christianity even beyond the limits of the Roman Empire. This was no doubt the *occasion* of giving to the surrounding nations a knowledge of the Christian religion, but it cannot be taken as a *cause* prompting them to submit to its precepts.

The wonderful charity of the faithful, not only among themselves, but also toward their enemies, was, beyond doubt, a powerful motive for many to join the Church, because it was easily seen that such charity was a supernatural, not a natural, virtue. The abundant alms distributed by Christians might have been, with many, a natural motive for professing the Christian doctrine, had they not had at all times before their eyes the danger of death, to which they exposed themselves by becoming Christians.

Gibbon urges the foolish argument of Julian the Apostate: The Christians are eager to receive all kinds of sinners into their communion. If there be, says Julian, a corrupter of female chastity, a murderer, a man guilty of the most atrocious crimes, let him come with confidence; as soon as water has been poured over him, he will be pure, and, should he fall again into the same crimes, he may expiate them by shaving his head and striking his breast. It is quite true that Christians did not refuse to admit even the greatest sinners into their fold; but the first and indispensable condition was, that they should mend their ways, and live up to the precepts of the Gospel. This fact, of itself, proves the divinity of a religion which was able to transform monsters of wickedness into models of virtue. Julian himself, writing to Arsacius, the pagan highpriest in Galatia (*Epist.* 49. Edit. Spanheim), urges him to exhort Pagans to imitate the holy lives of the Christians.

Another argument is the miraculous power which Christians were supposed to possess, and which induced many to embrace the faith. But whether or not Christians were endowed with this gift, could easily be tested; because these miracles were performed in the light of day, in the amphitheatre before hundreds of thousands of people—before the crowd surrounding the judgment-seat of persecution. The acceptance of the Christian religion on the evidence of miracles cannot be looked upon as an event brought about by natural causes.

Again, it is said, people are always fond of novelties, and easily follow them. This is true, if the novelties are in harmony with nature, not if they contradict it and exact great sacrifices without prospect of temporal good. Hence a love of novelty could not have influenced those who became Christians.

Finally, even the efforts of Paganism to crush the Church have been assigned as a natural cause for its spread, on the plea that persecution is sufficient to insure the perpetuation of an error. This may be true of some misguided persons, whom persecution, for a time, renders more obstinate: some of them may even brave death; but there still remains a great difference between such men and the Christian martyrs. The former may hold out for a while; but, should the persecution last, many will seek safety in emigration; others will submit, at least outwardly, to the ruling powers, or, if they see the least chance of success, they will have recourse to arms in order to enforce toleration, or become persecutors in their turn: never will they cherish feelings of charity toward their enemies, because meekness and love of enemies is not the characteristic trait of fanatics.

Very different was the conduct of the Christians. They had to suffer the most dreadful torments for three centuries; never did they, as a class, conform outwardly to the will of the persecutor; and yet the throwing of a few grains of incense on the brazier might not only have saved their property and lives, but procured them the favor of the ruling powers. They did not hate their enemies; they did good to them whenever they could. They allowed themselves to be butchered, though oftentimes they might have resisted successfully by force of arms. Those who suffered for their faith are not a few hundred, but many millions, of every age, and sex, and rank. Yet the number of the Christians, far from diminishing, swelled after each successive trial.

No parallel can be instituted between the propagation of the Christian religion and that of Mahometanism or the Protestant sects. Of the former we have said enough in the eighth chapter. Protestantism began by stripping Christianity of everything unpleasant to nature: penances, fasting, confession; it fostered spiritual pride, by making each one the arbiter of his own religion; it enticed the nobles and princes to embrace the new religion, by holding out independence from the salutary restraint of the Holy See, and the rich plunder of churches and monasteries; it allured priests and religious, by making away with their vow of chastity. What wonder, then, that, with motives such as these, many were brought to abandon the Church? Still, despite these enticements, Protestantism was soon checked in its growth, and, owing to the absence of a principle of unity, it rapidly broke up into a host of fragmentary sects. At present it is in a state of utter disintegration, many of its adherents drifting naturally into open unbelief, and yet persuaded that they are stanch Protestants. Another reason why the two cases (of Protestantism and Catholicism) are not parallel, is this: it is far more difficult to make people embrace a new religion totally at variance with the one professed before, than to corrupt a religion already in existence, by persuading the people that salvation can be had at less cost, and cloaking over this apostasy with the plausible name of reformation.

All attempts, therefore, to explain the spread and maintenance of the Christian religion on natural grounds are futile, and we are compelled to admit that it is of divine origin.

It remains now to show which of the many societies calling themselves Christian is the one founded by Christ: this will form the second part of the present treatise.

PART II.

INTRODUCTION.

JESUS CHRIST being the Messiah promised to the Jews, the religion He established on earth is the only true one, to be embraced and professed by all men. But, unfortunately, those who call themselves Christians do not all agree as to Christian Doctrine and practice; many rival churches exist, each claiming to profess the true title-deeds of the Divine Founder; yet of all these one alone can be true.

It is admitted on all hands by those who profess to be Christians, that Christ established on earth a Church, or a visible society of true believers; the New Testament speaks constantly of the Church as a visible association of the faithful, so much so indeed that to prove it were needless. The idea of a church whose outward action cannot be perceived, has long since been abandoned as untenable; for an invisible society which nobody knows, whose existence cannot be discovered, whose teaching and action cannot be laid hold of, is no society at all, and it is quite impossible for any one to join it. Hence all sects, whatever be the name by which they are known, form external associations, profess certain doctrines, use outward rites, and claim that their society is framed after the model drawn out in Holy Writ, and that they are the true Church.* Now, as it is impossible that all these rival churches, holding doctrines at variance one with another, can be *the* Church founded by Christ, we have to consult the records left us by the apostles and disciples of our Lord, if we want to establish its identity; forasmuch as its foundation is an historical fact, it can be proved by historical monuments alone.

Although the apostles did not leave in writing the whole of the teachings of Christ, but handed down by tradition many doctrines and practices, still the New Testament contains the main documents or title-deeds of the Church. The genuineness and authenticity of the Four Gospels have already been established; the Acts, the Epistles, and the Apocalypse stand on the same ground. In the second century of our era, according to Tertullian (*Cont. Marcionem*, lib. iv, capp. 2,

---

* It must, however, be admitted, that, though the Protestant sects have always kept up an outward organization and formed a visible society, the theory of the invisibility of the Church is intimately connected with their system, and is even at present taught by some of them. Those who pretend that the predestined or the just, or the predestined and the just alone, are the true members of Christ's Church, must needs hold that the Church is invisible; for here on earth it is impossible to know who is predestined and who is just. Others teach that the Church is partly invisible and partly visible; the invisible portion are the predestined or the just, or both together, and to this portion all the promises made by Christ to His Church belong exclusively; the other members of the sect form the visible body. Others again hold that, according to the promises of Christ,

4, 5; *De Præscript.*, cap. 36), these writings were publicly read in all the churches of Christendom, and acknowledged as the genuine production of the apostles.

But it should be observed that, although in the present controversy we use the writings of the New Testament, we are not, as yet, considering them as divinely inspired, but only as the faithful records of the teachings and actions of the apostles. The inspiration of the writings of the New Testament cannot be proved by historical criticism; it rests solely on the authority of the true Church. This remark suffices to set aside one of the chief arguments employed by Protestants against us, viz., that we fall into the sophism called by logicians *the vicious circle*. For, say they, you prove the Church from Scripture, and then Scripture from the Church. By no means. We prove the existence of the Church and her attributes from the New Testament, considered

---

the Church ought indeed to form a visible society; yet they maintain it may happen that this visibility be for some time very much obscured, or even disappear altogether. This last position all Protestants must necessarily take up: because, if it be true, as they pretend, that for many centuries the Church had fallen into idolatry and corrupted the faith; if her acknowledged head, the pope, be Antichrist; if, instead of being the spouse of Christ, the Church had become the harlot of Babylon, then, indeed, not only did the Church become invisible, but its existence must have ceased altogether. The only means of saving somehow the visibility of the Church would be to look upon the whole series of heretics, whom the Church always excluded from her fold, as the true Church of Christ, howsoever absurd and blasphemous may have been the doctrines they proclaimed. This has actually been held by some Protestants.

as a faithful historical record of what Christ and His apostles taught; then, having thus established the authority of the Church as a divinely appointed teacher, we learn from her that the Scriptures are inspired. Surely no flaw can be found in this line of argument.

EVIDENCES OF RELIGION.

PART II.

ON THE CHURCH ESTABLISHED BY CHRIST.

CHAPTER I.

DIVINITY OF CHRIST.

1. Importance of the Dogma of the Divinity of Christ.—2. Exposition of the Dogma.—3. Divinity of Christ supposed by the Economy of the Christian Religion.—4. Traditions of Pagan Nations.—5. Prophecies of the Old Testament proving the Divinity of the Messiah.—6. Assertions of Rationalists.—7. Divinity of Christ not invented either by St. Paul or by St. John.—8. Testimony from St. Matthew, St. Luke and St. John.—9. From St. Paul.—10. Traditions of the first Ages of the Church before the Heresy of Arius.—11. Solution of some Difficulties.

1. BEFORE investigating the nature and properties of the Church, it is necessary to inquire who Christ is. Is He merely a messenger sent by God, as Moses and the prophets were? Or is He something more than man? The issue of this question is of paramount importance: neither the institution of the Church, nor the powers and offices conferred upon her, can be rightly understood and duly appreciated, unless we possess a full

knowledge of Christ Himself. Who, then, is Jesus Christ? Arius dared to teach that Christ was a mere man, born in time, who, however, could be called God, for the many graces and superhuman powers vested in Him. Modern Unitarians hold the same doctrine. The Semi-Arians allowed the existence of Christ from all eternity, His similarity to God, and still they proclaimed Him to be a mere creature.

2. But the whole Christian Church has ever believed that Christ is true God and true man, the second person of the Holy Trinity, coequal with the Father and the Holy Ghost; He took upon Himself our human nature, to suffer and die for our redemption. In Christ, therefore, there are two natures entirely distinct: the divine and the human; but these two natures being hypostatically united, there is in Him one person only: the divine one, supplying the personality of the human nature. Thus the actions performed by the sacred humanity, though finite in themselves, are yet infinite in dignity and merit, since, owing to the hypostatic union, they belong in truth to the person of the Godhead; and Christ, who as God can say: I am the infinite Ruler and Lord of the universe, as man may also say: I have suffered and died on the cross.

3. The whole economy of the Christian religion necessarily supposes the divinity of the Redeemer; without it Christianity is meaningless.

Hence those who deny it, deny the Atonement also, one of the main pivots on which revolves our whole religious belief. Both the Jewish and the Christian revelation teach that man is a fallen being; that Adam, by transgressing God's command that he must not eat of the forbidden fruit, placed himself and his whole posterity in the power of the Evil One, and that neither he nor any of his descendants could, by their own efforts, break the chains that held them captive, nor regain the right to the heavenly inheritance forfeited by sin. Almighty God, taking pity on the human race immediately after the fall, promised to our first parents a Redeemer, who was to free them from the power of Satan, and reopen to them the gates of heaven. God might, indeed, have pardoned sin without exacting a full and rigorous satisfaction to His divine majesty; but He willed that a complete atonement should be made: the promised Redeemer was to suffer and die for the sins of man, and thus reconcile him to his Maker.

This was foretold by the prophets; this, too, was the reason of the rite of sacrifice instituted by God after the fall as a means of remission for sin; and this rite drew its efficacy from the sacrifice to be offered by the Redeemer, and was at the same time a public manifestation of the belief in the coming Messiah. But a mere human being, however perfect, could not have made this atonement; for, on the one hand, his actions, being finite, could never adequately satisfy the Divine Majesty offended by sin; on the other hand, being a mere child of Adam, and thus subject, like the rest of mankind, to the power of the Evil One, he himself would have stood in need of redemption, and could never have redeemed his fellowmen. To accomplish this work, it was necessary that God should become man. But might not an angel have been sent to redeem us? No; for, waiving the question whether angelic spirit might be hypostatically united to human nature, an angel's actions, being finite, could not give to God the atonement required by His divine majesty.

4. This was implied in the belief, not of the Jews only, but of all the nations of antiquity. If we analyze ancient religions, and separate the primitive traditions from fable and fancy, we discover everywhere the fall of man, the expiatory value of sacrifice, the expectation of a Redeemer not man, but God himself.

In the Zend-Avesta, the first man and woman are said to have been innocent, but Ahriman, the evil spirit, under the form of a serpent, brought about their ruin, and they are to be saved by Mithra the Mediator.

The same primitive tradition is found in India. Vishnu, incarnate under the form of Krishna, destroys the serpent Kalya.

The Chinese traditions contained in the Book Li-Ki inform us that man fell from his state of happiness through the instigation of the evil spirit, but a time will come when a complete restoration is to take place, brought about by a hero called Kiun-tse, a shepherd and prince, the most Holy one, the Universal Doctor and Sovereign Truth.

Plutarch, in his treatise on Isis and Osiris, tells us that, according to the Egyptian mythology, Typhon is the cursed one whom Osiris, a descendant of Isis, had overcome.

The Greek tradition is very beautifully given by Æschylus in his tragedy of Prometheus, who, for stealing fire from heaven, is chained to a rock, and constantly fed upon by a vulture. Io, the woman, is to be touched by God, and to conceive and bring forth a son, who is to free Prometheus by hurling from his throne the author of evil. But this son is not a mere man, for Mercury says to Prometheus: "Do not believe that such torments could ever cease, unless a god offer himself to take your place."

Alexander von Humboldt, in his *Vues des Cordillères*, informs us that, in the Mexican mythology, the mother of the human race is always placed in close relation with a serpent, and that other allegorical pictures represent a huge crested serpent cut to pieces by the great spirit Tezcatlipoca, or the personified Sun. (Conf. *Le*

Christ et les Antechrists, by V. Deschamps. Paris, 1858.)

5. That the Messiah promised to the Jews was not a mere man, but God Himself, is evident from the prophets and the Psalms of David. Micheas (v, 2,) not only predicts the place of His birth, but also His eternal generation, " His going forth from the beginning, from the days of eternity." Isaias (vii, 14) calls him "Emmanuel," God with us; and, in xxxv, 4-6, He is God Himself: "God Himself will come and will save you. Then shall the eyes of the blind be opened, and the ears of the deaf shall be unstopped. Then shall the lame man leap as a hart," etc. This evidently refers to the Messiah. The prophet, after having described in the fifty-third chapter the passion of our Lord, addresses the Gentiles in the following chapter, and bids them to rejoice, because they, too, shall be partakers in the blessings; and in the fifth verse he says: "For He that made thee shall rule over thee, the Lord of Hosts is His name: and thy Redeemer, the Holy One of Israel, shall be called the God of all the earth." The one hundred and ninth Psalm also bears testimony to the divinity of the Messiah. This Psalm, beyond a doubt, refers to Christ, because He who is spoken of is to possess the sceptre of Sion, to rule over all nations, to be a priest forever according to the order of Melchisedech; and both our Lord (*Matt.* xxii, 41-45) and

St. Paul, in his Epistle to the Hebrews, apply this text to the Messiah. But He who is spoken of in this Psalm is God, because He is engendered by God the Father from all eternity: "From the womb before the day-star I begot Thee."

Aggeus the prophet, to console the Jews returned from captivity, who were grieved at the inferior glory and magnificence of the second temple, tells them that the glory of this temple shall be far greater than that of the first, because the Desired of all nations shall honor it with His presence. But, if the Messiah was but a mere man, this would not have been verified, because the first temple was not only more magnificent, but, at its dedication, God by some visible signs showed His presence in it (2 *Paral.* vii, 1–3): "Neither could the priests enter into the temple of the Lord, because the majesty of the Lord had filled the temple." Now this did not happen to the second temple.

I have no intention of maintaining that the people possessed a clear idea of the divinity of the coming Messiah; I simply state that the prophecies had plainly indicated this doctrine. Still it cannot be doubted that those who had a deeper insight into the meaning of these prophecies, knew their significance. This is confirmed by the sayings and teachings of rabbis, preserved in the Talmud, the Targums, and other Jewish works of earlier date.

6. There are some who, though claiming to be Christians, deny that Christ is God; they do not want to find in the writings of the New Testament any mention made of the divinity of our Lord. A few texts, they allow, seem to give this appellation to the Reedemer; but these texts, they pretend, ought to be taken in a metaphorical sense. Other rationalists, on the contrary, affirm that the New Testament is very explicit in asserting the divinity of Christ; and hence they suppose that the Gospels were not written by the apostles or evangelists whose name they bear, but were composed much later, when the opinion that Christ is God had already taken root among many Christians sprung from Gentiles, who had found the germs of this doctrine in the philosophy of Plato. Others, again, affirm that neither Christ asserted that he was God, nor had the apostles at first any thought of teaching His divinity, but that either St. Paul or St. John was the first to start this idea.

7. The authenticity of the Gospels has already been established, and it is perfectly true that both St. Paul and St. John, in all their writings, clearly lay down the principle, that Christ is God. The latter wrote his Gospel for the very purpose of inculcating this dogma against the error of the Cerinthians; but neither he nor St. Paul invented the doctrine of the divinity of Christ. They could never have succeeded in

foisting it on the people, if all the other apostles taught a different doctrine. Had the first converts been told that Christ was not God, they would have strongly opposed the introduction of the new teaching; still no trace of any such opposition is to be found: the only controversy among the first Christians was about the necessity of circumcision. Hence the doctrine of these two apostles was in strict conformity with that of the others; nay, St. Peter, in his Second Epistle (iii, 15, 16), written a short time before his death, gives full sanction to all the writings of St. Paul.

8. St. Matthew, who wrote his Gospel before the other evangelists, testifies to the divinity of Christ. In the fifth chapter, Christ acts as the supreme lawgiver: "You have heard that it was said to them of old. . . but I say to you. . ." In the tenth chapter (37-40), Christ exacts from His disciples that submission, devotion, and love, which are due to God alone. In the sixteenth chapter (13-17), St. Peter confesses Christ to be the Son of the living God, and on this account he is made the rock on which our Lord builds His Church. In the twenty-second chapter (42-46), Christ proves His divinity from the words of the Psalmist: "The Lord said to my Lord: Sit thou at my right hand." In the twenty-sixth chapter, the high-priest adjures Christ by the living God to tell him whether He is the Christ, the Son of

God. Jesus answered: "Thou hast said it. Nevertheless I say to you, hereafter you shall see the Son of man sitting on the right hand of the power of God, and coming in the clouds of heaven. Then the high-priest rent his garments, saying: He hath blasphemed." The high-priest, therefore, understood that Christ called Himself the Son of God, not by any means in the same sense as all the just may be called the children of God, but in truth and to the letter; and on this account he dared to pronounce that Christ was guilty of blasphemy. St. Luke also testifies to the same truth. (See chaps. i, 35; vii, 47–50; xx, 41–44; xxii, 70.)

But the testimony of St. John is more explicit: "In the beginning was the Word, and the Word was with God, and the Word was God. . . All things were made by Him [the Word]: and without Him was made nothing that was made. . . And the Word was made flesh, and dwelt among us (and we saw His glory, the glory as it were of the Only-begotten of the Father), full of grace and truth" (i, 1–14). These words need no comment. Christ, who was made flesh, is the Word of God, the only-begotten Son of the Father, God Himself, by whom all things were created.

Christ is the *only-begotten Son*, whom the Father has given to the world, that whosoever believeth in Him may not perish, but may have life everlasting (iii, 16–18).

When Christ, on the Sabbath-day, had cured

the paralytic stricken for thirty-eight years, the Jews sought to kill Him, because He not only broke the Sabbath, but also said that God was His Father, making Himself equal to God (v, 18); Christ not only does not undeceive them, but He reiterates His assertion more strongly. He does all things which His Father does (v, 19); He, as well as the Father, gives life to whom He pleases (v, 21); He is the Supreme Judge of all men (v, 22); He claims the same honor as the Father; and he who does not honor Him, does not honor His Father (v, 23); He gives life everlasting to those who believe in Him (v, 24).

Christ, answering the question put to Him by the Jews, "Who art thou?" said: "The beginning, who also speak unto you" (viii, 25), and, "Before Abraham was made, *I am*" (*Ibid.* 58). He therefore attributes to Himself the ineffable name of God, and thus was He understood by the Jews, who, on this assertion, immediately set about stoning Him.

When Christ walked in the temple, on the feast of the dedication (x, 23, 24), the Jews said to Him: "How long dost Thou hold our souls in suspense? If Thou be the Christ, tell us plainly." To answer this question, Christ first appeals to the works He performs; then He tells them that they do not believe, because they are not of His sheep, who hear His voice, and follow Him, to whom He gives life everlasting, so that they shall not perish forever, because they were given to Him by the Father, and no one can snatch them from the hands of His Father; and then He adds: "*I and the Father are one.*" The Jews, hearing this, took up stones to stone Him. Jesus said to them: "Many good works I have showed you; for which of these works do you stone me?" The Jews replied: "For a good work we stone Thee not, but for blasphemy; and because that Thou, being a man, makest Thyself God." Then Jesus said to them: "Is it not written in your law: I said, you are gods? If he called them gods, to whom the word of God was spoken, and the Scripture cannot be made void, do you say of Him whom the Father hath sanctified and sent into the world: Thou blasphemest, because I said, I am the Son of God?" This answer of our Lord is alleged by Unitarians as a proof that Christ did not claim to be truly God, but that He called Himself the Son of God in the same manner as others to whom the word of God was spoken. But this is not the meaning of our Saviour, as may be clearly seen from the words He adds: "If I do [the works of my Father], though you will not believe me, believe the works: that you may know and believe *that the Father is in me, and I in the Father.*" Nor did the Jews understand that He retracted His previous assertion, because, precisely on account of these last words, they sought to take Him, but He escaped out of their hands (x, 22-39).

Christ calls Himself the Resurrection and the Life, who gives life everlasting to those who believe in Him. Now, to give to man life everlasting, or the eternal beatitude, belongs to God alone: for He alone can be the ultimate end of man (xi, 25).

Christ makes Himself equal to the Father (xii, 45), when He says: "He that seeth me, seeth Him that sent me."

In the fourteenth chapter, Christ requires of His disciples that, as they believe in God, they should also believe in Him (*v.* 1); He asserts that He is the way, the truth, and the life (*v.* 6); he that sees Him sees the Father (*v.* 9); He is in the Father, and the Father is in Him (*v.* 11); He sends the Holy Ghost, the Spirit of truth, to abide forever with His followers (*v.* 16, 17). It is true that in the same chapter He says, "The Father is greater than I;" but it is evident that this refers to His humanity: for He there speaks of His passion and death, and as God He could not die. Hence He adds: "And now I have told you before it come to pass, that, when it shall come to pass, you may believe (*v.* 29).

In the sixteenth chapter, Christ promises to His disciples to send them the Paraclete, who shall glorify Him, because, as He says, "He shall receive of mine" (*v.* 14); and He gives the reason: "All things whatsoever the Father hath are mine" (*v.* 15). He comes forth from the Father (*v.* 28).

In the twentieth chapter, Christ, breathing on His apostles, confers on them the Holy Ghost, and empowers them to forgive and retain sin. St. Thomas confesses Him to be his Lord and his God.

The same doctrine is embodied in the Epistles and in the Apocalypse, where Christ is called the Alpha and the Omega, the beginning and the end, who is, who was, who is to come,—the Almighty. (*Apoc.* i, 8; xxii, 13.)

It is worthy of remark that the four evangelists, and all the other writers of the New Testament, strongly insist on giving to Christ the title of "Son of God," because in it is really embodied the doctrine of His divinity, while at the same time, it points out the distinction of persons. The Jews understood this to be the meaning of the words of our Saviour and of the apostles: this is plain from the Gospel narrative. (*John* x, 33; *Matt.* xxvi, 63–66; *John* xix, 7, etc.) Had we, therefore, no other testimony to this doctrine than the title, "Son of God," given to Christ, it would be quite sufficient to prove His divinity: for Christ never intimated that the Jews misunderstood Him, nor does He seek to explain away this meaning; on the contrary, He always confirms it with the strongest expressions, as is evident from the texts already quoted.

9. St. Paul is not less explicit than St. John in proclaiming the dogma of the divinity of Christ.

He teaches that every one of us must stand before the judgment-seat of Christ: "For it is written: As I live, saith the Lord, every knee shall bow to me, and every tongue shall confess to God. Therefore every one of us shall render account to God for himself." (*Rom.* xiv, 10–12.)

To the Colossians he writes: "God hath delivered us from the power of darkness, and hath translated us into the kingdom of the Son of His love, in whom we have redemption through His blood, the remission of sins; who is the image of the invisible God, the first-born of every creature. For in Him were all things created in heaven and on earth, visible and invisible, whether thrones or dominations, or principalities or powers: all things were created by Him and in Him" (i, 13–16). These last words refute the cavil of Unitarians, who say that, since Christ is the first-born of every creature, He, too, must be a creature. As all things are created by and in Christ, whether angels and men, or material beings, He himself is not created: He is truly God, the image of His Father, coequal with Him. Besides, the creative act is such that it belongs to God exclusively, and cannot be communicated to any created being. In the second chapter (*v.* 9), St. Paul adds, that in Christ all the fulness of the Godhead dwells corporally, *i. e.*, really, not its mere shadow, but its very substance.

Again, Jesus Christ, " being in the form of God, thought it not robbery to be equal with God; but emptied himself, taking the form of a servant, being made in the likeness of men, and in habit found as a man. He humbled Himself, becoming obedient unto death, even to the death of the cross." Wherefore, " God also hath exalted Him, and hath given Him a name which is above all names: that in the name of Jesus every knee should bow, of those that are in heaven, on earth, and under the earth; and that every tongue should confess that the Lord Jesus Christ is in the glory of God the Father." (*Phil.* ii, 6–11.)

In the second chapter of his Epistle to Titus, St. Paul repeatedly speaks of Christ as God our Saviour (*v.* 10, 11, 13), as also in the third chapter (*v.* 4): "When the goodness and kindness of God our Saviour appeared."

In his Epistle to the Hebrews (i, 3), St. Paul asserts that Christ is the brightness of God's glory, the figure of His substance, who upholds all things by the word of His power. The main argument of the whole Epistle is to show that Christ is God.

Other texts might be cited in confirmation of this doctrine; but those already alleged abundantly prove not only that the apostles taught the divinity of Christ to their disciples, but that Christ Himself asserted the same. Now, Christ is undoubtedly a messenger sent by God, who proved His divine mission by His miracles, and principally by His resurrection; therefore, we are bound to believe Him. Were we to reject His testimony on this point, we should have to discard His authority on every other.

10. It need scarcely be proved that the belief in the divinity of Christ was common to all the faithful before the Council of Nicæa, in which this doctrine was solemnly declared and defined against the Arians. It is contained in the Apostles' Creed, which, from the first days of the Church, constituted the summary of the Christian faith. In it we profess to believe in God the Father, in His Son, Jesus Christ, and in the Holy Ghost; hence we confess their equality. We do not believe *in* the Church, we simply *believe* the Church. If the Son and the Holy Ghost were not equal to God the Father, we could not say, "We believe in," but only, "We believe" the Son, etc.

The same is evident from the Doxology: "Glory be to the Father, and to the Son, and to the Holy Ghost." The Church, therefore, always gave equal honor to the three Divine Persons. That the Doxology dates from the earliest times is attested by St. Polycarp, the disciple of St. John the Apostle, who expresses it thus: "Through whom (Jesus Christ) to Thee (God the Father), with Him in the Holy Ghost, glory now and in all future ages." St. Basil, in his works against the Arians, also proves that the Doxology was always in use among Christians.

Some modern infidels assert that St. Justin was the first who taught the divinity of Christ; but, for reasons already stated, this is impossible. All the faithful well knew whether they had been taught that Christ is God, or simply a messenger of God; hence they would never have accepted the teaching of St. Justin, had it been contrary to that already received by them. His doctrine would have been declared heretical, and rejected by the universality of the faithful. So far from this being the case, those who dared to contradict this article of belief were looked upon as heretics. St. Justin, moreover, did not teach this doctrine as a conclusion drawn from other principles, but as handed down by tradition. (*Dialog. cum Tryphone*, nn. 4-7.)

From the authentic acts of the first martyrs, we learn that they confessed the divinity of Christ. The Pagans themselves objected to the Christians that they, too, adored more than one God, since they adored also Christ as God. This appears from the testimony of St. Justin, of Origen (*Contra Celsum*), and from the Acts of the Martyrs. Pliny, writing to the Emperor Trajan, attests that the Christians honor Christ as God. Now, the Christians never denied the charge that they adored Christ, but they asserted that they worshipped but one God, because His

Son was of the self-same essence or nature as the Father.

11. A number of texts might, no doubt, be brought from the writings of the Antenicene Fathers, which, if taken apart from the whole context, could be used as arguments to show that they did not hold the doctrine of the divinity of Christ, though it is quite certain that they firmly believed it. Thus Tertullian, who wrote a work against Prazeas, in order to prove the equality of the three Divine Persons and the divinity of Christ, uses certain expressions which seem in direct opposition to this doctrine, such as, "The Son is a portion of the Father," "He had a beginning," etc. But these expressions, though somewhat bold, must not be taken separately: their meaning must be determined from the context. The only idea which Tertullian wished to convey by these forms of speech is, that the Son, the Word, was not without *origin*, but had received the divine nature, not by creation, but by generation, from all eternity, and that thus He possesses the same divine substance with the Father. Besides, before the Arian controversy, a number of words, such as, "person," "nature," "substance," "cause," "principle," had not yet received a determinate meaning; hence some of the Fathers used one for the other: *v. g.*, substance for person, cause instead of principle. Afterward, the meaning of these words was clearly deter-

mined, the better to meet the objections of the Arians. At any rate, when these ambiguous words of the Antenicene Fathers are taken in connection with the whole context, it is clear they express the Catholic doctrine.

CHAPTER II.

FIGURES BY WHICH THE CHURCH IS EXPRESSED IN THE NEW TESTAMENT.

1. The Church is a Kingdom.—2. A City.—3. A House.—4. A Temple.—5. Meaning of these Figures.—6. The Church is a Body.—7. What this Figure implies.—8. The Church a Sheepfold.—9. A Bride.—10. Parables referring to the Church.

THE Church founded by Christ is represented in Holy Writ under different figures, from which we may gather her nature and properties.

1. The Church is a kingdom.

a) The kingdom of heaven:—

Matt. iii, 2: "Do penance: for *the kingdom of heaven* is at hand." St. John the Baptist here speaks, as appears from the next verse, of the kingdom to be established by the Messiah.

Matt. xviii, 23: "Therefore is *the kingdom of heaven* likened to a king, who would take an account of his servants."

b) The kingdom of God:—

Mark i, 14: "Jesus came into Galilee, preaching the Gospel of *the kingdom of God.*"

Mark iv, 11: "To you it is given to know the mystery of *the kingdom of God;* but to them that are without, all things are done in parables."

This Christ said to His apostles, referring to the parable of the sower: consequently, He was alluding to the Church on earth.

Luke xxiii, 51 : " Who [Joseph of Arimathea] also himself looked for *the kingdom of God*."

c) The kingdom of Christ:—

John xvii, 36, 37: Christ declares that He is a king, and hence that He has a *kingdom* on earth, though not of the earth ; *i. e.*, that His kingdom is not of the temporal, but of the spiritual order.

e. The Church is called a city.

a) Apocalypse xi, 2 ; xx, 8: A holy city.

b) The city of the living God:—

Heb. xii, 22 : " But you are come to Mount Sion, and to *the city of the living God*, the heavenly Jerusalem, and to the company of many thousands of angels, and to the church of the firstborn," etc. That St. Paul is speaking of the call to the Church here upon earth, is evident from the twenty-fifth verse, in which he exhorts those whom he addresses not to neglect this call.

3. The Church is called a house.

a) Heb. iii, 6 : " But Christ [was] as the Son in His own *house:* which *house* are we, if we hold fast the confidence and glory of hope unto the end."

Heb. x, 21 : " And [Christ is] a high-priest over the *house* of God."

1 Tim. iii, 15 : " That thou mayest know how thou oughtest to behave thyself in *the house of*

God, which is the Church of the living God, the pillar and ground of the truth."

b) A spiritual house:—

1 Pet. ii, 5: "Be you also as living stones built up, a *spiritual house*, a holy priesthood, to offer up spiritual sacrifices."

c) A house containing vessels of every kind:—

2 Tim. ii, 19, 20: "But... the Lord knoweth who are His... But in a great *house* there are not only vessels of gold and of silver, but also of wood and of earth," etc.

d) The dwelling of God:—

Eph. ii, 22: "In whom you also are built together into an habitation of God in the spirit."

4. The Church is called a temple.

a) The temple of God:—

1 Cor. iii, 16, 17: "Know you not that you are the *temple of God*, and that the Spirit of God dwelleth in you? But if any man violate the *temple of God*, him shall God destroy. For the *temple of God* is holy: which you are.

b) The temple of the Holy Ghost:—

1 Cor. vi, 19: "Know you not that your members are the *temple of the Holy Ghost*, who is in you, whom you have from God; and you are not your own."

c) The temple of the living God:—

2 Cor. vi, 16: "What agreement hath the *temple of God* with idols? For you are the *temple of the living God*: as God saith: I will dwell in them

and walk among them; and I will be their God, and they shall be my people."

d) Though the architect of this temple be Christ (*Eph.* ii, 20-22), the apostles are also architects under Christ.

1 Cor. iii, 10: "According to the grace of God, that is given to me as a wise *architect*, I have laid the foundation: and another buildeth thereon."

e) The foundation of this temple is Christ:—

1 Cor. iii, 11: "For other foundation no man can lay, but that which is laid; which is Christ Jesus."

f) Yet the apostles are secondary foundation-stones:—

Eph. ii, 20: "Built upon the foundation of the apostles and prophets; Jesus Christ Himself being the chief corner-stone."

g) Christ is the corner-stone of the temple:—

Eph. (*loc. cit.*); Isa. xxviii, 16: "Behold, I will lay a stone in the foundations of Sion, a tried stone, a corner-stone, a precious stone, founded in the foundation." (1 *Pet.* ii, 6; *Luke* xx, 17; *Matt.* xxi, 42; *Acts* iv, 11; *Rom.* ix, 32, 33.)

The reason of Christ being the foundation and corner-stone of this spiritual building is given in Acts iv, 12: because in Him alone is salvation.

5. These figures portraying the Church show that she is an organized association, like a kingdom, a city, a house, which, being visible on earth,

because it is the light of the world, and the city placed on a mountain (*Matt.* v, 14), must possess, besides Christ the invisible Head, a visible authority on earth. The figures of a city and a house express the intimate union between the members of the Church, as well as her solidity; the word kingdom denotes her amplitude; and, if we take these figures in connection with the promises made in the Old Testament about the reign of the Messiah, they declare the universality, or catholicity, of the Church. There is question of *one only* kingdom, house, city, or temple; so that the Church of Christ is a body organized and *one*, not an union of several independent societies: she forms a single society, under the same invisible and visible authority. The figure of the temple shows the holiness of the Church, because not only is she founded on Christ, but she is the temple wherein dwells the Holy Ghost, the temple of the living God.

a) The Church is a body:—

Rom. xii, 4, 5: "For as in one body we have many members, but all the members have not the same office, so we, being many, are *one body* in Christ, and every one members one of another."

6. 1 Cor. xii: The apostle speaks first of the diversity of gifts in the Church, but all these proceed from one and the same Spirit, the Holy Ghost (4-11). All the members of the Church form one body, which is Christ (12), because into

one body we are baptized (13). These members are necessary one to another (14-26). But it is God Himself who has placed in the Church the various members, some superior to the others (28-30).

b) The head of this body is Christ:—

Eph. v, 23: "Because the husband is the head of the wife: as Christ is the head of the Church. He is the Saviour of His body."

Col. i, 18: "And He (Christ) is the head of the body, the Church."

c) The spirit or soul of this body is the Holy Ghost. (1 *Cor.* xii.)

7. The foregoing beautiful figure exhibits the intimate union between Christ and the members of His mystical body, the Church. But as Christ has but one body, so the Church must, of necessity, be *one*. Christ is the head of His body; but, as the body is visible, it must have, besides Christ the invisible Head, a visible one, as also principal members, which direct the whole body. These, according to St. Paul, are the apostles, prophets and doctors, whom God Himself has placed in the body. Those, therefore, who exercise authority in the Church are not constituted by the body, but by God; they do not wield a power which they receive from the members, but from the Holy Ghost, who acts with and through them (*loc. cit.* v, 4-11).

8. The Church is a fold.

THE CHURCH IS A SHEEPFOLD.

a) Isa. xl, 10, 11: "Behold, the Lord shall come with His strength, and His arm shall rule; behold, His reward is with Him, and His work is before Him. He shall feed His flock like a shepherd, and shall gather together the lambs with His arm, and shall take them up in His bosom; and He Himself shall carry them that are with young."

Matt. xviii, 12, 13: Our Lord compares Himself to a shepherd who, having lost one sheep, leaves the ninety-nine, and goes in quest of the lost one.

Heb. xiii, 20: "The God of peace, who brought again from the dead the great pastor of the sheep our Lord Jesus Christ."

1 Pet. ii, 25: "For you were as sheep going astray; but you are now converted to the Shepherd and Bishop of your souls."

b) The fold is but one:—

St. John x, 11 and 16: "I am the Good Shepherd. The Good Shepherd giveth His life for His sheep. . . . And other sheep I have, that are not of this fold: them also must I bring, and they shall hear my voice, and there shall be one fold and one Shepherd."

c) St. Peter, under Christ, has been constituted the visible shepherd of the whole flock.

St. John xxi, 15-17: Our Saviour, having thrice asked Peter if he loved Him, commissioned him to feed His flock. "Feed my lambs . . . feed my sheep."

d) St. Paul (*Acts* xx, 28) informs us that, besides St. Peter, other shepherds are instituted by the Holy Ghost to feed the flock of Jesus Christ.

9. The Church is called a bride, whose bridegroom is Christ. (*The Canticle of Canticles; Ps.* xliv; *Apoc.* xxi, 9; *Matt.* ix, 15; 2 *Cor.* xi, 2; *Eph.* v, 25.)

The last two figures also inculcate the unity of the Church, because there is but one fold, governed by Christ, the Supreme Pastor, who, since He was not to remain visibly on earth, appointed St. Peter and his successors as His own vicars, to whom He committed the care of His flock. The figure of the bridegroom and bride manifests the indissoluble union between both. Having united the bride to Himself, Christ never abandons her; He sanctifies her, as St. Paul says to the Ephesians (v, 26, 27), "by the laver of water in the word of life, that He might present her to Himself a glorious Church, not having spot or wrinkle, or any such thing, but that it should be holy and without blemish." The Church, therefore, always remaining the bride of Christ, cannot teach error, but must always be animated by the spirit of truth. The same follows from the figure of the Church as Christ's body, quickened by the Holy Ghost, the Spirit of truth and holiness.

10. We find also several parables referring to the Church: That of the sower (*Matt.* xiii);

the vineyard and the laborers (*Matt.* xx); the mustard seed (*Matt.* xiii); the leaven (*ibid.*); the pearl (*ibid.*); the net (*ibid.*); the wedding feast (*Matt.* xxii).

.. The two last parables deserve particular attention, for they show us that not the just only or the predestined are members of the visible Church on earth, but that among those who belong to the Church there are sinners who, remaining such till the end of their lives, are finally separated from the rest, and thrown into everlasting fire.

CHAPTER III.

INSTITUTION OF THE CHURCH AS RELATED IN THE GOSPELS.

1. The Calling of the Apostles and their Election.—2. Promises made to St. Peter alone.—3. To all the Apostles.—4. Fulfilment of these Promises.—5. The Mission of the Holy Ghost.—6. Presence of the Holy Ghost in the Church as a Body, and in the individual Members.—7. Corollaries: the Church is One.—8. The sole Teacher of Truth—9. She is indefectible and infallible in her Teaching.—10. Catholic.—11. Holy.—12. Apostolic.

1. THE facts related in the New Testament with reference to the institution of the Church, may be grouped under the following heads: the calling and election of the apostles; the promises made to them; the fulfilment of these promises, the day of Pentecost, or the birthday of the Church.

Christ, during the time of His public preaching gathered around Him many disciples (*Matt.* iv, 18–21; *ibid.* viii), and from among them He chose twelve apostles, who became His inseparable companions. (*Matt.* x; *Mark* iii; *Luke* vi.) St. Peter is named first on the list by the three evangelists, and Christ changed his name from Simon to Cephas, which is interpreted Peter, or a rock. (*John* i, 42.)

2. Christ promised to Peter, and to him alone, that he should be the rock upon which He would build His Church; to him also He gave the keys of heaven (*Matt.* xvi, 18): "Thou art Peter (a rock); and upon this rock I will build my Church, and the gates (or the powers) of hell shall not prevail against it. And I will give to thee the keys of the kingdom of heaven. And whatsoever thou shalt bind upon earth, it shall be bound also in heaven: and whatsoever thou shalt loose on earth, it shall be loosed also in heaven."

The building on a rock signifies the unshaken stability of the edifice, so that neither wind, nor rain, nor flood, nor storm can overthrow it (*Matt.* vii, 24-27); and, owing to this firmness of construction, the gates, or the powers, of hell cannot prevail against the Church.

3. Besides the promise made to St. Peter alone, there are others made to all the apostles. They were to become fishers of men. (*Matt.* iv, 19.) The meaning of this promise becomes clear from the parable of the net thrown into the sea.

Again, after the promise to St. Peter, He makes a similar one, though not the same, to the other apostles. (*Matt.* xviii.) He tells them that whatsoever they bind on earth shall be bound in heaven, and whatsoever they loose on earth, shall be loosed also in heaven. By this promise made to the apostles alone, and not to all the members of the Church, as the context shows, Christ did not revoke that which He had made to Peter alone: He did not constitute them the rock on which he was to build the Church; nor did He give them the keys of the kingdom of heaven in an especial manner. Hence the power and authority promised to the apostles suppose the promise made to St. Peter, so that they cannot exercise this authority independently of him, but must be subject to him, as the head of the apostolic body.

Moreover, Christ promised to His apostles that He would send them the Holy Ghost. The effusion of the Holy Ghost was already promised by the prophets (*Isa.* xliv, 3; *Jer.* xxxi, 33; *Ezech.* xxxvi, 26; *Joel* ii, 28); but this prophecy related to all the members of the new covenant. The apostles received the promise of the Holy Ghost in an especial manner. In the supper-room where Christ was alone with His apostles, to celebrate the Pasch, He promised to send them the Holy Ghost to teach them all truth, viz., all those truths which He had imparted to them in His teachings (*John* xvi, 13); and this Holy Ghost was to abide with them forever (xiv, 16). He was to strengthen them, that they might announce the Gospel to all nations (xv, 27). They received, therefore, the promise of the Holy Ghost to enable them to teach the doctrine of Christ infallible. This last promise was renewed after the resurrection of our Lord. (*Luke* xxiv, 49; *Acts* i, 4–8.)

4. Now as to the fulfilment of these promises:—

Christ, before His passion, had sent His apostles to preach in Judea, and conferred on them the power of expelling evil spirits and of curing all kinds of diseases (*Matt.* x, 1); but at the last supper, when He instituted the Holy Eucharist, He gave them the power to offer the sacrifice of the New Law (*Luke* xxii, 19): "Do this for a commemoration of me."

After His resurrection He conferred on them the power of forgiving sins.) (*John* xx, 23.) He delegated to them the same powers which He, as man, exercised on earth: "All power is given to me in heaven and on earth. As the Father hath sent me, I also send you." (*Matt.* xxviii, 18; *John* xx, 21.) They had, therefore, to continue His work here on earth. Hence He commissioned them to go and teach all nations, baptizing them in the name of the Father, and of the Son, and of the Holy Ghost, teaching them to observe all things whatsoever He had commanded them; and He added: "Behold I am with you (baptizing, teaching, etc.) all days, even to the consummation of the world."

The special promises made to St. Peter alone, were also realized at that time; for (*John* xxi, 15) our Lord confided to him the care of His whole flock, and thus conferred on him the authority of teaching, guiding and directing the whole Church.

5. The mission of the Holy Ghost:—

Christ, during His sojourn on earth, had, so to speak, gathered together all the materials for the building of the Church ; but the last form had not as yet been given to it. This was to be accomplished by the Holy Ghost; and, in consequence, the apostles were told to abide in Jerusalem, and to wait for His coming. On the day of Pentecost all those who were destined to form the nascent Church were gathered in the supper-room, and the Holy Ghost descended on them to infuse the living principle or soul into the organism constituted by Christ. The Holy Ghost was communicated to all those who were present, and, though the increase of sanctifying grace, and some external gifts, such as that of speaking different tongues, were imparted to every one, all did not receive the same powers. The apostles were strengthened, in order to the exercise of their authority in teaching and governing the faithful, while the others received the graces required for submission to the apostolical authority; and thus the Church was constituted a living organism.

Now, the Church is to exist on earth till the consummation of time; she has to continue the work of redemption inaugurated by Christ. Hence the powers conferred by Him on the apostles were to be permanent in the Church. This is evident, both from the nature of the Church, and the promises of our Saviour.

The Church must always teach the doctrines of Christ, and impart the sacraments instituted by Him for the sanctification of souls; therefore the power given to the apostles must be permanent. Besides, Christ promised to be with His apostles till the consummation of the world. (*Matt.* xxviii, 20.) Now, these words do not refer to the apostles considered merely as individuals; for the presence of which Christ speaks is not that which the saints enjoy in heaven, because it is limited to the consummation of the world, whereas the union of Christ with the saints in heaven is eternal. But the apostles were not to live on earth forever: they have long since passed to a better life; therefore, the presence of Christ with His apostles on earth till the end of time signifies that He will be with them, inasmuch as they, with their lawfully appointed successors, form one moral body, always living, teaching, baptizing and governing the faithful, who constitute the mystical body of Christ on earth.

Christ, moreover, promised His apostles that the Holy Ghost, whom He was to send them, should abide with them forever, to teach them all the truths He had imparted to them. Now, this presence of the Holy Ghost was necessary for the Church, not at the time of the apostles only, but at all times; and if this assistance was required to remind the apostles of the doctrines Christ had taught them, how much more so is it indispensable for those who have these truths handed down to them from the apostles through a series of many generations. The Holy Ghost, therefore, always teaches the apostles, inasmuch as they continue to live upon earth as a moral body in their legitimately appointed successors.

Wherefore, since the apostolic body always remains morally the same, though the individual members constituting it are ever changing; and since St. Peter was appointed by Christ the foundation of His Church, the centre of unity, the chief pastor of Christ's whole flock, St. Peter also continues to live on earth in his lawfully appointed successors, the Bishops of Rome,—for these alone have ever been recognized as his successors, and no others have ever dared to claim this prerogative,—and he ever exercises the powers intrusted to him by Christ.

6. The Holy Ghost, therefore, is always present in the Church, quickening it, making it a living and acting organism. By the grace of ordination He transmits the powers conferred on the apostles, and continues to teach the Church, to give efficacy to the sacraments, and to govern the mystical body of Christ. He also renders the ministry of the Church fruitful, so that there will always be a flock to be governed by the successors of the apostles.

The Holy Ghost is also present in the individual members of the Church, by the gift of faith and other graces, which enable them to perform salutary acts; and in those who are vivified by sanctifying grace, He dwells as in His temple. Still this presence in the individual members depends on the presence of the Holy Ghost in the Church as a living organism, because the gift of faith and sanctifying grace are imparted to the individual members of the Church by the ministry of the apostolic body.

7. From what has been said in this and the preceding chapter, the following inferences may drawn:—

There is but One Church. For, as we have seen, the Church forms one kingdom, one house, one city, one temple, one body. There is one Supreme Head, one Corner-stone; the whole is quickened by one Spirit. There is but one fold, one flock, one shepherd, one apostolic body, one visible head, appointed by Christ, for government is one only. Hence is excluded the idea of many independent churches, which, though professing contradictory doctrines, claim to form the one Church instituted by Christ. To belong to Christ's mystical body, it does not suffice to acknowledge Him; we must also observe all things which He commanded His apostles to teach; we must believe all their doctrines, for he only who believes what was preached by them, and is baptized, can be saved; he who believes not, is condemned. (*Mark* xvi, 16.) There is, therefore, no salvation to be found out of that one Church which Christ has instituted, because there is no other name given us but that of Christ whereby we can be saved (*Acts* iv, 12), and because He has lodged all authority and means of salvation in His Church alone.

8. As the Church is the sole teacher of truth leading to eternal life, she must be conspicuous, so that she may easily be known to all who seek after salvation. She must have a visible authority for all to obey, since Christ says that he who will not hear the Church is to be considered a heathen and a publican. (*Matt.* xviii, 17.) This visible authority is the apostolic body over which Peter, in his successors, presides till the end of the world. There must also be tangible means of salvation, such as baptism and other sacraments, by which the members are incorporated into the body of Christ and sanctified.

9. The Church must be *indefectible* and *infallible* in her teaching, because Christ is always with her: the Holy Ghost always abides within her, making her a living organism. As Christ and the Holy Ghost continue to teach through the Church, she must always teach the truth: were she ever to proclaim falsehood, the Holy Ghost would have abandoned her, and the gates of hell prevailed: and this Christ promised would never be.

10. The Church is *catholic*, or *universal*, because

the Messiah, according to the predictions of the prophets, was to unite all nations into one spiritual kingdom; because Christ willed that the apostles should teach all nations; and because, after Christ's coming, the Church alone possesses the means of salvation, and yet He came to save all mankind.

11. The Church is *holy*, because the Holy Ghost is the life-principle of Christ's body, and sanctifies the members belonging to it. The efficacy of the sacraments does not depend on the sanctity of the ministers appointed to distribute them, but on Christ and the Holy Ghost; for the ministers of the Church act in virtue of the powers conferred on them by the sacrament of holy orders; and the presence of the Holy Ghost in the Church, giving to this mystical body its life, its vigor, and its efficacy, is distinct from that presence by which the individual members are quickened. Hence the sanctity of the Church is not destroyed by the unworthiness of some of her ministers, nor by the sins and crimes of some of her individual members. All the members of the Church, so far forth as they belong to her, are holy, because the faith which unites them to her is a gift of the Holy Ghost, and the root or first principle of justification.

12. The Church is *Apostolic*, because Christ has confided to the apostles and their lawful successors the whole and universal power which He

Himself, as man, exercised upon earth. Hence none can wield these powers unless he be a member of the apostolic body, in union with the Church; for, as out of the Church there is no salvation, no means of salvation can be dispensed out of her communion. It follows, also, that there cannot be in the Church any extraordinary mission not derived from her authority; and that all who claim a mission to teach new doctrines, or to reform the doctrinal teaching of the spouse of Christ, are impostors.

From what has been hitherto said it is manifest that the Catholic Church alone is the true Church of Christ, and that no sect or denomination separated from her has a right to claim the title of Spouse of our Lord.

CHAPTER IV.

UNITY OF THE CHURCH.

1. Christ willed the Church to be one.—2. She is one in Faith.—3. This Unity is indispensable.—4. The Apostles insisted on it.—5. The Church always asserted it.—6. Unity of Charity without Unity of Faith insufficient.—7. Absurdity of Unity in fundamental Articles only.—8. It cannot be determined.—9. Unity in Sacraments.—10. In Government.—11. Unity of Government required by Unity of Faith.

1. ALTHOUGH the truth of the Catholic Church has been sufficiently established in the two preceding chapters, it will not be out of place to give a more detailed account of the properties of the Church established by Christ. These are contained in the confession of faith made by the Council of Nicæa: "I believe one, holy, Catholic, Apostolic Church."

Christ willed the Church to be one. As we have seen in the second chapter, the figures under which Holy Writ represents the Church always imply the idea of unity. The Church is a kingdom, which, though embracing many provinces, must still be one in unity of government. She is a city presided over by one magistracy; a house where all the members of the family are subject to the head; a temple likewise one; a body, the members of which, albeit various and distinct, are quickened by the same vital principle, and mutually dependent on one another, so as to form but one organism. Moreover, Christ prayed for the unity of the Church, and He established it as a criterion of His divine mission (*John* xvii, 20-23), and a mark by which His disciples might be recognized (*John* xiii, 35).

2. This unity requires unity of faith, of sacraments, and of government.

Unity of faith: for Christ came into this world to teach us the way of salvation, and through Him alone can we come to God. (*John* xiv, 6; *Acts* iv, 12.) We must, therefore, believe what Christ has taught us. But His teachings form a body of truths containing no contradictory doctrines, because truth is but one. Hence faith also must be one, according to St. Paul (*Eph.* iv, 5): One Lord, one faith, one baptism.

3. Were unity of faith not required, this would proceed from the fact that Christ taught contradictory doctrines, or that He proposed His doctrines in an ambiguous manner, or that He left us without the means of knowing His revelation; or, finally, that man is free to choose or to reject what he pleases from the Christian doctrine. These suppositions are all of them utterly groundless; for, were the doctrine of Christ contradictory, He would have been an im-

postor. He could not have spoken in a vague and ambiguous manner; being the Son of God, infinite truth, who came on purpose to show us the way to heaven, He could not leave us in doubt as to what He had said, and what He required of us. Moreover, He promised His disciples and their successors to send them the Holy Ghost, who should abide with them forever, teach them all truth, and suggest to them all that they had heard from Him. (*John* xiv, 26.) He told His apostles to go to all nations, and to teach them, and insist on the observance of all those things which He had commanded them. Hence He did not leave us at liberty to choose what doctrines we please, but, under pain of eternal damnation, we have to believe the whole of the doctrine. (*Matt.* xxviii; *Mark* xvi, 16.)

Nor can it be said that Christ has not afforded us the means of knowing His revelation; because he who wills an end, must necessarily also will the means; and, as Christ was sent by His heavenly Father, as He is one with the Father, He had most undoubtedly the power of giving us the means to reach the end He had in view: that is, He had the power of showing us the way of salvation. Besides, the Church is established in order that the unity of faith may be preserved, that we be not tossed to and fro like children, and carried about with every wind of doctrine. (*Eph.* iv, 11–16.) Christ also promised to be with His apostles, teaching and baptizing till the end of the world.

4. The apostles always insisted on this unity of faith. Thus St. Paul to the Romans (xvi, 17): "Now I beseech you, brethren, to mark them who make dissensions and offences contrary to the doctrines which you have learned, and to avoid them. For they that are such serve not Christ our Lord, but their own belly; and by pleasing speeches and good words seduce the hearts of the innocent." To the Galatians (i, 8) he writes: "Though we, or an angel from heaven, preach a gospel to you besides that which we have preached to you, let him be anathema." The same apostle commands Titus (iii, 10) to avoid, after the first and second warning, any man who is a heretic.

5. The Church, from the beginning, has always maintained this unity of faith by excommunicating those who dared to uphold any doctrine contrary to her teaching. Thus, in the earliest ages, the Nicolaitans, the Gnostics, the Encratites, the Valentinians, the Marcionites, the Montanists, the Novatians, the Donatists, the Sabellians, the Arians, the Nestorians, the Macedonians, the Eutychians, the Pelagians and others, were expelled from the Church.

6. Modern heretics, seeing a multiplicity of sects constantly arising among themselves, and yet being conscious that unity is required, pre-

tend that the bond of charity is sufficient. No doubt this union of charity is indispensable (*John* xiii, 34, 35), and constitutes one of the distinguishing characteristics of the Church; but it must be based on oneness of faith, for the human will is guided by the intellect, and where there is diversity of opinion, there cannot be conformity of will. Whenever men coöperate together, there must needs be uniformity of principles; if, therefore, they are to be united in religious matters, they must agree in admitting the same doctrines, otherwise no union is possible. The more men are attached to their religious belief, the more they will strive to uphold its tenets, and get the upper hand. They can agree with others of different religious views only in the supposition that they look upon their own peculiar doctrines as something of small account, and thus fall into the state of indifferentism which is the ruin of religion.* Now, Christ does not approve of this indifferentism, for He commissioned His apostles

---

* Men of different religions may agree in political matters and practise toleration about their religious belief, but they cannot agree in religion, unless they profess the same principles; so that they who discard all positive teachings, agree only inasmuch as they consider all positive doctrines entirely indifferent. The only bond of union which exists between the various Protestant sects is their hatred and opposition to the Catholic Church: when there is question of attacking her, they act as one man, but otherwise they are opposed to each other more or less in proportion as they adhere to their own peculiar opinions. The recent attempts made by the sects to form a bond of union were all based upon these two principles: indifferentism as regards their peculiar opinions, and hatred against the Catholic Church.

to teach all things which He commanded them, threatening with eternal damnation those who do not believe.

Hence St. Paul, exhorting the faithful to charity, bases this virtue on the unity of faith; for thus he writes to the Philippians (ii, 2): "Fulfil ye my joy, that you be of one mind, having the same charity, being of one accord, agreeing in sentiment." And to the Ephesians (iv, 3-6): "Careful to keep the unity of the spirit in the bond of peace. One body and one spirit: as you are called in one hope of your calling. One Lord, *one faith*, one baptism, one God and Father of all," etc.

7. Other heretics pretended that, for the unity of faith, it suffices to agree in the fundamental articles of Christianity. But this can by no means be held. Christ does not leave us free to choose what we wish to believe, but bids us believe all that He commanded His apostles to teach. (*Matt.* xxxviii.) The apostles always insisted on the confession of the whole truth they taught, and looked upon as separated from the Church those who denied but one article. (*Rom.* xvi, 17.) St. Paul (2 *Tim.* ii, 17, 18) considered Hymeneus and Philetus as heretics to be shunned, because they said that the resurrection is past already; and (1 *Tim.* i, 20) he delivered up to Satan Hymeneus and Alexander, because they had "made shipwreck concerning the

faith." The same rule was followed by the Church in the earliest succeeding ages. The Novatians, for instance, were condemned, because they denied that the Church had the power to absolve the repentant sinner from the crimes of adultery, murder, and apostasy, and because they rebaptized those who joined their sect; the Quartodecimans, because they refused to submit to the Council of Nicæa with regard to the time of celebrating Easter.

Every revealed truth is God's own word, and what God says is of the highest importance to man, and must be believed; so that it is impossible to make the distinction between fundamental truths and those which are not so. Were it the same for us to believe or not believe them, God would never have revealed them. Moreover, all revealed truth rests on God's veracity. Whosoever, therefore, rejects but one article, how irrelevant soever it may appear, impugns God's veracity, and is guilty of a great crime.

8. Besides, the various sects which had recourse to this subterfuge never could settle among themselves which were the fundamental articles required for their supposed unity of faith. Those established by one were rejected by another, and each one considered its own peculiar tenets as strictly fundamental. To say that those articles only are fundamental on which they all agree, is extremely vague: for hitherto they have never

been able to determine which sects this union should embrace. Those who deny the divinity of Christ might claim admittance into it; nay, even those who look upon the Bible as a myth, and reject all supernatural truth, still consider themselves good Protestants, and their title cannot be easily gainsaid. Truly such unity is a Babel; and if Christ did not intend to establish any other unity of faith, both His coming on earth and His teaching were perfectly useless.

9. Unity in sacraments is also required. The sacraments are means instituted by Christ, and confided to the Church, to be administered to the faithful for their sanctification. Hence the Church must always possess and distribute these means of salvation. The Church could not fail in the unity of sacraments without, at the same time, failing in the unity of faith. For the sacraments could be instituted by Christ alone, because He alone could attach invisible grace to outward signs. Therefore the sacraments belong to the dogmatical part of religion, or to the deposit of faith held by the Church.

10. There must be unity of government: for the Church is *one* visible kingdom, household, temple, city. But a kingdom is one, only inasmuch as it is governed by one authority; a household is one, because governed by its head; the city is one, because presided over by its magistracy. The members of a moral body are one, only by

means of the supreme authority constituting the bond of union, and directing all to the attaining of the end in view. Diverse associations cannot be called one society, simply because their end is identical, and the means the same; they can be called one only when directed by the same authority.

This single authority guiding the many members of the mystical body of Christ, cannot be Christ and the Holy Ghost alone, because their action on the Church is invisible, and is perceptible only by the tangible effects worked in and through the members. The Church on earth, though containing an invisible element, is still a visible society, using outward means to attain the spiritual end to which it tends; for she is a city built on a mountain, she is the light of the world. (*Matt.* v, 14-16.) She is the divinely appointed teacher of salvation, whom all must listen to and obey, who must therefore be apparent to the whole world. An invisible church or a visible church deprived of a visible authority, could neither be heard, nor could she be the guide of mankind: for none could know where she is to be found, nor what are her commands. The preaching of God's word, the sacraments, are visible means; therefore the authority of the Church preaching and administering the sacraments must also be visible.

Were the Church not a visible body, presided over by a visible supreme authority, the faithful could never form a society on earth: for no society can exist without some outward bond of union by which its members are made one, and without mutual coöperation to the same end. But how could they mutually coöperate, if there were no visible authority directing them to the one end? Nay, if the Church were invisible, Christ's mission on earth, His teaching, His founding a Church would be purposeless. Since, then, the Church is necessarily a visible body, it must be guided and directed by a visible authority whom all the members are bound to obey; for, as Christ said, he who will not hear the Church, let him be " as the heathen and publican" (*Matt.* xviii, 17); and this visible authority must be *one*, else the body, so far forth as it is visible, could not be *one*.

11. What is more, the unity of faith and of sacraments requires unity of government. For unity of faith demands unity in the teaching body, which supposes unity of authority; because in the Church those only can be invested with authority who are commissioned to teach, since it is from them that the faithful have to learn what they are to believe, and the means they must use in order to salvation, and the faithful must, therefore, submit to the divinely appointed teachers, and obey them in all things appertaining to faith.

THE UNITY OF FAITH.

Besides, when controversies arise, there must be a recognized authority to determine finally what is the true doctrine of the Church; otherwise the unity of faith would soon be lost, as happens with Protestant sects who repudiate such authority. This is the reason why Christ conferred on Peter and his successors the keys of heaven (*Matt.* xvi), and commissioned him to feed His flock. (*John* xxi, 15-17.) St. Cyprian, who was martyred in the year of our Lord 258, thus expresses this fact in his work on the unity of the Church, written in 251: " The first step taken begins by unity (*exordium ab unitate proficiscitur*), and the primacy is given to Peter, that the Church of Christ may be set forth as one, and the seat of doctrine (*cathedra*) as one " (cap. iv). (Conf. the whole passage translated in *The Evidence for the Papacy*, by the Hon. Colin Lindsay, p. 23.)

CHAPTER V.

CATHOLICITY OF THE CHURCH.

1. Foretold in the Old Testament and willed by Christ.—2. The End Christ had in View requires it.—3. It is simultaneous.—4. How it is simultaneous.

1. THE Apostles' Creed teaches us that the Church must be Catholic, since it contains this article: "I believe in the holy Catholic Church;" and this even the sects could not help keeping in their creed, though some, in order to avoid the word *Catholic*, translated it in the vulgar tongue, by saying: "I believe in the holy *Universal* Church," which, after all, is the same thing, *Catholic* meaning *Universal*.

The Catholicity of the Church was foretold in the Old Testament, as we have seen. (Part I, chap. xii.)

Christ willed that His Church should be Catholic, because He commanded His apostles to go to all nations and to preach the Gospel to every creature, and what Christ willed was realized: for to Him all power is given in heaven and on earth, and He promised to be with His apostles preaching and baptizing till the consummation of the world.

2. The end which Christ had in view required the Catholicity of the Church; for Christ is the Saviour of all mankind (1 *Tim.* iv, 10); through Him alone can we have life (*John* vi, 54); there is no other name by which we can be saved but the name of Jesus. (*Acts* iv, 12.) And, as Christ has lodged all the means of salvation in His Church, that Church must be of such a nature as to be easily known to those who do not wilfully shut their eyes against truth. Hence it is Catholic.

This property belonged to the Church from the very beginning of her existence. St. Paul writing to the Romans (i) rejoices that their faith is spoken of in the whole world. The apostles had received the gift of tongues, that they might announce the Gospel to all nations, and Tertullian (*De Præscript.*, No. 20) tells us that, having divided the world among themselves, they went to announce the same faith and doctrine to the nations. St. Irenæus, who was Bishop of Lyons in 177. testifies that in his time "the Church was diffused through the whole world, even to its extremities." (*Contra Hæreses*, lib. i, cap. x.) St. Justin (*Dial. Contra Tryph.*) says that there is no nation, whether Greek or Barbarian, whatever be its manners or customs, in which prayers are not addressed to God the Father in the name of Jesus sanctified.*

---

* A strong cumulative proof of the Church's Catholicity at her birth will be found in Father Thébaud's forthcoming work on *The Church and the Gentile World*. Hardy & Mahony, Philadelphia.

3. This Catholicity must be, not successive, but simultaneous; which means that the Church must, at one and the same time, be spread and known throughout the accessible parts of the globe. The Donatists, who arose in the beginning of the fourth century, separated themselves from the Church, because they did not wish to communicate with those who, during the persecution, had given up the sacred writings, though the latter had done penance and been reconciled with the Church; and in fact they did not hold communion with the churches which received back these repentant sinners. As their sect was found only in some parts of the north of Africa, they pretended that, though the Church of Christ ought to be Catholic, it might yet be so diminished in number as to be found only in a few provinces; but they were condemned, and their sect soon ceased to exist. The Catholic writers, as St. Augustine, St. Optatus, and others, who refuted their errors, laid particular stress on the fact that these heretics, being confined only to a corner of the earth, could in no way claim the title of *Catholic*. Truly, if the Church were so restricted in number, she would cease to be the light of the world, she could not be the teacher of mankind.

4. Yet this Catholicity, though necessarily simultaneous, does not imply that the Church of Christ should be dominant everywhere. Christ foretold that there would be heresies; that many

would refuse to listen to His word; that the Church would have to suffer persecution. Therefore He has not promised that all the nations of the earth should at all times profess the true faith. Consequently, for the Catholicity of the Church, it is sufficient that she be solidly established in many places, so that her preaching may be within the reach of those who do not wish purposely to stop their ears; that, where she is not established, notice of the truths proclaimed by her may be easily brought home to those who wish to save their souls. There are many countries where the majority, even the whole nation, is Catholic; in other countries, as in England, North America, North Germany, the Catholic Church, though not in the majority, is still so established that her preaching is open to all. Elsewhere, as in Sweden, Norway, Denmark, etc., the Catholic truth may be known to all those who wish to know it: and this may be said of almost every other heretical, infidel, or heathen country, because Catholic missionaries are preaching the Gospel everywhere. Nay, more: the very persecutions to which the Church is exposed are means used by God to spread the knowledge of her, and to attract the attention of those who are not within her pale. What is at present the case has always been so in former ages for the countries of the then known world.

CHAPTER VI.

SANCTITY OF THE CHURCH.

1. In what consists the Holiness of the Church?—2. The Unworthiness of some of her Members no Obstacle to her Holiness.—3. This Holiness must be made visible.—4. Proved by the Gift of Miracles.

1. THE Church, being Christ's mystical body, whose life-giving principle is the Holy Ghost, must of necessity be holy. She is holy inasmuch as she is a body, because she is quickened by the Holy Ghost, who gives efficacy to her ministry of preaching, dispensing the sacraments, and governing the faithful so as to lead them to eternal life. She is holy in her members, whether we consider those who are partakers of her authority, or those who are subject to it. The authority of the former is holy, because it is the same as was exercised by Christ in the flesh; the means used are holy, because instituted by Christ, and their efficacy depends, not on the personal merits of those who administer them, but on Christ Himself. She is holy in her members; for, though all those who are actually her members are not clothed with the gift of sanctifying grace, still all, so far forth as they belong to her, are holy, since

that by which they are united to her is holy and the effect of the Holy Ghost. For, in order to be a member of the Church, faith is required as well as subjection to the authority instituted by Christ. Now, faith is a gift of the Holy Ghost, which, though it does not of itself justify the soul, is still the foundation, the root of sanctification; subjection to the authority of the Church is also in itself holy.

2. Hence it follows that the unworthiness of some ministers in the Church cannot affect her holiness, since ministers are not the authors of grace and holiness, but merely channels through which these gifts flow to the faithful; and the efficacy of the ministration depends on the Holy Ghost. Nor is it required that all the members of the Church should actually be saints. Christ foretold that on earth the tares should grow together with the wheat. The whole economy of His new law supposes that there will be sinners needing forgiveness. He instituted the sacrament of the remission of sins, when He conferred on His apostles and their successors the power of forgiving sin. (*John* xx. 22, 23.) He told His apostles that, if any of the members of the Church should sin against his brother, he should first be admonished; if he did not heed this advice, he should be referred to the Church; and if he did not hear the Church, he should be banished from it. (*Matt.* xviii, 15 et seqq.) Hence there

will be in the Church those who stand in need of having their sins forgiven, and who, consequently, are not saints. That the Church always professed to have the power of forgiving sins, is obvious from the condemnation of the Novatians (A. D. 251), who denied that she could grant absolution to those guilty of adultery, murder and apostasy.

3. Holiness, though it be itself invisible, must still produce outward effects. The sanctity of the Church, inasmuch as she is a body, shows itself in the external effects of her life-principle, the Holy Ghost. Her preaching must ever be fruitful; she must always be gathering new members into her fold, implanting in them the principle of Christian life, and sanctifying them by her sacraments.

Our Saviour has foretold that the Church will always be persecuted; yet at the same time He has promised to be with her till the end of time, and that the gates of hell shall never prevail against her. Therefore, the Church must ever triumph over all her enemies, and every persecution is sure to crown her with new glory.

She must always bring forth both men and women, who, having renounced the world and its enjoyments, devote themselves exclusively to the service of God, or to alleviating the temporal or spiritual wants of their fellow-men, and this with the sole view of pleasing their Lord.

Christ has praised virginity (*Matt.* xix, 12);

St. Paul praises it (1 *Cor.* vii, 32-38); therefore the Church must foster those who, to consecrate themselves more closely to God, cultivate virginity.

The Church must also give forth saints who practise virtue in an heroic degree: for the model of our lives is Christ himself; He is the way, the truth, the life (*John* xiv, 6); He exhorts us to be perfect as our heavenly Father is perfect (*Matt.* v, 48). Hence there must always be in the Church those who strive after higher perfection than that which ordinary Christians reach, as the Church is instituted for the perfecting of the saints. (*Eph.* iv, 11, 12) This sanctity must also be manifested outwardly, both by extraordinary works of piety and charity performed habitually, and by miracles setting upon these deeds the seal of God's sanction.

4. The gift of miracles has been granted to the Church (*John* xiv, 12; *Mark* xvi, 17, 18); and, though it be not imparted to each individual member of the Church, there will in all times be some on whom God bestows this gift, that thus the promise of Christ be fulfilled. In the first ages of the Church the gift of miracles was given more abundantly, because more necessary then to counteract the lying wonders of Satan; yet it has not been withdrawn from her. Protestants contend that the gift of miracles ceased after the apostolic era, or at the end of the first **two or**

three centuries; but why should they have ceased, when Christ promised that the gift would be permanent in the Church? They were performed, it is said, for the sole purpose of establishing the Christian religion; this having been effected, they are purposeless. But how can this assertion be substantiated? From the writings of the Old Testament we learn that many miracles were wrought for the establishment of the law of Moses; but even when this had been done, and the whole nation worshipped the true God alone, there was no cessation of the miraculous gifts: we meet with them under Josue, the judges, the kings, after the Babylonian captivity. Nor were these miracles performed only for the defence and preservation of the Mosaic law: many are recorded in Holy Writ, tending solely to the benefit of private individuals, as that of Eliseus in favor of the Sunamitess. (4 *Kings* iv.) Now, if the gift of miracles did not cease in the Old Law, why should it cease in the New?

Besides, Christianity was not established all at once over the whole earth. One nation after another was brought within the fold of Christ during successive centuries, and there are many still to be converted. If miracles, as the apostle says, are for unbelievers, they are not converted without them; and miracles are as necessary for their conversion as they were for the conversion of the Greeks and Romans.

Christian writers in all ages of the Church have been constantly testifying to the existence of miracles; they state them not only on hearsay, but as eye-witnesses. To deny their testimony, to look upon them as guilty of wilful fraud, may be of the direst necessity to our opponents for bolstering up their theory; but it cannot be done without sapping the very basis of Christianity. If all Christian teachers were wilful liars, where, then, was the Spouse of Christ? Had our Lord so soon forgotten His promises, and given over His Church to the guidance of the Evil One? And if facts stated by eye-witnesses, whose trustworthiness can be questioned only by those who purposely seek to distort truth,—if facts attested by such a cloud of witnesses during all ages are to be set aside, what becomes of the Gospel miracles themselves? Surely, Protestants who wish to uphold the truth of the latter, and to deny the former, place themselves in a very awkward position. They cannot solve the arguments urged against them by unbelievers.

Every so-called Christian association, therefore, which grants that in its communion there are no miracles, confesses, by the very fact, that it is not the true Church.

CHAPTER VII.

APOSTOLICITY OF THE CHURCH.

1. The Church apostolic.—2. Material Succession alone not sufficient.—3. Apostolicity required by all ancient Writers.—4. No extraordinary Mission to teach new Dogmas, or reform old ones.—5. No Break in the Apostolic Succession to be feared.—6. The four Properties of the Church based on Unity.—7. The Church can never fail.—8. No dogmatical Reform needed in the Church.—9. The Promises made to the Church not conditional.—10. Reform of individual Members may at times be required.

1. THE Church, being one and the same at all times and in all places, must have preserved intact the power of teaching, administering the sacraments, and governing the faithful, which Christ conferred on His apostles and their legitimate successors. Hence the Church must be apostolic: which means that those who actually preside over her must have the power transmitted to them by an unbroken chain reaching back to the apostles.

2. But a mere material succession does not suffice. A bishop who has received his authority from a legitimate source, if he separates himself from the Church, by the very fact loses all power of teaching, administering the sacraments, and governing the faithful, so that he can no longer

transmit it to his successors. Though, by his separation from the Church, he does not lose his character of bishop; though he can, by the imposition of hands, transmit to others the character of bishop or priest, yet jurisdiction he has none, and he cannot confer on others what he himself does not possess. Because all the powers which Christ bestowed on His apostles are for the Church, and belong exclusively to her,—those, therefore, who exercise them, must necessarily be her members. She is the mystical body of Christ, which is one, undivided; He gives her life and activity; He quickens her by His presence and by the Holy Ghost, and this only inasmuch as she is His body. Hence, to participate in this life and activity, one must be incorporated into the mystical body of our Lord.

3. Such has been the constant teaching of the Church from the very outset. St. Clement, in his first letter to the Corinthians, writes thus: "God has sent Jesus Christ, and Jesus Christ has sent His apostles. These faithful ministers, having received the command from the mouth of their divine Master, . . . went everywhere to announce the kingdom of God; and preaching thus in the country and the cities, they chose the first-fruits of the new-born churches; and having tried them by the light of the Holy Ghost with which they were filled, they established these men bishops and deacons over those who were to

believe in the Gospel, and they ordered that after their death others equally tried should succeed in their ministry."

St. Irenæus (*Contra Hæreses*, lib. iv, cap. 30): "The knowledge of the apostolic doctrine, the antiquity of the Church, and the character of the body of the Church, is in the *succession of bishops*, to whom the apostles, in the Church of every country, have transmitted it, and which has come down to us without error." (Also *ibid.*, cap. 31; lib. iii, cap. 3.)

Tertullian (*De Præscript.* Nos. 20, 32, 36) appeals to this as the best argument for silencing heretics. Also Optatus Milev., *Contr. Parmen.*, (lib. 2); St. Cyprian, Epist. 86, *Against the Novatians*; St. Epiphanius, *Hæres.* 27; and others.

4. It follows, therefore, that no extraordinary mission can exist in the Church, either to proclaim new dogmas not taught by her, or to reform her dogmatical teaching. For Christ has promised His apostles and their lawful successors that the Holy Ghost would teach them all truth, and abide with them forever; He has promised to be with them teaching and administering the sacraments even unto the end of time. St. Paul, who was called to the apostleship in an extraordinary manner, had to receive his powers by the imposition of hands from those who had already received it from the apostles. (*Acts* xiii, 1–3.) To suppose the necessity of a dogmatical

reformation in the Church's teaching, is to maintain that Christ was unfaithful to His promises; that He abandoned the Church, and allowed the gates of hell to prevail against her.

5. It has been objected that we cannot know whether the apostolic succession is continued in the Church; for, to confer the sacrament of Order, the intention of the consecrator is required, and the recipient must be validly baptized. And is it not possible that some may have received Holy Orders who were not baptized; and how can we be certain the consecrators had always the intention of conferring this sacrament? And if a break occurred once in the nineteen centuries, who can say how widely it has extended? Were the Church a human institution, this difficulty would be insolvable; but, as she is a divine institution, we need not fear any break in the apostolic succession, for the simple reason that Christ is powerful enough to insure the means adequate to the fulfilment of all His promises.

6. The four properties of the Church mentioned above are closely and necessarily connected together, and they may all be reduced to that of *unity*. Catholicity is nothing but the permanency of the Church's unity in every time and place. Sanctity is the intrinsic principle from which this unity arises; for it produces and manifests the subjection of the faithful to the legitimate pastors of the Church, as also the efficacy of

the ministrations by which unity is preserved. Apostolicity is the extrinsic principle of unity, inasmuch as the same power of teaching, administering the sacraments, and governing the faithful, which was conferred by Christ on the apostles, is transmitted, by legitimate succession, to the actually existing pastors of the Church. Consequently the true Church must, of necessity, possess these four properties, and she cannot have one without simultaneously enjoying the three others; hence, also, the absence of one implies the absence of all the rest.

7. It follows, too, from what has been said, that the Church can never fail, but that she must exist in her purity unto the end of time. Christ has promised this perpetuity. He has built His Church on a rock, and has said that the gates of hell shall never prevail against her. But, if the Church could have fallen into either heresy or idolatry, the gates of hell would have prevailed; for, instead of sanctifying her children, she would have led them astray, and separated them from Christ. Christ has promised to be with His Church till the end of time: had she, therefore, taught error, He would have abandoned her, the Holy Ghost would not have abided with her forever,—a supposition which becomes blasphemy as soon as it is turned into an assertion. Besides, the Apostle St. Paul informs us that the Church, by means of the body of pastors, will ever

maintain the unity of faith, and, by the administration of the sacraments, consummate or perfect the saints, till the whole mystical body of Christ is completed in heaven. (*Eph.* iv, 11-14.) Hence the Church must always preach the true doctrine of Christ, and administer the sacraments instituted by Him for the sanctification of her members.

Moreover, the Church is the kingdom of Christ, whose reign is eternal. (*Dan.* ii, 44; *Luke* i, 32, 33.) The Church, therefore, can never fail. The Church is the mystical body of Christ, which He sanctifies by His own presence and by the action of the Holy Ghost; but Christ's body cannot perish; it must always teach truth: were it to teach error, it would no longer be His.

8. This is another reason why, in the Church of Christ, there can never be a necessity of reforming her doctrinal teaching. Those who laid claim to a call to reform the teaching of the Church, gave the lie to Christ. Had He allowed her to fall into error or idolatry, as was asserted by the self-constituted reformers of the sixteenth century, His promises would have come to nought, and the gates of hell prevailed. Instead of being guided by the Holy Ghost, the Church, at least for a long time, would have been overruled by the Evil One. Now, if Christ could not keep the promises He so clearly gave, then He would not be God, but an impostor, and the

whole Christian religion would be no better than Mahomet's.

9. The promises made to the Jews with regard to the temple, or to themselves as the chosen nation of the earth, were conditional, and depended for their fulfilment on their fidelity to God. Nay, their apostasy was predicted by the prophets. Not so the promises made by Christ: they imply no condition. He simply foretells that His Church will stand forever, and that in all times there will be a large number of His disciples spread over the world, and that He will remain with them unto the consummation thereof.

10. If at times a reform was needed, it was not a reform of the Church herself, nor of the generality of her members; because, in all times, even when holy men insisted upon reform, there were many saints, and a great number of the faithful practised all Christian duties. But a number of bishops and priests stood very much in need of a reform in their conduct; and the discipline of the Church, which in not a few places had been relaxed through interference of the temporal powers in ecclesiastical affairs, had to be brought back to its former vigor and purity.

CHAPTER VIII.

THE ROMAN CATHOLIC CHURCH ALONE HAS THE PROPERTIES OF CHRIST'S CHURCH.

1. Unity of the Roman Catholic Church.—2. She has always held the same Doctrines.—3. The Catholic Church could not vary in her Doctrines.—4. Definitions of Doctrine argue no Change.—5. Catholicity of the Roman Catholic Church.—6. Her Sanctity; she makes her Children holy.—7. Converts pagan Nations.—8. Fosters Virginity.—9. Produces Saints.—10. Whose Sanctity is confirmed by Miracles.—11. Her Stability.—12. Sects constantly lose Ground.—13. Calumnies against the Church refuted.—14. Apostolicity of the Church.—15. Antipopes no Break in the Apostolic Succession.—16. Nor is the great Schism of the West a Break.—17. Neither the Greek Schismatics—18. Nor Protestants can claim to be the Church of Christ.

1. THE Church which acknowledges the Pope, the Bishop of Rome, as her visible head and the vicar of Christ upon earth; in other words, the Roman Catholic Church possesses all the properties which belong to the spouse of Christ. She is one in faith, sacraments, and government. As to the last, there is no need of proof: the fact is self-evident, and granted by all. That there is unity of faith at present among all Catholics, to whatever nation they belong, is also beyond question; because all Catholics acknowledge the Church as the divinely appointed

teacher of truth, and they consider it a strict duty firmly to believe all the articles of faith which she sets forth. If anybody rejects even one article of her creed, he is by that very fact separated from her communion, and ceases to be a member of the flock. So much for the present; as to the past, her unity of doctrine is disputed by all heretics, since they all separated from the Church under pretence that she had changed the faith. From what has been said in the preceding chapter it is clear that no such change of doctrine can have occurred.

2. The sects, indeed, pretended to bring back the Church to her pristine purity of doctrine, but by this very presumption they gave the lie to Christ, as we have already shown. Called upon to state the time when new doctrines were introduced into the Church, they were at a loss to settle this point: some assigned one epoch, others another. But all in vain. They could never point to a single period when the dogmas impugned were not held in common by all truly Christian nations. And yet history has preserved for us a clear statement of every heresy which, in successive times, arose to rend the unity of the Church. We know their authors, the time when they began to proclaim their new doctrines, those who first withstood them, the councils which finally overthrew them. How, then, is it that there never arose any question about the doctrines which, as Protestants

assert, have been introduced into the teaching of the Church? She always kept strictly to the principle that nothing new in matters of faith is admissible, so that all heresies were condemned: how, then, could any new doctrine be broached without a most decided opposition in many places?

3. It will not do to say that these novelties were introduced *gradually* and *imperceptibly*. For, though many Catholic doctrines denied by Protestants surpass the natural power of the human intellect, still they are not mere theoretical views; they are the very foundation of Christian life, and are daily put in practice. The faithful, when receiving Holy Communion, could not but know whether what they received was merely a piece of bread eaten in remembrance of Christ's death, or the real body of our Saviour. They also knew what they had to do to obtain the remission of their sins: whether confession was required or not. They were aware of the practices of piety which had been taught them from their youth. How, then, could any innovation in the doctrine of the Holy Eucharist, the sacrament of Penance, and the other sacraments, be introduced without attracting the notice not only of the pastors of the Church, but of every Christian layman, whether learned or not? How could the practice of praying for the dead, of venerating the saints and their relics, be inaugurated

without contradiction, if it were opposed to the received doctrines?

The very ceremonies of the Church, used in her worship and in the administration of the sacraments, are based upon the doctrines she teaches. Thus St. Augustine proved against the Pelagians the dogma of original sin, by pointing to the exorcisms which are used even before the baptism of children.

Protestants, forsooth, came fifteen centuries too late; hence their claim to be the Church of Christ is absurd. The principal doctrines they reject are even now professed, not only by the schismatic Greeks, by the Jacobites, but also by the Nestorians, who separated from the Church eleven centuries before Protestantism was known. What they now hold about these doctrines must have been the common teaching of the Church: had it been a novelty brought in after their separation, they would never have accepted it; nay, they would have used this innovation as a most powerful and cogent argument to justify their seceding from the Church. The unity of doctrine, therefore, of the Catholic Church in all times is an historical fact which cannot be gainsaid, except by those who wilfully shut their eyes to the truth.

4. But the new definitions which were lately made about the Immaculate Conception of the Blessed Virgin Mary, and the Pope's Infallibility,—have they not changed the faith of Catholics?

By no means. The Church always taught these doctrines, but had not solemnly defined that they are in fact contained in the deposit of faith confided to her. There are still other doctrines which form part of the Catholic belief, but which as yet have not been solemnly defined. The Church resorts to these definitions only in the event of a serious provocation, when her silence would endanger the sacred deposit. As the solemn definition that Christ is the Son of God, true God and true man, which was proclaimed at the Council of Nicæa, did not change the faith of the Church, so the subsequent definitions, called forth by the false doctrines of heretics, have made no alteration in her teaching.

5. The Church is Catholic. She alone bears the name of Catholic; and it is a title which even her enemies allow her. If a stranger enters into any city where there are churches belonging to different denominations, and asks where the Catholic church is, neither Protestant, nor Jew, nor infidel, will point out any Protestant or schismatic church, but will direct him to the church which is in communion with the See of Rome. Of late, Protestants, belonging to the so-called English Church by law established, have endeavored to get themselves called Catholic; but this title is acknowledged by no other sect: in the eyes of all mankind, whether Catholics, Protestants, Jews or infidels, they rank with Protestants as they

really are. The Church's right to the name of Catholic is so evident that it need not be proved; for Catholics are spread all over the globe.

6. The sanctity of the Catholic Church may be shown by the following considerations. Any Catholic who lives up to the teachings of his faith enjoys the reputation of a holy man, even with the enemies of the Church. There are many upright men among Protestants, but these are so, not in virtue of their religion, which allows them to frame their own code of morality, but on account of their natural rectitude; whereas a Catholic leads a good life only inasmuch as he follows the precepts of his faith, and as soon as he grows negligent in the practice of his religious duties, he gradually ceases to be virtuous. There are no doubt many worthless Catholics; but they are such precisely because they do not follow the precepts of faith, and do not make use of the means of sanctification which the Church holds out to them.

7. The Catholic Church alone is capable of converting nations to the Christian faith, and not only of civilizing them, but of training them to the practice of every Christian virtue. No Protestant sect, however large its staff of well-paid missionaries, has hitherto been able to convert a single pagan nation, and imbue it with the principles of Christian life. The only success they can boast of is the conversion of the Sandwich

Islands; but this people, remarkable for their mildness of character, have not improved much since their conversion. They have, it is true, rejected idolatry, but they have also contracted some of the vices of the civilized nations with whom they have come in contact; so that, in a short time, the population, which on the arrival of the missionaries was 400,000, is now reduced to 50,000. The sterility of Protestant missions is an historical fact attested by many Protestant writers. On the other hand the Catholic Church, though unprovided with the ample pecuniary resources at the disposal of Protestant sects, and unseconded by the protection of governments, succeeds everywhere in forming new Christian Churches. The Greek schismatics have not as yet endeavored to send missionaries among pagan nations; the Russians, indeed, do try their hand at conversion, but the persuasion they use, principally against Catholics, is brute force.

8. The Church alone is able to foster multitudes of men and women who, for the love of God, renounce all worldly honors and enjoyments, and devote themselves entirely to practices of piety, and to assisting their fellow-creatures in their spiritual and bodily necessities. No Protestant sect has as yet been able to do as much. Some few attempts have been made of late, but with little or no lasting success: nay, the religious state of life is so repugnant to Protestant ideas,

that the Protestant masses have for it an instinctive detestation, and seek by every means to calumniate Catholic religious communities. The Greek schismatics have maintained religious communities both of men and women; but these do not devote themselves, as Catholic religious do, to alleviating the spiritual or temporal sufferings of others.

9. There have always been saints in the Catholic Church, whose sanctity has been proved by their works of charity, and confirmed by miracles due to their intercession. The Greeks still continue to venerate the saints produced by the Catholic Church before their separation from the centre of unity, but since that period they have not been able to produce new ones. Protestants have discarded every saint in the calendar, so far are they from pretending to form them; whereas the sanctity of many Catholics whom the Church has canonized is such, that even Protestants cannot help admiring them. They cannot but venerate the charity of St. Vincent of Paul; the zeal and labors of St. Francis Xavier; the sweetness of St. Francis of Sales; the courage of many martyrs who, in these latter times, have died for the faith.

10. Not a century goes by that does not witness the canonization of a number of holy persons, both men and women. Now, to obtain the honors of canonization is no such easy task as

Protestants may perhaps imagine. In the first place, it must be clearly proved that the candidates for the honors either died for the faith, or practised, during a considerable portion of their lives up to the moment of their death, all the Christian virtues in an heroic degree: which means that they practised them habitually, and even under the greatest difficulties. All the acts of their lives are minutely scrutinized; those who knew them most intimately are examined under oath; all their words and doings are thoroughly sifted; if any doubt arises about their virtues, if all their acts are not entirely blameless, the cause is at an end: their canonization will never take place. Then their holiness must be proved by true miracles: nor is any miracle so easily admitted as some suppose; the witnesses must be in sufficient number, they must be altogether unexceptionable; the fact itself which they attest must be of such a nature as not to be explainable by any natural causes. As long as there remains any doubt whether natural causes may not account for it, it is set aside.

But Popish miracles, we are told, are mere old women's stories, unworthy of belief. No doubt those who will never take pains to examine the miraculous facts which happen even in our days, who reject them *a priori*, because they imagine that they are impossible, or that miracles were performed only by Christ and His apostles, cannot discern them. Those who close their eyes cannot be expected to see the sun shining overhead. Were they but to examine carefully the numerous miracles which have lately been performed at Lourdes in France, they would see clearly and evidently that miracles have not ceased in the Church. Christ, as was proved already, both promised to His Church and conferred on her the gift of miracles. In the Gospel of St. John (xiv, 12) He says: " Amen, amen, I say to you, he that believeth in me, the works that I do he also shall do: and greater than these shall he do." It is evident that Christ speaks here of miracles, and that the promise is not restricted to the apostles alone: " And these signs shall follow them that believe [the preaching of the apostles]: In my name they shall cast out devils; they shall speak with new tongues; they shall lay their hands upon the sick, and they shall recover." (*Mark*, xvi, 17.) To maintain, therefore, that miracles can no longer take place, is to gainsay the words of Christ. In fact the same objections which Protestants bring up against the miracles in the Church, are urged by infidels against the Gospel miracles.

11. The sanctity of the Church is also proved by her unshaken stability, for this shows that she is not a human, but a divine institution, whose life and strength come from above. Many a time have Protestants ventured to predict the downfall of what they were pleased to call the

harlot of Rome, because, according to human prudence, there seemed no further hope for the Church; yet she has always come off triumphant, the losses sustained in one place having been more than compensated in another. Especially in our days all the powers of earth have conspired against her. False science is arrayed in opposition to her, by the invention of pretended facts, or the distortion of true ones. Yet all in vain. The Pope, though at present a prisoner in the Vatican, is more loved and respected by Catholics than when he was in the zenith of his temporal power. Catholics are everywhere more courageous, more zealous, more united, than they have been for many ages. All so-called scientific theories, invented by the enemies of the Church to destroy her, are overthrown one after another by infidels themselves, each of whom is eager to invent a new system with which to demolish those of others; and in this fraternal by-play they are uniformly successful. Hence the result of such attacks is always to strengthen still more the Church's position.

12. All other religious denominations, on the contrary, are continually losing ground; many of their adherents drift into infidelity, or at least into total indifference about religious matters. Many clergymen of the English, the Swiss, the French, the German, and other Protestant churches, are avowed unbelievers, and openly

reject the whole supernatural order. The Russian Church, though supported by the Tsar, is undermined by many sects, which are increasing every day. The Protestant sects, in spite of their efforts to form a union among themselves, are daily splitting up more and more in opposite directions; and their very attempts at union weaken their hold on any positive doctrine, as this union could be brought about only by discarding all positive teaching.

Reflecting minds among Protestants must understand that the common hatred which all the sects, together with the Jews and infidels of every description, profess for the Church, is a sure mark of her divine origin. All, though opposed to one another, readily unite when there is question of fighting the Church. A member of any denomination may change his religion as often as he pleases; he may even become avowedly an infidel, and give up all religions, without drawing upon himself the animadversions and obloquy of Protestants; but let him become a Catholic, and straightway he raises a fearful storm: he is ostracized by his former friends, he is shunned as a man bereft of his senses. He may have been a loose liver before, and his return to the Catholic Church may have brought him back to the path of virtue: it is all one to his friends. They would prefer his keeping up a dissolute life rather than see him mend his ways by becoming a Catholic; nay, they would sooner.

have him renounce all religion than embrace the
true faith. Protestants rejoice in seeing Catholics
led astray, even though they know that such apostates will most likely turn rank infidels: in their
eyes anything is better than being a Catholic.
If a Catholic sets himself up in opposition to the
authority of the Church, whatever his motives
or the religious maxims he takes up with, he is
extolled to the skies as a man of liberal mind and
superior merit. Now, this blind hatred against
Catholicity, common to all the sects, cannot come
from the spirit of truth, nor can it be accounted
for on mere natural principles.

13. But it is pretended that the Church teaches
and approves many horrible doctrines, such as:
" The end justifies the means;" " No faith is to be
kept with heretics;" " The Church sells pardon,
by which is granted a license to commit sin," etc.
Were the Church to teach such doctrines, all
Catholics would be ready to forsake her. Protestants have often been challenged to prove their
calumnies; but in vain. We need not prove the
contrary: every Catholic child who has studied
the Catechism, knows that these assertions are
barefaced lies. Protestants themselves should
understand that their cause is desperate indeed,
if they have no other weapons than calumny
to defend it with.

14. The Church is apostolic; for the bishops
who are at present governing the Church hold

their powers by legitimate succession from the apostles. To show this, we have but to trace the succession of the Apostolic See of Rome, with which all Catholic churches must agree, and in which is placed the plenitude of jurisdiction; because Christ gave to Peter and his successors the keys of heaven, the power of binding and loosing on earth, of feeding all His sheep and lambs, and of confirming his brethren in the faith. To this succession the ancient writers of the Church appealed as to the most conclusive and convincing argument, as was stated in the preceding chapter. Now, the continued and uninterrupted succession of the Bishop of Rome is an historical fact beyond dispute.

15. But what of the Antipopes? By the very fact that they were known as Antipopes, who, in opposition to the legitimately appointed and acknowledged successors of St. Peter in the See of Rome, pretended to exercise the supreme power, the succession was not, and could not be, broken by them. There is no need of refuting the fable of Pope Joan, for this has long since been exploded by a number of learned Protestant writers. It is not supported by any contemporaneous author: an obscure mention of this fiction occurs, for the first time, two hundred years after the event, and this not positively, but as a hearsay. Such a remarkable event could not but be known to the whole world, and, as there were always enemies

of the Popes, would certainly have been mentioned somewhere in contemporary chronicles. But, even had it been true, it could not have broken the chain of succession. The fable states that the woman was mistaken by all for a man of great learning and piety; and hence, during the two years and a half that she is said to have been thought to be the Pope, the Holy See would simply have been vacant, and the Pope chosen after her would have been the lawful successor of St. Peter.

16. During the schism of the West, when there were two Popes, and at one time three, the true succession did not fail: for the Popes in Rome were indeed lawfully elected, and those of Avignon were intruders. But, as there were in the minds of many Catholics doubts as to the identity of the real Pope, the Church, who, in such a case, has the right to decide this point, asked of the two pretenders, and of the Pope in Rome, to abdicate. This last did so, as well as he who was chosen by the Council of Pisa, and Peter de Luna, who refused, was abandoned by all his adherents, and excommunicated; then Martin V was chosen and acknowledged by the whole Church. The legitimate succession would have ceased, if the Church had suppressed the Roman See, or if the Pope of Rome had no longer been acknowledged as the successor of St. Peter; but this was never done.

17. From what has been said, it is plain that no heretical or schismatical denomination has a right to claim the title of Spouse of Christ. We need not speak of the heresies of the first ten centuries: they have all disappeared. A few remnants of Nestorians and Eutychians, or rather Monophysites, may still be found in the East, but no one will have the hardihood to proclaim that either of them is the true Church.

The Greek schismatics cannot claim to be the Church of Christ, because they are wanting in Catholicity; neither have they any true unity, since they separated from its centre, the See of Rome. They do not form one church, because the Russian Church, besides being subject to the Tsar, even in spiritual matters, is independent of the Church of Constantinople; and the Church of the kingdom of Greece has also seceded from the latter. They have rejected the centre of unity, the supremacy of St. Peter, which they acknowledged up to the time of the schism, and which they reaffirmed in the Council of Florence. The Russian Church remained united to Rome even much longer.

18. As to the Protestants, they have no shadow of unity, save their common hatred of the Catholic Church. Each sect has its own peculiar tenets; each acts independently of the other. None of them can claim either Catholicity or apostolicity. When Luther began to preach

his doctrine, the whole Christian world professed the Catholic faith; even the schismatic Greeks repeatedly condemned his teachings, as well as those of every other Protestant sect. That Church, therefore, from which all other sects separated, must be the true one; else, there is no Church at all, and Christianity is a dream.

CHAPTER IX.

TEACHING AUTHORITY OF THE CHURCH.

1. The Church must have an Authority.—2. Different from that of civil Society.—3. Not confided to the Faithful.—4. An external Teacher required in the Church.—5. The teaching Body must be infallible, because it must be authoritative.—6. Without Infallible Teaching no Faith possible.—7. Christ willed the Church to be infallible.—8. The Church always claimed Infallibility.—9. Infallibility not opposed to Science.—10. Galileo.—11. The Church not opposed to Civilization.—12. The Church may be known even to the Unlettered.—13. How Children and the Ignorant come under the Teaching of the Church.—14. Infallibility does not give Rise to civil Intolerance.—15. The Inquisition.

1. FROM what has been stated in the above chapters, it is plain that Christ has established His Church as a visible society, whose principal aim is to glorify God, by teaching mankind the road to salvation, and affording it the means of attaining that end. Now, every society must have an authority; without it society is utterly impossible. Authority is one of its essential elements; the members forming it are its material part; but authority communicates to it its real existence; it constitutes its living principle, its bond of union; through it society is capable of action and development. The Church, therefore,

must also have an authority instituted by Christ Himself. But, as the Church belongs to the supernatural order, it must be guided from above; still its authority cannot be only the invisible authority of God, nor only the continued assistance of Christ, who governs His Church by the action of the Holy Ghost. Besides this invisible guidance there must also be a visible authority, which, directed by the Holy Ghost, presides over the visible Church, and to which all her members must be subject. The existence of such an authority has also been sufficiently proved in the preceding chapters.

As Christ willed His Church to be Catholic, and one in faith, sacraments and government, it is plain that she cannot be looked upon as an aggregation of many independent churches, each one presided over by its own independent authority, whose only bond is their common belief in Christ; since this would constitute not one, but many churches. The unity of a society depends, not on oneness of end,—for various societies may pursue a common end,—but on the unity of government, which leads the members to this common end. Much less could the Church be one, if the several independent churches, though professing to believe in Christ, were to hold contradictory doctrines.

2. The government of the Church, and the authority invested with this governance, must of

necessity be quite other than the government and authority of civil society. The authority of the latter is, no doubt, of divine institution; yet the form of government, though often determined by anterior facts, depends in a great measure on the will of the members that concur to form a civil association. Anterior facts may likewise, at times, determine the subject to be invested with the exercise of authority; but the people may also be its depositary, and confer it either on a monarch or on a body of men, restricting its exercise more or less. Not so with the authority of the Church. It has been instituted by God Himself, not in a general way, like that of civil society, but in a special manner; its form of government has been determined, the transmission of its powers specified; the main laws by which it is to act have been laid down by Christ, and He has promised it His special assistance; He also appointed the means to be used for compassing the end He had in view.

3. The power to govern the Church was not communicated to the faithful, but to the apostles and their lawfully appointed successors; for, to them alone Christ said: "All power is given to me in heaven and on earth: as the Father hath sent me, I also send you. Receive ye the Holy Ghost: going therefore, teach ye all nations," etc. (*Matt.* xxviii, 18, 19; *John* xx, 21, 22.) St. Paul tells us that the bishops have been placed

by the Holy Ghost over their flocks in order to rule them (*Acts* xx, 28), and that the apostles were instituted by Christ to maintain the unity of faith and to perfect the saints. (*Eph.* iv, 12, 13.)

Moreover, the powers exercised by the ministers of the Church are not mere natural or human powers; they belong to the supernatural order, and, consequently, no one can possess them unless they be communicated to him in a special manner by a special rite instituted by Christ: and this was to be done by the apostles and their lawful successors, on whom alone these powers were conferred. So that the body of the faithful do not participate in the government of the Church, but they are subject to it; their having been incorporated into the Church by the sacrament of baptism does not invest them with the powers of the priesthood, as Luther asserted; it makes them simply members of the Church, and gives them the right to participate in the spiritual blessings bestowed by Christ on His mystical body. It is not the faithful who make the Church; else, she would be only a human institution. Christ Himself is her maker, and she communicates to those who join her the privilege of membership. The government of the Church, therefore, is not democratic; it is not one in which the people delegate the ruling power to officials chosen by themselves, and whose authority they may restrict at pleasure.

The same appears also from the end Christ had in view in instituting the Church. This end is to enable mankind to glorify God. For this purpose the Church has to teach us to worship God; it has to impart to us the knowledge of those truths which we must know in order to reach our final destiny, and of the means we must use to secure it. The authority must therefore be vested in those only who have received from Christ a commission to teach; because all those who wish to be saved must submit to this teaching. But the commission to teach was given to the apostles and their lawfully appointed successors. They alone, therefore, are invested with authority in the Church.

The faithful who enter the Church by the sacrament of baptism, come into her, not as teachers, but as learners; they are bound to submit to the teaching imparted to them, and hence are subject to the teaching body established by Christ.

At present we speak of the authority of the Church in general; in a subsequent chapter we shall treat of the subject in whom, according to Christ's institution, the plenitude of this authority resides.

4. It is evident that God might have taught every man by an interior illumination of the mind, for He is the Lord and Master of all things, and can act with his creatures as He pleases. Yet God has not willed it so. Christ came from

heaven to establish an external teaching: else, both His mission and the establishment of a visible Church were quite useless. Christ not only taught mankind by word of mouth, but He commanded His apostles to go and teach all nations, and obliged all to submit to this teaching under pain of eternal damnation. (*Mark* xvi.) And though the interior illumination of the Holy Ghost is absolutely necessary to make an act of faith, God willed that the truth to be believed should be proposed externally by those who have been invested with the power of teaching, as St. Paul informs us (*Rom.* x, 14): "How shall they call on Him in whom they have not believed? Or how shall they believe Him of whom they have not heard? And how shall they hear without a preacher? And how shall they preach unless they be sent?" This, though denied in theory by our adversaries, is admitted in practice on all hands; for all the sects make use of preaching to maintain themselves, and gain new converts: all, except the Quakers, admit a ministry.

5. But the teaching body appointed by Christ must be infallible in its teaching. For the apostles are commanded to teach all nations the truths which Christ revealed, and all are bound to believe them under pain of eternal reprobation. Now, there are only two ways of teaching: either by argumentative demonstration, or by authority. The first way is impossible; for not only are the

majority of mankind incapable of being thus instructed, and wanting in the leisure and facilities requisite for such studies, but the truths revealed by Christ cannot be demonstrated by philosophical arguments, since they surpass the reach of the human understanding. The pastors of the Church must, therefore, teach authoritatively. But, to teach thus, it is necessary that the teaching body be infallible; for our intellect cannot be compelled to admit anything as true, unless it be either made evident, or proposed by such authority as cannot be gainsaid. Now, the pastors of the Church cannot show any intrinsic evidence of the truths they set forth; therefore, as the only alternative, their authority in teaching must be infallible. Had we the least reason to suspect that their teaching might perhaps be false, we could never be compelled to listen to it, nor would Christ have threatened with eternal damnation those who refuse to believe.

6. Without this infallible authority to teach, faith would be impossible, unless God were to impart an immediate revelation such as He vouchsafed to St. Paul. Faith is a firm and unshaken assent given to truth because revealed by God, who can neither be deceiver nor deceived. To believe, we must have certainty of the truths proposed. But God does not speak to us immediately. He only enlightens our intellect and strengthens our will, to enable us to give our firm assent to the

truths revealed. The teacher appointed by Christ to convey these truths to the mind is the Church; therefore her teaching must be such as to leave no doubt about the truths proposed by her; in other words, she must be infallible. Were she not infallible, could we entertain the least doubt about her teaching, certainty would be impossible, opinions more or less probable alone remaining: there would be no real faith.*

7. Christ conferred this infallibility on His Church: for He built the Church on a rock, so that the powers of darkness shall never prevail against her. (*Matt.* xvi.) Therefore, she can never teach error: for, being established by Christ to teach us salvation, she would cease to do so were she to teach falsehood, and the Evil One would have conquered her. Christ promised to be with His Church till the consummation of the world (*Matt.* xxviii); but so long as Christ remains with her, she cannot fall into error. The Holy Ghost continually teaches her all revealed truth (*John* xiv, 26); therefore, she will ever be a truthful teacher. The body of the pastors of the Church has been instituted by Christ to pre-

---

* We do not deny that heretics who, through no fault of their own, are ignorant of the infallible authority of the Church, may, with the assistance of God's grace, believe with supernatural faith some of the doctrines revealed by Christ; but, as Cardinal Franzelin says (*De Divina Traditione et Script.*, p. 590. Romæ, 1870), this knowledge they unwittingly derive from the Church which they do not know. Cardinal de Lugo (*Disput.* xii, §§ 50, 51, *De Fide*) maintains that not only heretics, but even Jews and Mahometans may, with

serve the unity of faith, and to perfect the saints (*Eph.* iv); but unity of faith cannot be kept up by falsehood, nor can the saints be perfected by error. The Church is the body of Christ, quickened by His Spirit, the Holy Ghost, the Spirit of truth. She is the bride of Christ, and, as such, she remains forever united to Him; but so long as this union between Christ and the Church lasts, she cannot fail either in truth or in sanctity. She is, according to St. Paul, the pillar and ground of truth (1 *Tim.* iii, 15); therefore, she must be infallible in her teaching.

8. Moreover, the Church has always claimed and exercised this prerogative of infallibility. In every age she has condemned as heretical any teaching opposed to her doctrines, and has constantly exacted from her children not only external submission to her teaching, but also the interior assent of the mind.

9. The infallible teaching of the Church is not opposed to the progress of science, nor does it narrow the mind and fetter its activity. The Church does not interfere with true science; she allows us full scope to investigate the laws of nature, and to apply our conclusions to useful

---

the grace of God, elicit some true acts of faith; but the dogmas they thus believe they receive through tradition, which tradition is derived from the true Church, and reaches even unto them: *Sed dogma hoc ex traditione habent, quæ traditio processit a vera Ecclesia fidelium et ad eos usque pervenit.* But, if the tradition of the Church were not in itself infallible, could it reach them so as to enable them to make a true act of faith?

purposes. Real science must, of necessity, be based on truth; its deductions must also be true. Now, truth cannot be opposed to itself, since all truth is founded on God. Hence true science cannot be opposed to faith. The Church condemns only deductions unwarranted by the facts from which they claim to proceed, and this only so far they are opposed to her teaching. Now, all deductions which clash with her teaching must, of necessity, be false, because opposed to the truths revealed by God. By condemning such conclusions, she lends a strong helping-hand to science, for she points out the landmarks that lead to truth, and so prevents us from going astray.

The mind is made for the knowledge of truth; it does not make truth, but finds it, and hence it must submit to it. The mind is not at liberty to embrace falsehood; we are not free to say that two and two make five. The necessity of submitting to truth, far from cramping our intellect, perfects it. Thus the teachings of the Church, though pointing out the road we have to follow in our philosophical investigations, do not impose any restraint on our intellects: they simply shield us from falling into error, and afford us a sure means of reaching the truth. Enemies of the Catholic Church, in urging this difficulty, suppose that the Church is no more than a human institution. Were this the case, their objection would be quite reasonable, for no human authority can prescribe limits to the mind; but, as the Church is the divinely appointed teacher, their objection falls to the ground.

What has been the result of the free inquiry claimed by Protestants? Materialism, Pantheism, Positivism, Socialism, Communism, the denial of even the first principles of reason. Many Catholics have of late fallen into these same errors, but, by doing so, they have ceased to be Catholics. Protestants, on the contrary, only follow out their own principles, when they become infidels. By rejecting the teaching of the Church, and proclaiming the right of private judgment, they have deprived themselves of the means of effectually stemming the torrent of these errors; though they wish to defend revelation, they are powerless, and infidels look upon them, not as enemies, but as allies—they consider them as having made the first breach through which they themselves may enter to destroy the stronghold of revelation. They acknowledge as a real foe the Catholic Church alone, against whom all their attacks are directed.

10. There is no need of dwelling on the condemnation of Galileo. Historical records have clearly shown that, if he was condemned for upholding his new scientific theory, it was not precisely on account of the theory itself, as it had already been advocated by Copernicus, but for persistently supporting his opinion by Holy Writ.

Had he left the Bible out of the question, and confined himself to propose the motion of the earth as a mere scientific hypothesis, he would not have been interfered with. In fact, at his time, it was no more than a mere hypothesis: the grounds on which he based his theory were unsound; the real proofs of this system were discovered afterward. Besides, it can enter into the mind of no well-informed man that this condemnation was an infallible utterance of Holy Church: it was merely a disciplinary enactment, wisely given, because too great an abuse had been made of Holy Writ; and the act was withdrawn when the theory had settled down on a more solid basis. Protestants always forget to mention that when Kepler, who established his theory on solid principles, was expelled from Protestant universities on account of his teaching, Julius de Medicis, a Catholic prince, favored him, and the Catholic Republic of Venice offered him a chair in the University of Padua.

11. Well, we are told, enough of Galileo! but is not the Church opposed to modern civilization and progress? The Pope, in the Syllabus (*Prop*. 80), condemns those who say that the Roman Pontiff may and ought to reconcile himself and come to terms with progress, liberalism, and modern civilization. This is undoubtedly true; for this so-called modern civilization is not a genuine, but a sham pagan civilization, which

insists on material improvement, and advocates the superiority of the temporal over the spiritual order,—nay, destroys the latter altogether. The Pope can never sanction this: were he to do so the Church would cease to be the teacher of mankind. In upholding, as the Pope is bound to do, the independence and supremacy of the spiritual order, he is a stanch advocate of true liberty.

12. It has been objected that the Church, before she can be recognized as a teacher divinely appointed by God, must first be known as such her titles must be examined. This requires a great deal of study; and therefore even the authority of the Church cannot be known to the ignorant, the unlettered, who have neither time, nor opportunity, nor sufficient knowledge, to institute such an inquiry. This objection is weak. The Church is sufficiently conspicuous to all who do not wilfully shut their eyes. Her unity, her vitality, her fruitful labors, the effects produced on those who sincerely follow her teachings, are evident to all; her miraculous existence, in spite of all persecutions, cannot but make an impression on every reflecting mind; hence, no great study is required to know her and acknowledge her titles. To establish her claims scientifically, no doubt demands an amount of investigation of which the majority of mankind are incapable; but such a scientific inquiry is by

no means necessary to make people know her as a divine institution.

13. But how do children and the ignorant come under the infallible teaching of the Church? They hear the truths only from their parents or their parish priests, who certainly are not infallible teachers. This is true. But they know that the doctrines contained in their catechism are approved by the bishop of the diocese, who, being in communion with, and subjection to, the Pope, the head of the Church, teaches in unison with the whole Church: and thus the infallible authority of the Church reaches them also.

14. Does not this dogma of infallibility give rise to intolerance? To dogmatic intolerance, yes; because the true Church must oppose error. To civil intolerance, no. The Church does not claim the right of forcing those who are out of her pale, to embrace her doctrines against their will. Those who join her must do so of their own accord.

15. But what of the horrors of the Inquisition? No Protestant writer who attacks the Catholic religion fails to parade them before his readers, to excite their indignation against the Church. Yet, when calmly examined, all these declamations are quite aimless. The Inquisition, considered fairly, not in the distorted Protestant view, may be taken under a threefold aspect:—

First, as a mere ecclesiastical tribunal, to which it belongs to inquire into heresies, to judge those who spread them, and pronounce sentence upon them, inflicting ecclesiastical penalties on the guilty. Such a tribunal is absolutely necessary, and belongs by right to the bishop of the diocese. No religious society professing any set of positive doctrines can do without it, and all, without any exception, have adopted it in one form or in another. A total disregard of all positive doctrine can alone bring about the abolishment or neglect of such an institution.

Secondly, the Inquisition may be viewed as an ecclesiastico-political tribunal. When the Roman commonwealth became Christian, the emperors, adopting into the code of laws the canon law of the Church, looked upon heretics as disturbers of public order, and treated them accordingly. The Arian emperors applied these laws to harass and persecute Catholics; yet when, in 385, a Catholic emperor condemned heretics to death, this act excited the indignation of many bishops. When, after the disruption of the Roman empire, true Christian states were founded, and the Catholic religion was considered by the nations as one of the fundamental laws of the State, heretics were held guilty, not only of a crime against God and the Church, but also of rebellion against the State, and of conspiracy against the constitution; the more so, because the heresies of the West were not like the subtleties of the Greeks who dealt in abstract conceptions—they took a practical form, and affected the body politic itself. No wonder, then, that the authorities of the State should punish such heretics as offenders in the civil order. But as the State cannot be judge in religious matters, the tribunal to which these causes were deferred was, of necessity, a mixed court: the Church had to investigate and pronounce about the heresy; the secular judges applied the penalties inflicted by the State.

The spread of the Albigensian heresy led to the introduction of a special tribunal to check it and punish the guilty. The institution of the Inquisition, properly so called, dates from the Council of Toulouse in 1229, and it soon was adopted in other countries; but, though it had to deal with turbulent heretics, who attacked Catholics wherever they could, destroyed churches and monasteries, murdered priests and religious, and committed other unheard-of barbarities, even Protestant writers cannot find any tales of horror about the cruelties supposed to have been inflicted by inquisitors on convicted heretics.

Lastly, we have the Spanish Inquisition. After the conquest of Granada, Ferdinand and Isabella were induced to establish a tribunal for the trial of heretics, but especially of apostates, who, in order to remain in the country and keep their property, had embraced Christianity, and afterward returned either to Judaism or Mahometanism, and were in continued correspondence with the enemies of the State. Pope Sixtus IV empowered the two sovereigns to set up this Inquisition, but his intention was that the tribunal should be similar to those in vigor in other countries. This intention was not carried out. The Inquisition soon became a mere political tribunal; it was censured by several Popes, who sought to mitigate its rigors, to maintain for the accused the right of appeal to the court of Rome, to save the property of the condemned for their children, but in vain. The Inquisition made itself, if not *de jure*, at least *de facto*, independent of Rome; every nerve was strained to thwart any appeals to the Holy See, and Rome's endeavors to correct abuses were rendered fruitless; so much so, that Pope Leo X had to excommunicate the inquisitors of Toledo. The Popes at least succeeded in preventing the introduction of the Spanish Inquisition into Italy. Now, in the very teeth of such facts, it is absurd to make the Church and the Popes responsible for the acts of an institution in practice purely political.

As to the horrors of the Spanish Inquisition, they have been greatly exaggerated. That it was blamable, is plain from the action of the Popes; yet it was very far from being that bloodthirsty tribunal which Protestants delight in describing; and if we compare it with the Inquisition as practised under Elizabeth, James, Charles I and Charles II, against Catholics in England and Ireland, it seems almost certain that to the latter might justly be awarded the palm of cruelty. Nor can we place any reliance on the assertions of Llorente, though a Spaniard, and for some time connected with the Inquisition. He pretended, indeed, to quote from documents; but having, as he admits, destroyed them purposely, so that his statements cannot be verified, he has, by so doing, forfeited the confidence of posterity. The Inquisition had recourse to torture: true, but all tribunals in those times resorted to this practice. The accused were not confronted with their accusers; yet even this might find excuse, if we reflect that oftentimes persons of the highest rank were brought before the inquisitors, and the influence of the accused or of their adherents was such that they could easily have revenged themselves on the accusers, had they known them personally; but the points of accusation, with their proofs, were always handed over to the accused, that he might justify himself. At all events, whatever may be said against the Spanish Inquisition, the Church has nothing to do with it. A tribunal of the Inquisition existed in Rome, but its procedure was quite different from that of Spain, and even Protestants cannot light upon any horrible tales to tell about it.

CHAPTER X.

THE BIBLE NOT SUFFICIENT TO CONSTITUTE THE INFALLIBLE TEACHING OF THE CHURCH.

1. The Authority of the Church necessary to know that we have the whole Bible.—2. Its Inspiration can be proved only by the Church.—3. Vain Attempts of Protestants to prove its Inspiration.—4. The Authority of the Church required for the Understanding of the Bible.—5. And for knowing whether the vernacular Copy is conformable to the Original.—6. The first Christians had no Bible.—7. With the Bible alone, Christ would have poorly provided for His Church.—8. Objections from Scripture.

1. PROTESTANTS not belonging to the rationalistic school, with the exception of Quakers, admit the necessity of an external infallible teacher; but they pretend that this teacher is the Bible, which, being the word of God, is infallibly true. Though we readily admit that the Bible is the word of God, the Bible *alone* cannot be the teacher appointed by Him to impart to us the knowledge of the truths we have to believe, and the duties we have to practise, in order to save our souls. We require the infallible teaching of the Church, to know that the Bible is the word of God. Had we not her infallible testimony, we could not know that there is a Bible; and Protestants, who reject this testimony, have lost the means of proving the

authenticity of all the parts of Holy Writ, and its divine inspiration. St. Augustine, in his Epistle, *Contra Epist. Fundament.*, says: "I would not believe the Gospel, unless moved thereto by the authority of the Church." We may, indeed, applying the rules of sound criticism, establish the genuineness of many parts of Holy Writ; we may also prove the authenticity of the same, with regard to the main facts therein contained; but, independently of the authority of the Church, we can never establish the authenticity of all its parts, and, without her, it is utterly impossible to show that it is inspired by the Holy Ghost.

Nay, more; Protestants, rejecting the testimony of the Church, cannot proceed to prove the authenticity of the Bible as to its parts; for the authenticity of a book must be shown by the uniform testimony of all the generations up to the very time when this book was written. Now, this testimony is given by the Church alone, as regards the New Testament; for, though some pagan authors mention some of the Gospels, and allude to some parts of the other sacred writings, they never testify to the genuineness and authenticity of the same in the form in which we have them now. Even early Catholic writers do not agree in these statements: more than one of the books actually contained both in Catholic and Protestant Bibles were by some considered doubtful. It was the Catholic Church alone that determined the canon of Holy Writ; on her authority were the apocryphal Gospels, and other writings attributed to the apostles, separated from those which are genuine.

She alone preserved the Sacred Scriptures, and, were we to believe Protestants, she did so with such jealous care that the laity were never allowed to have a glimpse of them; so much so, that Luther is supposed to have met with a Bible by chance, and to have been extremely astonished at seeing it for the first time. However, it is an undeniable fact that to her care alone we owe its preservation. Protestants did not receive the Bible at the hands of an angel, but from the Catholic Church. If, therefore, the authority of the Church is not trustworthy, there is no means of proving that we have at present the genuine word of God.

Protestants cannot say that the providence of God preserved the Bible from being corrupted; for, if God, notwithstanding His promise to be with the Church unto the end of time, and that the gates of hell shall not prevail against her, allowed her to fall into idolatry for many centuries, and to corrupt entirely the deposit of faith, as Protestants assert,—who can vouch for the purity of the Bible which, according to them, contains the whole doctrine of faith, and was wholly in the custody of the Church? If she altered the dogmas of faith, may she not equally

THE INSPIRATION OF THE BIBLE. 313

have tampered with the sacred writings? It will not do to have recourse to the bibles preserved by Greek schismatics, or by the sects which in former ages separated themselves from the Church; for, as these sects admit almost all the doctrines which Protestants reject as so many abominations, viz.: the sacrifice of Mass, the real presence of our Lord in the Holy Eucharist, the prayers for the dead, the seven sacraments, the veneration of saints and holy relics, etc., we must say that, if they agreed with the Church in corrupting the dogmas of faith, we may also suppose that they concurred with her in altering the sacred text.

2. But, even if critical arguments were sufficient to prove the genuineness and authenticity of the Scriptures and all their parts, without the authority of the Church the inspiration of the same could never be proved. The Bible itself does not assert that it is inspired. St. Paul, indeed, says that all Scripture divinely inspired is profitable to teach, to correct, to instruct in justice, but he does not tell us which are the divinely inspired books; and, moreover, he speaks of the writings of the Old Testament, not of the New: for, when he wrote this Epistle, but few books of the latter were as yet written, and, besides, he speaks of the Scriptures which Timothy had known from his infancy, which, as it is plain, could be only the writings of the Old Testament,

whose inspiration was attested by the authority of the Jewish priesthood. (2 *Tim.* iii, 15, 16.) At most it might be said that St. Peter, numbering among the Scriptures the Epistles of St. Paul then written, asserts their inspiration (2 *Epist.* iii, 15, 16); but this does not help us much, because we must have the authority of the Church to vouch for the inspiration of this very Epistle of St. Peter, and the more so as Eusebius of Cæsarea informs us that this Epistle was, even in his time, looked upon by many as doubtful.

The Holy Ghost does not inspire every individual who reads the Bible, to make him know whether the book he reads is inspired or not. In the first ages of the Church many pious Christians held as inspired several writings attributed to the apostles, which the Church by her authority discarded, and which are not comprised in the canon of the Catholic Bible, nor in the Protestant versions. Luther rejected the Epistle of St. James, which he called an epistle of straw; and yet it is found in Protestant Bibles. There must, therefore, be an external authority that determines which books are inspired and which are not; and this authority can be none other than the Church.

3. Protestants, to prove the inspiration of the Bible, bring forward only intrinsic arguments; they speak of the spiritual taste experienced in reading it, the sublimity of the conceptions

therein contained, the effects which the Bible has produced in the world, and the like. But to all these arguments the Turks might reply that they too experience spiritual taste in reading the Koran, that many sublime conceptions are contained in it, and that it has exercised a great influence on many nations. And if the Protestant answer that many absurd things are found in the Koran, the Turk, no doubt, would reply that to his mind there appear also such things in the Bible. How, then, could a Protestant, by mere internal arguments, convince a Turk, or any unbeliever, that the Bible is truly inspired? There are contained in it many mysteries surpassing the limits of the human intellect, which can be credible only when it is known that God really inspired the sacred penmen who stated them. As to the conversion of mankind, it is owing not to the reading of the Bible, but to the preaching of the Church. Protestants, by spreading the Scriptures among infidels, never have succeeded in converting them; the only result they have attained is to render Christianity ridiculous in the eyes of pagan nations. It is a notorious fact that the Chinese very willingly accept the Bibles offered them, and then sell them to their shoemakers, who turn them into Chinese slippers.

Other Protestants think it enough, for proving the inspiration of any book of the New Testament, to show that it was written by an apostle, because the apostles were commissioned to teach the Gospel, and because they were more than the prophets, who were inspired writers. But the apostles were commissioned to *preach*, not to write. If a book is proved to have been written by an apostle, we may say with certainty that it contains nothing but truth; but this is not sufficient for inspiration, because inspired writing must be not only true, but dictated by the Holy Ghost. Besides, St. Mark and St. Luke were not apostles; and yet they are inspired writers.

Moreover, Protestant theologians have made sad havoc of the Scriptures. Using the liberty claimed by them of interpreting the Bible by private judgment, many set aside as spurious not only verses and chapters, but whole books; some consider all the miraculous facts as purely mythical, others deny altogether that the Bible is inspired.

4. Even if the inspiration of Holy Writ could be proved independently of the infallible authority of the Church,—a supposition which we cannot grant, but which, for argument's sake, we will allow for a moment,—the authority of the Church would still be required. The Bible contains many sublime teachings, which surpass the capacity of the human mind. As St. Peter says of the Epistles of St. Paul (2 *Pet.* iii, 16), there are in them "certain things hard to be understood, which the unlearned and unstable wrest,

as they do also the other Scriptures, to their own destruction." There must therefore be an infallible authority to explain the true meaning of these difficult passages, and, in the event of a controversy, to pronounce authoritatively, and thus prevent the spreading of erroneous doctrines. Were this authority wanting, there would be no means of knowing what Christ has revealed, and thus His mission on earth would be frustrated. Protestants boast that the Bible is clear, that it can be understood by every one who reads it with a prayerful mind, because the Holy Ghost suggests to him the true meaning. If this be true, why, then, are there so many sects? Every sincerely religious soul should understand the Scriptures in the same manner. Yet experience shows that this is not the case. There are countless sects, all pretending to read Holy Writ in a prayerful spirit, all claiming to find their special tenets in it. Not only do the sects which exist nowadays appeal to the Bible to prove their opinions, but all the heretics who have arisen since the earliest ages have ever done the same. Each sect pretends that it alone possesses the true meaning of the sacred deposit—that all the rest are wrong. Who shall decide amid such confusion? All equally appeal to the Bible; all claim to be enlightened by the Holy Ghost. Had Christ not established an infallible authority to decide these controverted points, the Church would be a real Babel of confusion, and infidels would be justified in deeming Christianity a gigantic imposture not worth the consideration of a reflecting mind.

5. But there are still other reasons which show the necessity of an infallible authority. Protestants, when asserting that the Bible alone is the rule of faith, must necessarily hold that each one is obliged to form his own creed by reading the Bible. Every one, therefore, must institute a critical examination to settle which are the canonical books; whether the Bible he has in his possession is or is not corrupted or interpolated; whether it is a faithful translation of the original text. Now, this is a serious matter, because not only Catholics assert that the Bibles which are in the hands of Protestants have been corrupted in various places, but Protestants also attack the versions made by other sects: they say that texts have been wilfully changed to suit particular views. It is a notorious fact that Luther added the word *alone*, so as to make the sacred text say, " By faith *alone* are we saved;" and when called upon to account for this change, he replied: " Thus I will it, thus I command it: let my will stand for a reason." Every Protestant should, therefore, test his own translation, and compare it with the original. He will thus be obliged to study the Hebrew, the Chaldee, the

Syro-Chaldaic, and the Greek languages. When he has mastered these tongues, and compared his version with the original, he should read the Bible with care from first to last, and extract therefrom the sum of the dogmas he has to believe, and of the moral duties he has to perform, for nowhere will he find a compendium ready made in Holy Writ: and yet unless he has done all this, he cannot make an act of faith. What, then, will the unlettered do? How can they ever come to the knowledge of what they have to believe? True, they get their Bibles from their ministers or from their own church, which also gives them a catechism, where they are supposed to find everything needful to salvation; but this very fact shows that the Bible alone is not the rule of faith, since the unlettered must trust their own peculiar church to receive the Bible as an inspired book, and to receive the sum of the doctrines they have to believe. It is, indeed, the practical, commonsense way of proceeding, for otherwise this class of persons could never know what they have to hold; but it is in contradiction with Protestant principles, and a refutation of their own position: and, unfortunately, these poor people can never make an act of faith, for the authority which hands them their Bible and catechism is, on their own confession, not infallible. They must pin their faith to the sleeves of their individual ministers.

Besides, if every one is to read the Bible for himself, and determine therefrom his own creed, what is the use of the Protestant ministry? Its functionaries can claim no special powers to teach, since they profess to be liable to err in their teaching; the sacraments they have retained may be administered by any of laity, as they reject the sacrament of Holy Orders. In fact, Quakers are the only consistent Protestants.

6. According to Protestant principles, we must have the whole Bible, if we wish to know what we have to believe. How, then, could the first Christians have known their faith? At the beginning they possessed the Old Testament only. In course of time the Gospels and Epistles were written and addressed to particular churches and individuals; and as they had to be transcribed by hand, a considerable delay must have intervened before these writings could be communicated to all the churches. St. John wrote his Gospel about sixty years after the resurrection of our Lord, and yet Christianity flourished and spread everywhere—many had died for their faith: and all this was done without their having the whole Bible. Therefore the Bible was not the only rule of faith. If it was not then the only rule of faith, it cannot be now; else the Church which Christ has founded would have undergone a great and radical change.

7. Lastly, we must say that, were the Protestant principle true, Christ would have provided very badly for His Church. At His time very few persons knew how to read; books were costly things, when the art of printing was unknown. Christ, therefore, should not have said to His apostles, "Go ye to the whole world, and preach the Gospel;" He should have given some such message as this: "Write the Bible, teach the nations to read and write; then spread the Bible far and wide for the conversion of mankind." Now, this the apostles never thought of doing; they simply *preached* the Gospel. Besides, Christ should have revealed to His apostles the advantages of the printing-press, to insure more ready circulation to their books, at reduced prices, for the benefit of the poor. Unhappily, nothing of the kind occurred; they had no Bible societies to spread the word of God; they confined themselves to preaching, and so do their successors. And, alas for Protestantism! the printing-press made its appearance full fourteen centuries after Christianity.

8. However our Lord says (*John* v, 39): "Search the Scriptures, for you think in them to have life everlasting." But it should be first proved that this reading is right, and that the word *search* expresses a command, and not rather a fact; the Greek text, which is the original, points rather to the latter meaning. But, be this as it may, of

what Scriptures does our Lord speak? Evidently of the Old Testament, since the New one was not in existence. And they had to read the Scriptures, not in order to know the doctrine which Christ taught, but to ascertain that He was the promised Messiah. We also bid Protestants read the Bible, not to find out all the doctrines which Christ taught, but in order to make them know that He instituted a Church to teach the way of salvation.

The Jews of Berea (*Acts* xvii, 11) are praised, because they daily searched the Scriptures whether the things which Paul announced to them were so. Undoubtedly; but there was question of the motives of credibility alone. They wanted to know whether the prophecies contained in Holy Writ were fulfilled in Christ; but, in reading the Old Testament, they were not to search for the doctrines they were to believe: these they had to receive from St. Paul.

Protestants accumulate a number of texts which speak of the interior teaching of the Holy Ghost; they refer to St. John (1 *Epist.* ii, 27), who says: "You have no need that any man teach you: but as His unction teacheth you of all things." The interior teaching of the Holy Ghost is, indeed, absolutely necessary, because without His assistance we cannot perform a single salutary act; but, besides this internal teaching, external means are required. If the teaching of the Holy Ghost were alone sufficient, the Bible itself would be superfluous. Now, this external teaching is not the Bible alone, but principally the authoritative teaching of the Church. Even St. John, in the preceding verse, refers to doctrines taught by himself.

CHAPTER XI.

PRIMACY OF ST. PETER.

1. The Church must have a supreme visible Authority.—2. Independent of the civil Power.—3. The Government of the Church not aristocratic.—4. The Church a Monarchy.—5. The supreme Power vested in St. Peter and his Successors.—6. Primacy promised to St. Peter by Christ.—7. The Church built on St. Peter.—8. Keys of Heaven promised to him.—9. Fulfilment of the Promise.—10. St. Peter exercised this Primacy.

1. HAVING described the authority of the Church in general, we have now to speak of the person in whom this authority principally resides. Every complete and independent society must be governed by a supreme authority, which, in the exercise of its powers, is not subject to the interference of any other upon earth, and from whose decision there can be no appeal. Now, it is evident that the Church instituted by Christ is a society complete and independent, because it has been formed by God Himself, from whom it received its own authority ; and to this authority alone does it belong to prescribe the means by which, in accordance with the laws given by Christ, its end is to be attained.

2. No civil power whatever has a right to interfere with the legislation and government of

the Church, because on the one hand the commission to teach was not conferred by Christ on kings, princes, or magistrates, but on the apostles and their successors; on the other hand, the Church being Catholic, her power extends over the whole world, while the jurisdiction of a state is confined to the limits of that state. Besides, the end proposed for the Church is quite different from the one to which the state is destined. The latter aims at promoting and preserving the temporal external order only; the Church leads mankind to their last end, which is supernatural and eternal; and as all things here below must be subordinate to the last or final end of man, it follows, of necessity, that the Church is above the state, that the latter must be subject to her in all things which concern either directly or indirectly the supernatural order. Hence the Church can in no way be dependent on the state; she must possess her own supreme and independent authority.

3. It has already been shown that the form of government in the Church, as constituted by Christ, neither is nor can be democratic. It has also been proved that Christ commissioned His apostles and their successors to teach authoritatively all those things which He had commanded them, obliging all to submit to this teaching under pain of eternal damnation. The successors of the apostles are the bishops lawfully appointed, as has always been held by the Church from

the very beginning, and as appears from Holy Writ. (*Acts* xx; *Eph.* iv, etc.)

It may now be asked whether the supreme authority of the Church does not reside in the collective body of pastors, so that in government the Church be an aristocracy. This has been asserted by Presbyterians or Calvinists, who, though acknowledging no bishops, pretend that the governing power resides in the body of presbyters or ministers. The Jansenists admit the divine institution of bishops; they also grant that the Bishop of Rome, by divine right, presides over the episcopate; but they maintain that the real supreme authority is vested in the body of bishops, and that the Pope is merely the first among equals, or nothing more than a president presiding over the deliberative assembly of the Church when actually in session, or acting as the chief of the executive power of the Church, but under her control. The Gallican doctrine also tended to deny that the government of the Church is a true monarchy; for, though its upholders confessed that the Bishop of Rome held from Christ the supreme jurisdiction over the Church, they virtually denied his supremacy. Because, as has been already stated, the supreme power in the Church must, of necessity, reside in him who is, or in those who are, commissioned by Christ to teach infallibly the doctrines to be believed, and the means to be used for obtaining the end in view. Hence, as Gallicans said that the dogmatic decrees of the Popes were infallible only inasmuch as approved of by the bishops, and that a general council was superior to the Pope, it followed as a necessary consequence that the supreme power, though generally exercised by the Pope, was in fact vested in the collective episcopate, and that the government of the Church must be aristocratic.

4. But reason, the experience of past ages, the traditional doctrine of the Church, and the records of the New Testament, show unmistakably that the government of the Church, in the present order of Providence, neither is nor can be an aristocracy, but is and must be a monarchy. The supreme ruler of the Church, though having no superior on earth, is, of course, bound to govern the Church in accordance with the fundamental laws enacted by Christ Himself; still in him the supreme power resides. Were it vested in the episcopal body, the unity of the Church would not be sufficiently guarded; for, if a large number of bishops were to separate from the Church, as happened at the time of the Arian heresy, there would be no sufficient means left for the faithful to know which of the two parties represents the Church. National antipathies and prejudices would tend to form national churches, and these would inevitably fall under the sway of the temporal power: witness

the fate of all the churches separated from the Holy See. Were the episcopal body invested with the supreme power, the government of the Church should be carried on either by the whole body of bishops, or by a number of delegates. Now, this has never been the government of the Church. General councils have been held, the decrees of which were considered binding on all the faithful; and yet these councils were not only convoked by the Popes, and presided over by them or by their legates, but the decisions of these councils became binding only inasmuch as they were sanctioned by the supreme authority of the Holy See. Besides, these general councils are few in number, if we consider the length of the Church's existence. Nor can the bishops form a permanent parliament to administer the affairs of the Church; because, according to the laws in vigor from the very first, bishops have to reside in their respective dioceses, to govern the flock confided to their care.

We shall now proceed to prove the supremacy of St. Peter both from Holy Writ and the writings of ecclesiastical authors.

5. Our divine Saviour having asked His disciples what they thought of Him, St. Peter answered: "Thou art Christ, the Son of the living God." And Jesus, answering him, said: "Blessed art thou, Simon Bar-Jona: because flesh

and blood hath not revealed it to thee, but my Father who is in heaven. And I say to thee: That thou art Peter; and upon this rock I will build my Church, and the gates of hell shall not prevail against it. And I will give to thee the keys of the kingdom of heaven. And whatsoever thou shalt bind on earth, it shall be bound also in heaven: and whatsoever thou shalt loose on earth, it shall be loosed also in heaven." (*Matt.* xvi, 16–19.) This text, the meaning of which is obvious, has been tortured in the strangest way by Protestants so as to avoid acknowledging the supremacy of St. Peter and his successors. These words evidently confer some prerogative on St. Peter, as a reward for his confession; and this reward is, that St. Peter should be the rock on which Christ was to build His Church. The word which in the English version is translated by Peter, in the language used by our Saviour is the same as *rock*, for Kepha (Peter) means *rock*, so that our Saviour said, "Thou art a *rock*, and upon this *rock* I will build my Church." Calvin, to elude the force of this text, said that Christ, in saying the words, "*and upon this rock*," pointed to Himself; but this is absurd: it is an interpretation unwarranted by the text, and in contradiction with it. Bloomfield, a Protestant commentator (*in hunc locum*), says that nowadays almost every [Protestant] expositor of note holds the Catholic interpretation, *i. e.*, that these words refer to Peter. In fact, the demonstrative pronoun *this* refers to the preceding member of the sentence. Moreover, the rock of which Christ speaks is he to whom was said, " And I will give to thee the keys of the kingdom of heaven," which undoubtedly refers to St. Peter; for this second part of the promise is strictly connected with the first, and is simply a consequence or explanation of it. Add to this that the promise made to Peter to be the rock on which Christ was to build His Church, was already foreshadowed by the change of name from Simon to Cephas (Kepha) or *rock*. (*John* i, 42.) For the changing or giving of a name by God Himself, always indicates the conferring of some privilege or prerogative signified by it. This appears from the change of Abram to Abraham, of Jacob into Israel, and from the name of Jesus given to our Lord. Lastly, all ancient writers are unanimous in stating that Peter is the rock on which Christ built His Church. (Tertullian, *De Præscript.*, cap. 22; Origen, *in Exodum Hom.* V, n. 4; *Commentar. in Matt.*, n. 139, *et passim;* St. Cyprian, *Epist.* 55 *ad Cornel. Papam*, n. 7; *Epist.* 69, n. 8; *Epist.* 71, n. 3, etc.; Gregory Nazianzen, *Orat.* 32, n. 18; Ambrose *in Ps.* xl, n. 30; Id., *De Fide*, lib. iv, 56; and others.)

6. Let us now examine the meaning of this promise. The metaphor, *rock*, is used to express strength, solidity, stability. Thus it is often used in Holy Writ. (Vid. *Ps.* xxvi, 6; *Ibid.* xxxix, 3;

Ps. lx, 3, etc.) Besides, our Lord had already explained this metaphor (*Matt.* vii, 24–27), and His meaning is also clear from the words which follow in the text we are now examining: "And the gates of hell shall not prevail against it."

The metaphor, *gate*, in the Oriental languages signifies *power;* hence, the expression for the Turkish empire, "The Sublime Porte." Thus it is used in Gen. xxii, 17; Gen. xxiv, 60; Judges v, 8; Ps. cxlvii, 13; Isaias xlv, 2, etc. The word *hell*, in the Hebrew *scheol*, signifies death, the grave, the place of the damned. Hence, the gates of hell mean the domain of death, or rather him who has the power of death, Satan. He is the great enemy of the Church who will always strive to overthrow it, but his efforts will ever be frustrated; for, the Church being solidly built on a rock, he can never prevail. Peter, therefore, is the rock to which the Church on earth owes its solidity, its unshaken stability. Now, the stability of the Church is preserved, inasmuch as she always keeps the unity of faith, administers the sacraments for the sanctification of her members, and preserves the government instituted by Christ; and as she owes all this to Peter, the rock on which she is built, Peter is the centre of unity of the Church, and her supreme head.

7. Protestants say that not Peter himself is the rock, but his faith. If they mean faith in the abstract, we deny their assertion, because the

text in question does not admit this interpretation. Our Saviour speaks to Peter personally; him He calls a rock, not his faith; hence He is to build His Church on Peter, not on his faith. Besides, no writer of the earliest ages of Christianity, giving the literal meaning of the word *rock* used in this text, ever dreamt of such interpretation; a few, besides the literal meaning, said that, *in an allegorical sense only*, the word *rock* means faith.

But if Protestants mean that Christ built His Church on Peter always confessing the true faith in his successors, we may readily grant this explanation, because it was given by many Fathers, and is not in contradiction with those who simply say that Christ built His Church on Peter. Peter is the foundation of the Church, inasmuch as he is the centre of unity, and thus always upholds the true faith of Christ, to which all the faithful must adhere in order to be members of His mystical body. (Vid. St. Hilary, *De Trinitate*, lib. ii, nn. 36, 37; St. Epiphanius, *Hæres.*, lix, 7; St. Chrysostom, *Homil.* 54, in *Matt.*, nn. 2, 3.)

However, according to St. Paul (1 *Cor.* iii, 11,) "other foundation no man can lay but that which is laid; which is Christ Jesus." This is perfectly true. Christ is *the rock*, for He, by His power and grace, sustains the whole building; but this does not exclude the visible foundation laid down by Christ himself, viz., Peter and his successors, whose stability and solidity depends entirely and solely on our Lord. Christ is also our true pastor, the bishop of our souls (1 *Pet.* ii, 25); and yet the Holy Ghost has placed other pastors and bishops in the Church. (*Acts* xx, 28.) Nay, St. Paul calls all the apostles foundations, whose chief cornerstone is Christ (*Eph.* ii, 20), although they are not foundations such as Peter, but only secondary ones, they themselves resting on him.

8. The keys of the kingdom of heaven which Christ promised to give to St. Peter, express *power:* among the Jews such was the signification of this metaphor. The kingdom of heaven signifies the Church on earth, for thus our Saviour often used this expression. Now, the keys not only express *power*, but *supreme power*. (*Isa.* xxii, 19-22; *Apoc.* i, 17, 18; *Ibid.* iii, 7; *Ibid.* xx, 1.) The words which follow are also clear: "Whatsoever thou shalt bind," etc. These bonds, which are to be tightened or loosed, are either moral precepts binding the consciences of the faithful, or the guilt of sin from which they are freed by the power of the Church; and Christ puts no restriction, for He says explicitly *whatsoever*. He, therefore, grants to Peter the fullest power of binding and loosing all those moral bonds, according as it may be necessary or useful for attaining the Church's appointed end. Now, these keys were given to Peter alone, for Christ spoke to him, and to him only: "And I will give to thee," ... "Whatsoever thou," etc. Had He meant

all the apostles, he would have said, "I will give to *you*," . . . "Whatsoever *you*," etc. It is urged that, as Christ had asked all the apostles what they thought of Him, Peter answered in the name of all, and that, consequently, the words of Christ are addressed to all the apostles. But the text cannot bear this interpretation. Christ speaks to Peter alone; him alone He calls a rock; his name alone is changed; to him the keys are given.

Again, it is said, Christ gave the keys to the Church: but this, too, is contrary to the text. He had mentioned the Church just before; assuredly, had He meant to give the keys to the Church, He would have said, *And I will give to it.* The keys were, of course, given to Peter, not for his own personal benefit, but for that of the Church: as he is the visible foundation on which she is built, the supreme power and jurisdiction was conferred on him, in order that he should maintain in the Church the unity of faith and government. Still, the keys were really *intrusted* to him.

But did not the apostles receive the same powers? Did not our Saviour say to all the apostles: "Whatsoever you shall bind upon earth, shall be bound also in heaven; and whatsoever you shall loose upon earth, shall be loosed also in heaven"? (*Matt.* xviii, 18.) Yes; but by these words the apostles were neither made the rock on which the Church is built, nor did they receive the keys of the kingdom of heaven, nor did Christ revoke the privilege already granted to Peter alone. Hence, if now they are made partakers of the powers conferred on Peter, they do not receive them in their fulness, nor can they exercise them independently of him. Their jurisdiction as apostles was not, indeed, restricted as that of the bishops, who are their successors in the episcopate, but not in the apostleship; yet they also depended on Peter, who was constituted the head of the Church, and the centre of unity.

Before His passion our Lord said to Peter: "Simon, Simon, behold Satan hath desired to have you, that he may sift you as wheat; but I have prayed for thee that thy faith fail not, and thou, being once converted, confirm thy brethren." (*Luke* xxii, 31, 32.) Our Saviour speaks not only of the trials to which His disciples were to be subjected through the malice of Satan during His passion, but of the many persecutions they would have to undergo throughout all ages; because, although He predicts that Peter would deny Him, and that the rest of the disciples would abandon Him, yet He has prayed for Peter in a special manner that his faith should never fail, and He commands him to confirm his brethren after his conversion. Hence, as Christ willed that Peter should strengthen and confirm the faith of the apostles, that they might resist the attacks of

Satan, He constituted Peter the head of the apostles and of the whole Church. The word *confirm* is used by sacred writers in the sense of affording strength and protection against the assaults of the Evil One. (Vid. *Acts* xiv, 21; *Ibid.* xv, 41; 2 *Thes.* ii, 16; 1 *Pet.* v, 10.) This is so plain that the Protestant commentator, Alford, says: " The use of this word (confirm) and the cognate substantive *thrice by Peter* in his two Epistles, and in the first passage in connection with the mention of *Satan's temptations*, is remarkable."

9. The powers promised to St. Peter were conferred upon him by Christ after His resurrection. When, after having been asked three times by our Lord if he loved Him, Peter had answered each time in the affirmative, he was twice told to feed Christ's lambs, and once to feed His sheep. (*John* xxi, 15-17.) Now, the flock of Christ is all the faithful, or His Church: as He, therefore, intrusted to Peter's care not only the lambs, but also the sheep, and this without any restriction, He constituted him the pastor of His whole flock, investing him with all the powers necessary to fulfil that office; that is to say, He commissioned him to lead, to protect, to punish, to govern, the flock or Church.

The words, *pastor* and *to feed*, are often used in Holy Writ to signify *supreme ruler*, and *to rule* or *govern.* (Vid. 2 *Kings* v, 2; *Isa.* xl, 11; *Ezech.* xxxiv, 23, 24; *Mich.* v, 2-4.) Again, where in the

Latin and vernacular versions we read *to rule*, the Greek has *to feed, to pasture*. (*Ps.* lxxix, 2; *Matt.* ii, 6: *Apoc.* xi, 5, etc.) Even profane authors gave the name of shepherds to rulers. (Vid. *Iliad, passim.*) Christ, therefore, constituted Peter His visible representative, His vicar upon earth. (Conf. Leo Magnus, *Serm.* iii, *De Natali;* St. Cyprian, lib. *De Unit. Eccles.; Ecclesia Orientalis in Epist. ad Symmachum Papam*, Labbe, *Act. Conc.*, tom. iii, col. 1205.)

10. That St. Peter really possessed this primacy and also exercised it, is clearly indicated in Holy Writ. The Gospels, when they give the list of the apostles, place Peter always at the head. St. Paul (1 *Cor.* xv) states the witnesses of Christ's resurrection, and names Peter first, apart from all the rest: as he does not enumerate these witnesses according to the chronological order, he gives us to understand that he cites them according to the order of authority. St. Paul also confers with St. Peter before he begins to preach the Gospel, though he had obtained the knowledge of the truth by special revelation. (*Gal.* i, ii.) As long as St. Peter is with the apostles, he always takes the lead in everything that is done. In Acts i, he has another apostle elected to replace Judas; in Acts ii, he is the first to announce the Gospel on the day of Pentecost; in Acts iii, he performs the first miracle in confirmation of Christ's resurrection; in Acts v, he pronounces

sentence against Ananias and Saphira; in Acts viii, he condemns the first heresy, that of Simon Magus; in Acts x, he is the first who admits Gentiles into the Church; in Acts xv, it is he who, in the Council of Jerusalem, gives the final decision: St. James and the others simply approve of what he has defined.

The whole Church always held the See of Rome to be the first, the principal Church, the mother of all churches, because St. Peter was its first bishop: nay, the churches of Antioch and Alexandria were always held to be the first in dignity after Rome, because they were founded by St. Peter.

Protestants object that St. Paul resisted St. Peter (*Gal.* ii), and hence that he could not have acknowledged him as his superior. To this we reply that, in the first place, it is not quite sure whether the Cephas of whom St. Paul speaks is really St. Peter: many deny their identity, whilst others admit it. But supposing that St. Paul really rebuked St. Peter, it does not follow that the latter was not his superior; because, when great interests are at stake, even an inferior might rebuke his superior. St. Cyprian (*Epist.* lxxi, n. 3) says: "Nor did Peter, whom the Lord made the first, and on whom He built His Church, act insolently and arrogantly when Paul afterward disputed with him about circumcision; he did not say that he held the primacy, and was to be obeyed by those who were new and came after, nor did he despise Paul because the latter was at first a persecutor of the Church." And St. Augustine (*De Baptismo contra Donatistas*, lib. ii, cap. 2), quoting this passage of St. Cyprian, adds: " The apostle Peter, in whom the *primacy of the apostles* is preëminent by so singular a grace, when acting about the circumcision differently from what truth required, was corrected by the apostle Paul."

CHAPTER XII.

THE SUCCESSOR OF ST. PETER IN THE PRIMACY.

1. St. Peter's Privilege permanent in the Church.—2. The Bishop of Rome the Successor of St. Peter.—3. Proved by History.—4. False Decretals.—5. St. Peter was Bishop of Rome, and died there.

1. IT is plain that the prerogatives conferred on Peter by our Lord were to be permanent in the Church; for they were not granted him as a mere personal favor, but for the good of the mystical body of Christ. St. Peter is the foundation on which the visible Church is built; hence, as long as the edifice is to last, so long must the foundation endure. Now, the Church on earth is to remain till the end of the world. But, as St. Peter was not to live on earth during all this time, he continues to live in his successors. The primacy was instituted to preserve the unity of the Church, which is one of her essential properties. (Irenæus, lib. ii, *Contra Hæres.;* Opt. Milev., lib. ii, *Contra Parm.;* St. Jerome, lib. i, *In Jovin.;* St. Augustine, *In Ps. Contra Part. Donati;* St. Cyprian, *De Unit. Ecclesiæ.*) But this unity is to last till the end of time. The Church, therefore, can never be without Peter's primacy. The Church

must preserve the same form of government which Christ has instituted; else her intrinsic constitution would change: so that, Christ having instituted the primacy, it must endure in the Church. Surely it is absurd to contend that Christ conferred the primacy on Peter only during the lifetime of the apostles who, confirmed as they were in grace, did not so much need to be presided over by one of their number, and that this primacy should cease precisely when, the apostles being dead and gone, it was most urgently needed.

2. But who is the successor of St. Peter? The answer is very easy. The supreme power must necessarily reside in him who from the very beginning claimed and exercised it, and whose claim was always acknowledged. The constitution of the Church was not framed by human agency, but given by Christ Himself; and as He alone could invest man with those spiritual and supernatural powers for the attainment of the end in view, the Church could not transfer the supreme power from the episcopate to any particular bishop, supposing the episcopal body had indeed been invested with it by Christ; for, in doing so, the Church would have changed her own constitution, and would have ceased to be the Church instituted by Christ, because a radical constitutional change affects the very nature of a society. Now, history shows, as we are about to prove, that the Bishops of Rome

always exercised the supreme power in the Church; they, therefore, are the lawful successors of Peter in the primacy. Their powers are derived, not from the Church, but directly from Christ; nor can these powers ever be restricted by the episcopal body. The person who is to succeed St. Peter in the primacy is, of course, to be chosen in accordance with the recognized laws sanctioned by the supreme authority of the Church; but the individual thus appointed receives his powers from Christ: and they are the very same which St. Peter possessed as head of the Church.

Our adversaries say that the Bishops of Rome gradually usurped the supreme power; but they cannot historically substantiate their statement. They do not see that, by maintaining this view, they destroy the very existence of the Church, since, after such usurpation, acquiesced in by all Christians, for many centuries, the Church as instituted by Christ would no longer exist—she would have become a mere human institution, and the powers of darkness would have succeeded in destroying the mystical body of Christ. On this theory, at the time of the so-called Reformation, there would have been no Church of Christ, and therefore nothing to be reformed, but everything to be created anew.

In truth no usurpation could have been possible, because it would have been strenuously resisted by every bishop at the very outset. Both the natural desire of preserving a legitimately conferred authority, and the promptings of faith not to allow the order laid down by Christ to be interfered with, would have moved them to stern resistance. The history of the first ages of the Church does, indeed, record many instances of bishops who put themselves in opposition with Rome, but these were heretics condemned by the Church; on the contrary, those who maintained the purity of the faith always acknowledged the high prerogative of the Roman See.

3. That the Bishop of Rome, or the Pope, always exercised the supreme power in the Church from the very beginning, is an historical fact which can be gainsaid by those only who are intent on purposely falsifying history.

St. Ignatius, who died a martyr at the beginning of the second century, in his Epistle to the Romans calls the Church of Rome the *presiding* Church.

St. Irenæus, who died at the beginning of the third century, and who had been a disciple of St. Polycarp, in his *Contra Hær.*, lib. iii, cap. 3, n. 2, says of Rome: "It is necessary that the whole Church,—that is, the faithful of the whole world,—should be in communion with this Church, on account of its more powerful authority, in which [Church] the faithful of the whole world have preserved the tradition that comes from the apostles." This text, being so important, has been attacked most severely.

It has been said that in the sentence, *Ad hanc Ecclesiam . . . necesse est convenire*, the last word is not to be taken in the sense of *agreeing*, but that it means that all should *visit* Rome on account of its greater eminence.

This is a childish cavil. Never were all the faithful obliged to go to Rome; and besides, St. Irenæus gives the reason of his *necesse est*, viz.: because in the Church of Rome the apostolic tradition has been preserved.

It is also urged that the tradition was preserved in Rome precisely because so many from other countries visited it, and hence the faithful taught Rome, not Rome the faithful; but this is contrary to what St. Irenæus says in the words which precede this text. He there teaches that, to know the true doctrine of the Church, it suffices to consult Rome, and then assigns, as a reason for this, the words we have quoted.

Others pretend that the saint meant only the faithful living near Rome. But then he would not have said *omnem Ecclesiam*, every Church, nor *undique*, from all parts, from every quarter.

It is true that the original Greek text of St. Irenæus has been lost, but we know that the Latin text is a faithful translation of the original.

St. Cyprian, martyred A. D. 258, in his letter to St. Cornelius (*Epist*. lv, n. 14), calls the Roman See the See of St. Peter (*cathedra Petri*), the principal Church from which sprang the unity of the priesthood, to which perfidy can have no access.

The same, in his book, *De Unitate Ecclesiæ* (cap. iv), says: "What Peter was, the other apostles were also: endowed with an equal fellowship of honor and power; but the first step taken begins by unity (*exordium ab unitate proficiscitur*), and the *primacy* is given to Peter, that *one* Church of Christ and *one* teaching authority (*cathedra*) may be set forth." (Vid. *supra*, cap. iv, *in fine*.) The saint distinguishes between the apostleship which all the apostles equally shared, and the primacy which belonged to Peter alone. (Vid. St. Optatus, lib. ii, § 2; lib. vii, § 3; St. Ambrose, *In Ps.* 40, n. 30; *In Ps.* 43, n. 40; St. Epiphanius, *Hær.* li, n. 17.)

This also appears from all those ancient writers who, to prove the divine institution of the Church, deem it sufficient to appeal to the series of the Bishops of Rome, the successors of St. Peter.

The same is attested by the facts which show the exercise of the supreme powers of the Holy See over the whole Christian world. St. Clement settled a difficulty at Corinth, though at that time St. John the apostle was still alive. When St. Victor, who died A. D. 197, had either excommunicated, or threatened with excommunication, some bishops of the East, on account of their refusal to submit to a decree about the time when the feast of the Pasch should be celebrated, St. Irenæus, in expostulating with the Pope, alleged, not the absence of jurisdiction, but the rigor of the sentence.

Julius restored to their sees St. Athanasius and other bishops of the East, who had been deposed by the Arians; and the historians of those times state that this was the exercise of a legitimate right, not a usurpation of power. Socrates says that Julius intervened on account of the prerogative of his see, and that the Arians acted against the canons, because they held a council without the approbation of the Pope. Theodoret affirms (lib. ii, cap. 4) that Julius acted in accordance with the canons in reprehending the Arians, because they had presumed to judge the See of Alexandria, which could be judged by the See of Rome alone. Nay, even the leader of the Arians acknowledged the supreme power of the Pope, since, according to St. Epiphanius (*Hær.* 68), Ursacius and Valens went to Julius to give an account of their error and crime. St. Athanasius, in his letter to Pope Felix, says: "The Bishops of Rome have been intrusted with the care of all the churches, in order to come to his (Athanasius's) assistance." St. Basil (*Epist.* 52 *ad Anastas.*): "It has seemed just to write to the Bishop of Rome, that he may know our affairs, and interpose his sentence." St. Chrysostom, having been unjustly deprived of his see by a council held at Constantinople, appealed to Pope Innocent, who, after investigating the matter, deposed and excommunicated Theophilus, the chief opponent of St. Chrysostom, and this sentence was acknowledged by the Emperor Arcadius.

We have also the acts of authority exercised by the Roman Pontiffs with regard to Nestorius, Eutychius, Dioscorus, Accacius, Photius, and others, by which it may be seen that the Popes exercised jurisdiction not only in the West, as patriarchs of the same, but that their authority extended over all the churches of the East, whether patriarchal or not; and that this authority was acknowledged as lawful by the Patriarchs of Antioch and Alexandria and the Bishops of Constantinople. These latter, after the transfer of the seat of empire to their city, always affected more or less the second place in the hierarchy, which they obtained at last by favor of the Holy See. Now, it is evident that, had this assumption of power been a usurpation on the part of Rome, these prelates would never have yielded obedience, but would have resisted to the utmost. They very often showed their proud and unbending temper; so that their submission to Rome during the first ten centuries could be owing to nothing less than the firm persuasion that it was required by revealed truth.

This doctrine is confirmed by all general

councils. In the Council of Ephesus (*Act* ii), the Roman Pontiff is called the head of the council, and shortly after (*Act* iii), it is said that Peter, in his successors up to this time, and always, lives and pronounces judgment. In the Council of Chalcedon (*Act* ii), the Fathers say: "Peter has spoken by the mouth of Leo." It is also a well-known fact that all the earlier councils, though held in the East, were presided over by papal legates, who took precedence over all the patriarchs in the order in which they signed the decrees of the council, and that these decrees were sent to Rome to be ratified by the Pope.

4. The False Decretals, about which Protestants speak so much, did not confer any new dignity or prerogative on the Bishops of Rome: they embodied the discipline and practice of the Church, as these had ever been; nor were the canons and decisions themselves forgeries: the forgery consisted only in attributing some letters, canons or decrees to Popes and councils of earlier times. These decretals were not needed to establish the power of the Pope, because, when they appeared, this power already existed. The reason why many were deceived at first and thought them genuine, was precisely because they introduced no innovations in the discipline of the Church.

5. Many Protestants, hoping to make a clean sweep of our whole argument, assert that St. Peter was never Bishop of Rome, and that he did not

die at Rome; their logical inference being that the Popes are not his successors. This argument, ingenious though it be, is unfortunately wanting in truth. It is, in fact, refreshingly ridiculous to impugn an event attested by innumerable witnesses, whose names, starting from the very time when that event took place, have come down to us in an unbroken line without contradicting voice for more than one thousand four hundred years. All the ecclesiastical writers of antiquity proclaim the Bishops of Rome to be the successors of St. Peter: none of the heretics of the earliest ages ever dreamt of questioning this fact. Protestants who, without one historical record to back them, presume to deny this fact, do not deserve a hearing: their case must be bowed out of court.

But, say they, St. Peter wrote his Epistles from Babylon, and this shortly before his death. (2 *Pet.* iii, 1; *Ibid.* i, 14; 1 *Pet.* v, 13.) "The Church," these are his words, "that is in Babylon, elected together with you, saluteth you." There is no historical record which attests that St. Peter was ever in Babylon, the capital of Chaldea. Hence, if he mentions Babylon, it is a figurative expression for the city of Rome. Papias, cited by Eusebius in his *History* (lib. ii, cap. 15), says: "Peter, in his first Epistle, which he wrote in Rome, mentions Mark, and in it he calls Rome Babylon in a figurative sense." (*Hieronym. in Libro de Viris Illustrib. in Marcum;* S. Leo, *De Natali Apost.*)

CHAPTER XIII.

INFALLIBILITY OF THE POPE AS HEAD OF THE CHURCH.

1. All must agree in Faith with the Pope.—2. What is meant by Infallibility of the Pope.—3. Proofs. The Foundation of the Church.—4. The Centre of Unity.—5. This Doctrine held by the Church.—6. Gallicanism false.—7. The Pope's dogmatical Decrees cannot be reformed by the Church.—8. Unity of Faith demands this Infallibility.—9. Objections: St. Cyprian.—10. Liberius.—11. Honorius.—12. Councils examined the Decisions of the Popes.—13. Bad Popes.—14. Usefulness of General Councils.—15. The Decrees of the Vatican Council did not change the Relations between Church and State.

1. FROM what has been proved in the preceding chapter, it is evident that the Pope, the Bishop of Rome, being the successor of St. Peter, is the head of the Church, the Vicar of Christ upon earth, the centre of unity, with whom all must agree in faith. See St. Irenæus, St. Cyprian, cited in the preceding chapter. St. Optatus (*Contra Parm.*, lib. vii, cap. 3) says: "He who erects another see against that of Peter is a schismatic and a sinner." St. Ambrose (lib. i, *De Pœnit.*, cap. 7): "They who have not the faith of Peter are deprived of his inheritance." (Vid. St. Jerome, *Epist.* 15ª *ad Damas.*) St. Maximus, Patriarch

of Constantinople, in his letter to the Oriental bishops, says: "All nations which have sincerely accepted the Lord, and all Catholics who everywhere profess the true faith, look upon the power of the Roman Pontiff as upon the sun, and rightly; because we read that Peter, by God's revelation, first professed the true faith when he said, 'Thou art Christ,'" etc.

The Roman Pontiff, therefore, is the doctor and teacher of the whole Church, as was defined in the Council of Florence, at which the Eastern bishops were present. It follows, therefore, that he, acting as the head of the Church, never erred, nor can err; or in other words, that he is infallible when he officially speaks *ex cathedra*.

2. When we say that the Pope is infallible, we do not mean that he is impeccable, or, in other words, that he cannot fall into sin; nor do we pretend that all he says is free from error. The Pope is a man, like the rest of us; he may, no doubt, be mistaken, he may hold false opinions about many things, and manifest them. Many persons may be far more learned than he is, not only in profane sciences, but even in theology. Were the Pope, as a private doctor, to publish books, we should not be bound to hold that whatever he might thus publish is infallibly true: in such a case we are free to examine his assertions, and reject them if we find solid reasons for so doing. But we say that when he acts, not in his private

capacity, but as head of the Church, and defines any truth appertaining to faith or to morals, he, not in virtue of his own intellectual superiority, but by the assistance of the Holy Ghost, is incapable of falling into error. And this prerogative is a necessary consequence of the principles laid down in the two preceding chapters.

3. St. Peter, with his successors, is the visible foundation on which the Church is built; hence all the faithful, whatever be their dignity or position, must rest on this foundation. Now, the foundation of a building gives strength and solidity to it; and the strength and solidity of the Church consists in her unity of faith, sacraments and government. The Church, therefore, must find in Peter and his successors the necessary means of maintaining inviolate the unity of faith; consequently, St. Peter and his successors must be infallible. Were it otherwise, we should be obliged to look out for another foundation for the Church, on which her solidity might depend. But there is none other laid by Christ. Therefore the Roman Pontiff, as successor of St. Peter, must always teach the true faith to the whole Church; in other words, he must be infallible when speaking *ex cathedra*.

4. St. Peter and his successors are the centre of unity; but this they can be only inasmuch as all must agree with them in the same faith, so that those who wilfully teach doctrines in opposi-

tion to theirs separate themselves from Catholic unity. Now, there could be no obligation to submit to their teaching, unless they were infallible; because the mind cannot be compelled to admit as true aught else but what is either evident, or proposed by infallible authority.

5. This is the constant doctrine of the ancient ecclesiastical writers and councils. Thus Origen (*in Matt.* xvi) says: " It is evident, though it be not expressly stated, that the gates of hell cannot prevail either against Peter or against the Church; for, were they to prevail against the rock on which the Church is built, they would also prevail against the Church." St. Chrysostom, in his commentaries on the same text, says: "God alone can be the cause that the Church built on a fisherman does not fall, though exposed to many storms." (Conf. St. Jerome, *Epist.* xv, aliter lxvii, *ad Damasum;* Gelasius, *in Epist. ad Anastas. Imperat.*) Pope Hormisdas made all the Oriental bishops subscribe the following formula: " The first rule of salvation is to keep the true faith, and not to swerve from the tradition of the Fathers. Because we cannot pass over the sentence of our Lord Jesus Christ, who says: ' Thou art Peter, and upon this rock I will build my Church.' This word has been proved by its effects, for *in the Apostolic See the Catholic religion has always been kept inviolate.* . . . Hence, following in all things the Apostolic See, and upholding

all its constitutions, I hope to be worthy to be with you in the communion which is that of the Apostolic See, *in which is the entire and true solidity of the Christian religion,*" etc. This formulary was approved in the Eighth General Council, held in 869 at Constantinople, to put down the Photian schism. The same conclusion is drawn from the councils cited in the foregoing chapter. The Council of Ephesus testifies that it is through the Roman Pontiffs that Peter imparts truth to those who seek it.

6. The Gallicans did not deny that the Pope is the head of the Church, that his dogmatic decrees must be received with respect, not by the faithful only, but also by the bishops taken individually; but they pretended that these decrees became infallible only inasmuch as they were approved by the majority of bishops either assembled in council, or dispersed over the world. This opinion, which was condemned in the Vatican Council, has always been rejected by the Church. For it is evident that it must be the foundation of the Church and her centre of unity, which gives to her unity of faith and unshaken stability. The infallibility, therefore, of the Church's teaching depends and is grounded on her foundation. Now, this foundation is not the episcopal body, but Peter and his successors; therefore the infallibility does not rest on the body of pastors, but on their head, the Pope.

Besides, Peter and his successors have received from Christ the commission to teach the whole Church *authoritatively*, which means *infallibly;* for they have to feed the whole flock of Christ—they have to confirm their brethren in the faith. But if the dogmatic decrees of the Roman Pontiffs were not infallible, it would not be Peter that would feed the whole flock, but part of the flock that would feed him; it would not be he that would strengthen the brethren in the faith, but rather the brethren that would strengthen him.

7. Moreover, Gallicans granted that all must accept with reverence the decrees given *ex cathedra;* and even bishops, taken singly, had to respect them. Therefore, the consent of the bishops must always, of necessity, follow such dogmatical decrees: because, on the one hand, even before the decision of the Vatican Council, the great majority of bishops firmly believed the infallibility of the Pope; on the other, those who, before the last council, opposed such *ex-cathedra* decrees, could not do so except by an act of disobedience to the head of the Church. Now, it is absurd to say that the only means of reforming a dogmatical decree of the Pope, supposing such a decree could be erroneous, is the commission of a sinful act. That bishops sinned, even before the late definition, when they opposed a papal dogmatical decree, is evident from the condemnation of the eleventh proposition of the

Synod of Pistoia; and the constitution of Clement XI, *Vineam Domini* (which was admitted by the whole Church, and which, consequently, even according to Gallican principles, is an infallible pronouncement), requires that all, without exception, should not only observe a respectful silence, or give only a provisional assent, but that they must give a full internal assent to the apostolic constitutions. Therefore, he who refused this assent, even were he a bishop, sinned mortally, and, from the nature of his sin, he did no more represent the Church.

8. Furthermore, the unity of faith would be exposed to the greatest dangers, if the consent of the bishops were required to give the seal of infallibility to the dogmatical decrees of the Pope. For, suppose a great number of bishops profess heretical doctrines, as happened at the time of the Arian and Eutychian heresies, the faithful, before the holding of a general council, would have no means of knowing what is the true doctrine of the Church, and might easily be led into error. But if, as St. Ambrose says, "Where Peter is, there is the Church," all danger is averted.

Lastly, there is not a single instance in the history of the Church of any dogmatical papal decree having been corrected or abrogated by a subsequent Pope, by a council, or by the episcopal body. Those who resisted such decrees either submitted, or were cut off from Catholic communion.

9. Let us now examine some historical facts which have been alleged against this doctrine.

St. Cyprian resisted the decree of St. Stephen about not rebaptizing heretics, and still he is venerated as a saint; therefore, he could not have looked upon the Pope's dogmatical decrees as infallible. But St. Augustine remarks very justly that St. Cyprian is a saint, not because he withstood the Pope, but because he suffered martyrdom in the Church. As to his conduct, we must say either that he acted in opposition to his own principles laid down in his work on the unity of the Church, or, what seems more probable, that he did not look upon the rescript of the Pope as a dogmatical decree, and thought the rebaptizing of heretics a mere disciplinary custom, which might and should be retained: for, though he did not then conform to the Pope's decision, but with his whole provincial council resisted it, he did not separate himself from the unity of the Church. Certain it is, however, that the Pope's decree was afterward ratified by the Council of Nicæa.

10. Liberius is said to have subscribed an Arian profession of faith, forced thereto by the persecutions of the Arian emperor, Constantius. Were we obliged to grant this fact, it would prove nothing against our thesis. A Pope, yielding through human frailty to the threats of persecutors, does not act as head of the Church, in

which capacity alone he is infallible. But, that Liberius did not sign any heretical profession of faith, is proved by the joyful ovation he received from the Roman people on his return. They had refused to have anything to do with Felix, though a Catholic, because he had been thrust upon the See of Rome by the Arians, whom they detested. How much more would they have abhorred Liberius, had he yielded so far as to sign an heretical confession of faith! It is known, too, that Constantius was induced to send Liberius back to Rome on account of the persistent solicitations of the Roman ladies, and not because the Pope had yielded to his wishes. The story of his subscription originated with the Arians, who invented it to deceive Catholics.

11. But Honorius was condemned as a heretic by the Sixth General Council. Let us suppose that the acts of the council have not been interpolated by the Greeks,—a feat of which they were by no means incapable, as in the same council some of their number were found to have altered certain texts of the Fathers. If, then, Honorius was condemned,—which fact is granted by many Catholic writers,—we say with all Catholics, and this on solid grounds, that he was condemned, not because he taught heresy, much less because he proposed an heretical doctrine to the Church, but simply because he had been negligent in suppressing the Monothelite heresy, and

thus was condemned as one who favored heresy; men of that stamp being also called, in the style of the day, heretics. He was deceived by Sergius, Bishop of Constantinople, and sanctioned the policy of suppressing all discussion about one or two wills in Christ. This was his only fault. That his letters were not positively favorable to the heresy, appears from the fact that Sergius did not make use of them, and that they remained unknown till they were exhibited at the council. Besides, the very letters which formed the basis of accusation against Honorius, contain the true Catholic doctrine, because in them he says expressly: "We are bound to confess that in the one Christ both natures are united in natural unity, active and acting in unison one with the other; the divine nature operating what belongs to the Godhead, the human executing what things are of the flesh."

12. Some councils have examined the decisions previously given by Sovereign Pontiffs, not as if they were doubtful, but in order to add to them their own solemn sanction. In the Council of Chalcedon the letters of St. Leo were immediately approved by the following acclamations: "Anathema to him who does not believe thus!" "Peter has spoken through Leo!" If, then, the council afterward examined these letters, they did so for no other purpose than the better to convince those who were infected with the

poison of heresy. The Popes, Celestin, Leo and Agatho, sent their letters respectively to the Councils of Ephesus, Chalcedon and Constantinople, as a rule to be followed by the bishops, with strict injunctions to their legates not to allow anything relating to faith, in these letters, to be called in question. And in fact not a single definition of a Pope, acting as head of the Church, can be pointed out as having been rejected by a council.

13. There have been bad Popes. Well, and what of that? The prerogative of infallibility in matters of faith and morals does not depend on the individual sanctity of the Popes. It is not a mere personal privilege, but one granted for the good of the Church. That a few Popes were blameworthy in some of their actions, cannot be denied; yet modern historical criticism has shown that many crimes imputed to Popes were mere calumnies invented by their enemies. Were the Church a human institution, and had the Popes, as Protestants pretend, usurped the power of imposing upon the Church their own wills, the bad Popes who, according to Protestant tradition, were steeped in every crime, would, no doubt, have used their power to proclaim such principles as would countenance their dissolute lives. Has any thing of this kind ever happened?

14. From what has been said it follows that the Pope is superior to general councils, since he is

the head of the Church, the centre of unity, the doctor and teacher of all the faithful; hence, also, no council can be looked upon as legitimate, unless it be convoked by the Pope, presided over by him or by his legates, and all its decrees must receive his sanction. Of what use, then, are general councils, if the Pope is infallible without them? Councils are necessary, not to decide what is of faith, since this may be done, and has often been done, by the Pope alone, nor have the decisions of councils any binding force apart from his sanction; but they are necessary to give greater weight and solemnity to the defined dogmas of faith, and to show more palpably the common agreement, in matters of faith, among the members of the Church. This necessity was still greater in former times, when means of communication were far more difficult and far less rapid than at present.

15. We may here remark how absurd is the pretext of contemporary persecutors of the Church, who, to palliate their unjust aggressions against her, pretend that, since the definition of the Vatican Council, the relations between Church and State have been changed by the proclamation of Papal Infallibility, and that civil governments must take steps to guard against the possible aggression of the Pope. The Pope, at present, has not a jot more power than he possessed when his name was Peter or Linus.

Practically, his infallibility was always recognized, *theoretically*, some presumed to assert that it was based upon the consent of the bishops; and in relation to the State, it makes very little difference, or rather none at all, whether the true doctrine or the Gallican error be upheld, since, in both cases, the decisions of the Pope are infallible, whatever be the ground on which this infallibility ultimately rests.

CHAPTER XIV.

RELATIONS OF CHURCH AND STATE.

1. The Church superior to the State.—2. The normal Condition of a State requires Union between Church and State.—3. No Encroachment to be feared on the Part of the Church.—4. The Deposing Power of the Popes.—5. The State cannot impose any Religion.—6. When the State has, by a social Act, embraced the true Religion, it has a Right and is bound to protect and defend the Unity of Religion.—7. Toleration, and its Limits.—8. The Laws of Marriage not to be interfered with by the State.—9. The State cannot educate Children.—10. Has no Right to impose a Tax for the Support of mere secular Schools.—11. Liberalism.—12. So-called Catholic Liberalism.—13. Absurdity of this Theory.—14. Its Fundamental Error.

1. THE Church, being a society instituted by God with the object of leading mankind to salvation, must, in all things belonging to her, be independent of civil society, as we stated above. The supreme authority of the State in its own sphere is also independent; yet as its laws, to be just, must of necessity be founded on the laws of eternal justice, it depends on the Church, so far forth as it is obliged to take from her the standard on which it has to frame its own laws, the Church being the divinely appointed teacher of the moral law. No law of any state, framed in opposition with her teaching, can be binding on

the conscience of man; because such a law is opposed to the law of God, and we must obey God rather than man. This proposition can be denied by those only who either deny God's existence or His providence in human affairs, and thus acknowledge no higher law than the will of kings or peoples; or at most by those also who, while admitting God and His providence, ignore the divine institution of the Church, and recognize no other principles of right and justice than those deduced from the natural law.

2. The normal condition of society requires that both Church and State should act in harmony, that there should be union between them. This union consists neither in the absorption of the State by the Church nor in the subjection of the Church to state control, but in the mutual coöperation of both, each remaining in its own sphere. The Church has to legislate on all matters belonging to faith and morals; she does not frame laws relating to purely secular concerns; she proclaims only the rules of right and justice revealed by God, in accordance with which the state's legislation must be. The state, taking for its guidance this revealed law, may enact its own laws, and adopt what measures it deems fittest to attain the end of civil society; and as long as it remains within its own sphere, it neither will nor can be interfered with in the least by the authority of the Church. The duty

of the state is not only to protect all its citizens in the full enjoyment of their legitimate rights, but it must also lend its assistance to the Church by securing her liberty of action.

3. As the Church is a visible association, as she has to deal with men made up of body and soul, she must, of necessity, make use of material means. Hence it may happen that both Church and state have to legislate on the same subject. Oftentimes the limits of the respective jurisdictions are clearly indicated: for instance, in matrimony. As to the matrimonial contract itself, its impediments, all cases arising therefrom, they belong to the Church alone, because matrimony is a sacrament; but, as for the civil consequences of marriage, the laws of inheritance *ab intestato*, they belong to the jurisdiction of civil authority. When, in doubtful cases, a collision of rights might arise, it is evident that, to preserve the union between both powers, the state must yield to the Church, since she is the higher power, and she alone is competent to determine the limits of her own jurisdiction.

No fears need be entertained that the Church ever will encroach upon the rights of the state, and curtail its authority; because, not being a human institution, she is guided by the Holy Ghost. If any of the local authorities of the Church presume to interfere unduly with the rights of the state, the Pope will ever be ready to restrain their ambition. Moreover, the Church wields a spiritual power only; she has not, as the state has, material force at her disposal; hence, as history amply testifies, the encroachments of the civil power are the only dangers threatening the harmony between Church and State.

4. But what about the power, exercised by the Popes in the Middle Ages, of deposing kings and freeing subjects from the duty of allegiance? Is not this an evident encroachment of the spiritual power? This objection in the mouth of so-called liberals sounds rather strange, considering that they assume the people to possess an inherent right to deprive their rulers of the supreme authority, whenever they think they have reason to be dissatisfied with them: it would be more logical if urged by regalists, who uphold the absolute inviolability of kings or emperors. However, the exercise of the deposing power argues no undue interference of the Popes with temporal rulers. By consulting history, we find this power was used only in the case of princes abusing their authority and trampling underfoot all laws, human and divine; and by this very act of deposition, acknowledged, moreover, and acquiesced in by all Christendom, the Popes showed themselves the most strenuous supporters of the legitimate rights of the people.

This power was never claimed either by Popes

or any other Catholics as an arbitrary power which could be exercised at will. No temporal ruler could be interfered with, as long as he did not deviate from the laws of right and justice. Nor did the Popes exercise this right directly: it was rather an arbitration, the pronouncing of a juridical sentence, which declared that, since the temporal ruler had evidently proved unfaithful to his coronation oath, the people, on their part, were absolved from their oath of allegiance; for, though authority is not the result of a compact, still it cannot be denied that the prince is bound, either by explicit compact with the people, or at least by an implied one, to discharge faithfully the duties connected with the possession of the supreme authority, which, though coming from God, is instituted for the good of the community.

It is also beyond dispute that, in all Christian nations, kings, dukes or princes, at their coronation, had to take an oath that they would protect the Church, uphold the constitution and the legitimately established rights of their subjects; and the oath of allegiance was taken by the vassals of the prince only after he himself had taken his. It was, therefore, but natural that, when a king violated his oath, the authority of the Pope, the divinely appointed guardian and interpreter of the moral law, should be appealed to, that he might decide whether the violation of the oath was such as to free the subjects from their oath of allegiance.

We quote the words of His Holiness Pius IX on this very subject (Address to a Literary Society, July 30, 1871.—taken from *The Vatican Decrees*, by Cardinal Manning, chap. ii, n. xii):—

"Among all other errors, that is malicious above all, which would attribute [to the infallibility of the Popes] the right of deposing sovereigns, and of absolving people from the obligation of allegiance. This right, without doubt, has been exercised by the Supreme Pontiffs from time to time in extreme cases, but it has nothing to do with the Pontifical Infallibility; neither does it flow from the infallibility, but from the authority, of the Pontiff.

"Moreover, the exercise of this right in those ages of faith which respected in the Pope that which he is, that is to say, the supreme judge of Christendom, and recognized the benefit of his tribunal in the great contentions of peoples and of sovereigns, was freely extended (by aid, as was just, of public jurisprudence, and the common consent of nations) to the gravest interests of states and of their rulers.

"But altogether different are the conditions of the present time from the conditions [of those ages]; and malice alone can confound things so diverse, that is to say, the infallible judgment, in respect to truths of divine revelation, with the right which the Popes exercised in virtue of their authority when the common good demanded it."

Nowadays the people have taken into their own hands the right of deposing kings, and they exercise it mercilessly and unsparingly, in accordance, not with the rights of justice, but with the promptings of their own unbridled passions. As long as both kings and peoples recognized the right of arbitration, which, when there is question of the laws of right and justice that cannot be settled by any human tribunal, the Pope, as supreme head of the Church, naturally possesses,—so long the thrones of kings rested on a more solid basis than at present, and the people had within reach a far more efficient means to check the exercise of arbitrary power than what the self-assumed right of revolution can afford.

5. The state has no right to impose a religion on its subjects, because it has no right to teach *authoritatively* or *infallibly*. And though those who are invested with supreme power may have embraced the true religion, they cannot compel their subjects to profess it; for even the Church, the divinely appointed teacher of truth, cannot, by external means, force any one to submit to her authority who has never been subject to her. Nor can the state prescribe a common external worship, because this must be the external manifestation of the inward belief, else it were mere

mummery. But this inward belief cannot be exacted by the state; therefore it cannot make any outward form of worship obligatory.

But when a state, by a social act, has accepted the true religion, it may exact from its citizens that religious unity be not assailed by any overt act; because this unity is necessary in order to perfection in the workings of society. True religion teaches the principles of right and justice; it unites the minds and wills of subjects, and thus strengthens the bond of union among all the members of the state; it acts on the subject, to make him yield obedience to civil rulers for conscience' sake, and not merely on account of threatened punishment; it guides rulers in the path of wise and just government. Where there is not this unity of true religion, there is the germ of disunion; still more so, if the various sects are strongly attached to their own religious opinions. If, on the contrary, they care little about religious matters, this indifference will also extend to the moral obligations inculcated by religion, and these will soon be set aside; so that even the laws of the state will not be obeyed except through fear of temporal disgrace and punishment. A false religion professed by all the members of the state may, for a time, exert its influence on the people; but true and lasting perfection can never be attained through the instrumentality of falsehood.

6. When a state, by a social act, has embraced the true religion, the teachings and laws of the latter naturally form the basis of its constitution; and as those who, by overt acts, endeavor to undermine the government, are justly punished by the supreme authority, so may those be punished who, in a state which professes the unity of true religion, strive by overt acts to subvert this unity: for this attempt strikes at the very root of the civil constitution, and thus necessarily tends to bring about a revolution. This truth is substantiated by history: nowhere has heresy been introduced into *a Christian state* without causing civil discord.

7. But those who, in a state so constituted, have never embraced the true religion, can by no means be compelled by external means to do so: all that the state can require of them is not to attack, by overt acts, the socially established unity of religion. The state could never compel them to change their religious belief; hence, their refusal to embrace the religion socially professed by the rest of the nation is not a social crime, and cannot be punished by civil authority.

As the state has no right to impose upon its subjects any religion, so neither has it the right to proscribe any, unless it be one which inculcates teachings and practices *evidently* tending to subvert the natural principles of right and justice, or morality. The first part of the proposition is plain;

for the state, as such, cannot define which is the true religion, so as to compel its subjects to accept such definition. The other part is also evident; for, though the state is incapable of teaching religious truth, it has the right to preserve its own existence, and can check whatever tends to its own destruction.

Hence a state which has not, by a social act, embraced the true religion, must protect all citizens of whatever sect or denomination in the free exercise of their religion, provided the teachings of that religion be not evidently opposed to the public order of society. A state which has embraced a false religion by social act, might no doubt be led, with a view to preserving religious unity, to act like a state professing the truth ; but it has no right to do so. Error cannot claim the rights of truth, and the reason is plain : the motives of credibility alleged by false religions can never be truly convincing, while those on which the true religion justifies its position are such as to furnish real certainty. Whosoever professes a false religion must, necessarily, be led by reflection to doubt the truth of its teachings, and hence not only has he the right, but he is in duty bound, to embrace the true religion as soon as he has found it ; contrariwise, he who has embraced the true religion can never entertain a reasonable doubt concerning it, and hence can never have the right to change it.

From the principles just laid down it is plain that a state which, by social act, has embraced the true religion, may prohibit the publication of books, pamphlets or newspapers attacking the unity of faith, while other states have no right to do so: they can proscribe only those writings which attack the primary principles of morality, and tend to destroy the public order of society.

8. Marriage has always been considered as something sacred; it is only modern infidelity which looks upon it as a mere civil contract. The Catholic Church teaches that it is a sacrament; hence the laws of marriage cannot be interfered with by the state. At most it might exact certain formalities to be gone through, in order to extend to wedlock the protection of the civil law; but it has no right to declare null and void any marriage which is declared valid by the Church.

9. Since it is of great importance to the state that the citizens be well educated according to their different conditions of life, it has a right to *promote* education; but it cannot arrogate the right of educating, because it does not possess the gift of infallibility. Mere secular education is not enough for youth, as not the mind only, but the heart too, must be trained; nay, in this training of the heart lies the paramount province of education. Now, the right training of the mind and will cannot be had apart from religious

teaching, because the principles of right and justice are necessarily based on religious principles, and the will of a child must be influenced by religious or supernatural motives: if these motives be set aside, there remains nothing to mould the young heart with but self-interest, and this is quite unequal to the task of forming virtuous men and women. But the state cannot teach religion; therefore it cannot assume the functions of education. Its province is simply to assist parents in having their children educated according to the principles of the religion the parents profess.

10. It follows, therefore, that the state has no right to impose taxes in support of common schools, from which all religious training is banished. Were citizens to show negligence or unwillingness to support their own schools, the state might, perhaps, order a tax for the maintenance of schools; but in this case it would be bound to distribute such funds *pro rata* to the different religious denominations for the keeping-up of denominational schools. It is well known that secular education in godless schools is advocated by those who aim at the destruction of every religious principle; and no fitter means could they have chosen for compassing this end, as appears by the results obtained where such schools have been in operation for some time. Unfortunately many Protestants, though they cannot fail to see

that an education of this kind subverts their own religious tenets, nevertheless keep up this system, simply because denominational schools are favorable to Catholics.

These godless schools are advocated on the ground that, in a country where a mixture of religious creeds exists, all religious teaching must necessarily be excluded from common schools supported by the state. But this excuse is merely another proof that, in this matter, the state has neither power nor aptitude to legislate.

It is, therefore, the duty of every right-minded citizen who has at heart the religious training of his children, to oppose this wretched scheme of godless education, and not to allow liberty of conscience to be trampled upon by making education compulsory in schools where God is ignored.

11. Liberalism condemns this Christian view of union between Church and State, as if opposed to progress and modern civilization. Materialists, Pantheists, and Rationalists scout the idea of a union between Church and State, because, denying, as they do altogether, the supernatural order, they deem the Church a mere human institution, not based on objective truth, but the fanciful creation of a few enthusiasts. They, indeed, allow each individual the liberty to believe what he pleases, but they do not consider any religious association as having independent rights. If they permit it to exist at all, it must be under the

complete control of the state, like any other civil corporation. Although starting from an absolutely false principle, they are at least logical in their deduction. But regalists and supporters of Cæsarism, who, admitting the Church as a divine institution, still claim the right for civil authority to control her, fall into the most absurd contradiction, affirming as they do the subordination of the supernatural to the natural order, and seeking to usurp powers which Christ conferred exclusively on His apostles and their successors.

Another class of Liberals seem, on the one hand, to grant the existence of the Church as a divine institution, and consequently her independence; though, on the other, they practically deny it, since they claim the total independence of State from Church, according to the new formula invented by Cavour: "*A free Church in a free state.*" The Church may, with their kind permission, regulate her own internal concerns, define dogmas, proclaim laws, but she must confine herself to the interior of her temples and sacristies; she must never presume to judge the laws proclaimed by the state, even though they should be in flagrant opposition to her teaching. To the state it belongs to regulate education, to legislate about matrimony, to administer the property of the Church, if indeed she be allowed to possess any. All external acts must be controlled by the State, so that the Church can do no more than what statecraft is willing to permit. This is about the sum of the liberties granted by these Liberals to the "*free Church in a free state.*" The final outcome of such policy is the same as what follows from denying to the Church the very right of existence.

12. There are even liberal Catholics who, though in theory they admit that the state is inferior to the Church, and should be subordinate to her, in practice hold this doctrine impracticable and inconvenient. The state, they say, ought to be separated from the Church; for, if there be union between the two, the state will ever strive to subject the Church to its own control. To prove this, they appeal to history, and show how much the Church had to struggle against the encroachments of the civil power. The Church, therefore, should be freed from all interference of governments, to be at liberty to develop herself according to her own constitution. The Church, after all, does not need the protection of the temporal power; all that she requires is to be let alone. Wherever the Church is really separated from the state, as in the United States, she flourishes and spreads her influence more and more. Hence they applaud the efforts made nowadays to uproot everywhere the last remnants of union between Church and State, in order that the Church may be entirely emancipated. They maintain that full liberty should be granted to all other religious

denominations, even in countries altogether Catholic; for, say they, on what reasonable grounds can Catholics claim freedom in Protestant countries, if they themselves deny to Protestants the right of practising their religion in Catholic states?

13. This theory, though very plausible in appearance, is devoid of truth. The condition of civil society may indeed be such that the Church will be satisfied if she be let alone, as may happen in countries where the majority of the citizens are non-Catholics, and she may no doubt flourish under these circumstances, provided the liberty granted by law be not merely nominal, but real; for the Church, being under the guidance of the Holy Ghost, may prosper even when exposed to the worst persecutions, as she prospered during the first three centuries of the Christian era. But it is false that such a state of things is to be considered the normal condition of civil society with regard to the Church, and that therefore it should be introduced even in Catholic countries where the union between Church and State still exists. No state can be governed, unless its laws be based upon the principles of right and justice: and these can be fully known only through divine revelation, of which the Church is the divinely appointed guardian and interpreter. The state, therefore, must be subordinate to the Church, and accept from her the principles of divine law,

that it may be enabled to frame its own laws in accordance with those of God. To assert that the state is entirely independent of the Church, is tantamount to holding that it is independent of God, and need not be subject to His law.

It cannot be denied that, where the union of State and Church was recognized, temporal rulers have oftentimes endeavored to subject the Church to their own control, or to use her as a means of furthering their ambitious projects; but the attempt at fettering the Church is sure to be still oftener made where such union does not exist. All the efforts of the present to separate Church from State aim principally at subjecting her altogether to civil power; and even in the United States, where the constitution forbids all meddling in religious matters, attempts are constantly made to thwart the action of the Church on education. Besides, in pronouncing judgment on union of Church and State, it is very unfair to look exclusively at the comparatively rare evils arising from the abuse of this union by the temporal power, and to lose sight of the great benefits derived from it by both State and Church.

14. The fundamental mistake of these liberal Catholics lies in supposing that falsehood has the same right to exist and spread its influence as truth. This is much akin to the Manichean heresy: for, if error and falsehood possessed the same rights as truth, the evil spirit, father of lies,

would have the same rights as God, author of truth, and consequently would be independent of, and equal to, Him in power. Error must at times be tolerated by society; the Church herself has not the right to compel by force those who never joined her communion, to abandon their errors. Yet this is no warrant for saying that error has a right to exist. All right is derived from God, and He, the fountain-head of all truth, necessarily detests error and cannot approve it. The Church instituted by God to lead mankind to truth has the most undoubted right to proclaim it everywhere to all mankind, and no human power is privileged to impede her action. It is not only her right, but her duty, to shield her children from error, and use for this purpose every means given her by God. On the contrary, error can never claim this right.

THE END.

INDEX.

Aaron's rod, 64.
Abbeville, stone implements of, 142.
Abuses in religion, 40, 41.
Abydenus, 149, 151,
Accacius, 347.
Achior, 125.
Acrostic of the Erythræan Sibyl, 157.
Acts of the Martyrs, 224.
Adad, 111.
Agatho, Pope, and the Council of Constantinople, 360.
Aggeus, 168, 213.
Albigensian heresy, 307.
Alexander the Great, and the Sabbatic year, 124 ; and the High-priest Jeddoa, 166.
Alexandria, Christian school at, 195 ; Church of, 338, 347.
Alford's commentary on "Confirm thy brethren," 336.
Alluvial deposits of the Nile, 146.
Ambrose, St., on the Pope, 356.
America, peopling of, 150.
Amiens, stone implements found at, 142 ; peat formation at, 145.
Angels, 58 (note).
Antinicene doctrine, 223, 225.
Antioch, church of, 338, 347.
Antipopes, 288.
Apes, absurdity of man's supposed descent from, 6.
Apollonius of Tyana, 176.
Apostles, supposed hallucination of, 182 ; trustworthiness of, 187-191 ; promises made to, 237 ; powers conferred on, 239 ; permanency of these powers, 240 ; told, not to write, but to preach, 321.

Apostles' Creed, 223.
Apostolic succession, no break to be feared in, 271.
Aramean tongue, pseudo-primitive gospel in the, 176.
Arians, 250, 346, 356.
Arius, 208.
Artapan, and the crossing of the Red Sea, 125.
Assyrian clay libraries, 134.
Athanasius, St., 346.
Atheists, 51 (*see* Infidels and Rationalists).
Atlantis, 150.
Atomic theory of philosophers, 13.
Atonement, revelation necessary for, 90 ; the atonement, 209.
Attributes of God, 24.
Augustine, St., on demon worship, 80 ; on the end of man, 87 ; on the six days of the creation, 129 ; on the acrostic, 158 (note) ; on St. Jerome's translation of the Bible, 178 ; on the spread of Christianity, 193 ; on the Donatists, 260 ; on the ceremonies of the Church, 278 ; on the Bible, 311 ; on the primacy of St. Peter, 339, 340.
Australia, savages of, 138.
Authenticity, definition of, 114.
Authoritative teaching necessary for the masses, 88-90.

Babel, tower of, 157.
Babylonians, 124 (note).
Basil, St., on the Doxology, 223 ; on the Roman See, 346.
Bear, the naked, 145.
Berosus, chronology of, 132-135.

INDEX.

Bible, the, not sufficient to constitute the infallible teaching of the Church, 310–323.
Bloomfield's commentary on "Thou art Peter," etc., 329.
Borsippa, 152.
Bos primigenius, 145.
Boucher de Perthes, 143.
Brazilians, 149.
Brixham Cave, 144.
Brutes have instinct, not reason, 33, 34.
Buchner on dogmas, 42.

Callisthenes, 134.
Calvin and Jansenius, 47, 48 (note).
Calvinists, 326.
Cambyses, 135.
Canonization, difficulty of, 282.
Catholicity of the Church, 258–261; the name of Catholic belongs to the Church of Rome alone, 279.
Causality, principle of, 17; argument for its objective reality, ib.; its application, 18.
Cave-men, 144.
Cavour, 376.
Celsus, 175.
Cephas, Paul withstands, 338.
Ceremonies of the Church based on the doctrines she teaches, 278.
Cerinthians, 212.
Chalcedon, Council of, and the Pope, 348, 359.
Chaldeans, 77; their tradition of the deluge, 149.
Charity, the bond of, insufficient for the unity of the Church, 250.
Cheops, curious facts about the pyramid of, 137–139.
Chinese, originally monotheists, 86; their chronology, 139; their tradition of the deluge, 148; their tradition of a Redeemer, 211.
Christ, divinity of, 207–226; two natures, one person, 208; He is the corner-stone, 230; the head of the mystical body, 232; why His Church must have, besides His headship, a visible authority, 255.
Christianity, spread of, proves its divine origin, 192–201; embraced all classes of society from the very first, 195; obstacles in its way, 196–201.
Chronology of Scripture, 130, 147.
Chrysostom, St., 346, 353.
Church, proving the true, 205–206; the Church must and may be easily known, iv, 255, 259, 261; figures by which she is described, and their meaning 227–235; the Church a spotless bride, and therefore infallible, 234; parables referring to the Church, their significance, 235; institution of the Church, 236–246; unity, 243, 247–257; visible authority and infallibility, 244; catholicity, 244, 258–261; holiness, 245, 262–267, 282; apostolicity, 245, 268–274; perpetuity, 272; she needs no doctrinal reform, 273; the promises made to the Church are not conditional, as were the promises made to the Jews, 274; the Roman Catholic Church alone has the notes of Christ's Church, 275–291; Catholics now more united than they have been for ages, 285; teaching authority of the Church, 292–309; Church not a democracy, 295; nor an aristocracy, but a monarchy, 325–328; infallibility of the Church, 297–309; relations between Church and State, 363–380.

INDEX. 383

Cicero, 87, 157.
Civiltà Cattolica, 38, 143.
Clement, St., on apostolicity, 269; settles a difficulty during St. John's lifetime, 345.
Common Schools, 374.
Confucius, 139.
Constantinople, Bishops of, 347; general council at, 354.
Converts, ostracism of, supposes a preternatural hatred of Christ's Church, 286.
Core's rebellion, 121.
Councils, General, (see infallibility); usefulness of, 361.
Creation not "unthinkable," 22.
Credentials of God's messengers, 57.
Cuneiform characters, 152.
Cyprian, St., 132, 270, 337, 338, 340, 344-345, 357.
Cyrinus, 172 (note).

Dan, city of, 112.
Daniel, unpopular with rationalists, 166; could not be an impostor, 167; absurd subterfuge of Rationalists, 168.
Darwinism, 6, 34, 147; has at least strengthened the proofs of the unity of the human race, 150.
Decretals, False, 348.
Definitions of the Church not new doctrines, 279.
Deluge, 95, 147-150.
Demonstration an inadequate means of imparting moral truth, 88-90.
Demon-worship, 33.
Denmark, peat deposits on the coast of, 146.
Deposing power, the, 366-369.
Deucalion, 149.
Diodorus of Sicily on Berosus, 134; on Egyptian chronology, 136.
Dioscorus, 347.

Dogmas, Buchner and Page on, 42.
Donatists, 250-260.
Doxology, the, how St. Polycarp expresses it, 223.
Dragon, star a of the, 138.

Ebionites, 175.
Edomite kings, 111.
Egyptians, 77; why they would not be inclined to record Mosaic miracles, 125; their chronology, 135-139; civilization, 147; tradition about a Redeemer, 211.
Elizabeth, Queen of England, her Inquisition, 309.
Elk, the great, of Indian tradition, 145.
Elohim, use of the name, 127.
Encratites, 175, 250.
Encroachments, 365, 379.
English Inquisition, the, 309.
Ephesus, Council of, and the Pope, 348, 354.
Epicurean philosophy, 84.
Epiphanius, St., 270, 346.
Eratosthenes, 136.
Error has no rights, 379.
Esdras reconstructs the Jewish nation, 116.
Etudes Religieuses, 141.
Eupolemus, 152.
Eusebius, 125, 149, 151, 152, 179, 180, 193, 349.
Eutychians, 250, 290, 347, 356.
Evidences of Religion, scope of the work, iii; not necessary for an act of faith, iv; division of the work, v.
Evil spirits, 64; do not know the future, 75; worship of evil spirits, 79, 80.
External rule, necessity of an, owing to man's passions, 90.
Extinction of species, time unknown, 144.
Ezechias, 134.

Fanatics, difference between, and martyrs, 189, 199.
Facts vs. surmises, 139.
Faith defined, 298; how Protestants and even Jews and Mahometans may make acts of faith, 299 (note).
Felix, Pope, 346.
Fetichism, 79, 80.
First principles denied, 2; induction impossible without, 3; importance of, 36.
Florence, Council of, 351.
Foe-Koue-Ki, 157.
Fo-hi, 80.
Forests of North America, 146.
Forgiveness of sin, 263.
Fourth Eclogue of Virgil, 157.
Free-will, 34.
Fundamentals, the theory of, agreement in, 252-254.
Future, the, unknown to finite intelligences, 74.

Galileo, 302.
Gallicans, 326, 354, 362.
"Gates of Hell," meaning of, 331.
Gaubil, Father, 148.
Gauls, mythology of the, 81.
Gelasius, 353.
Genealogies in St. Matthew and St. Luke, 180.
Gentiles, gathering of the, 159.
Genuineness, definition of, 103.
Geology and the Mosaic record, 128-132, 139-150; facts vs. surmises, 139; not all changes gradual, 146.
Germans, mythology of, 81.
Gibbon's natural explanations of the spread of the Gospel, 196-198.
Glaciers, 148.
Glasgow, canoes dug up in, 146.
Gnostics, 175, 250.
God, His existence acknowledged by mankind, 4; the natural law, admitted by all men, supposes the Lawgiver, 4; this universal voice cannot be attributed to passions, prejudices, or fraud, 5—or to ignorance or fear, 6; existence of God proved from the existence of contingent beings, 7 —from the order of the universe, 8-10; God, a physical cause, 18; not unknowable, 19; not anthropomorphic, 20; not necessitated to create, 23; God contains all perfections, 23; His attributes, 24; our duties toward God, 52.
Golden age, the, 95.
Gospels, genuineness and authenticity of the, 172-183; apocryphal gospels, 174; characteristic fact concerning the veneration in which the Gospels were held in the early ages of Christianity, 178; a general answer to the difficulties of the Gospels, 181.
Greeks, primitive monotheism of the, 86; tradition of a Redeemer, 211.
Greek Schismatics divided, 290.

Haliburton, 138.
Hebron, 113.
Heliopolis, priests of, 125.
Heretics, early, excommunicated, 250.
Hermes, the Books of, 85, 86.
Herodotus, 136, 147.
Hierocles, 175.
Holy Ghost, the soul of the Mystical Body, 232, 242; Holy Ghost promised, 238; mission of the, 240; interior teaching of the, 322.
Honorius, Pope, and the Sixth General Council, 358.
Horace on idols, 78.
Hormisdas, Pope, his formulary for the Oriental bishops, 353.

INDEX.

Human race, age of the, 130–147; unity of the, 150.
Humboldt on Mexican traditions, 211.

Ice-period, 148.
Idolatry, various forms of, 77–82; without the intervention of evil spirits, it is a riddle, 79; a crime, 99.
Ignatius, St., martyr, on the Roman See, 345.
Immaculate Conception of the Blessed Virgin, definition of the, 278.
India, Bhagavata Pourâna, 148.
Indifferentism a crime, 49, 50; the basis of the union of sects, and the ruin of religion, 251.
Induction impossible without first principles, 3.
Infallibility, definition of Papal, 278; without infallibility faith impossible, 298; infallibility of the Church, 299–309; infallibility of the Pope, 350–362; general councils, 354, 356, 358–360.
Infidels, difficulty of grappling with modern, 1; their fear of miracles, 63; their ridiculous explanations of the Mosaic miracles, 120; their wild theory about the apostles, 181; they refute one another, 285 (see Rationalists).
Infinite number, absurdity of an, 7.
Infinite series, absurdity of an, 15, 16.
Innocent, Pope, and St. Chrysostom, 347.
Inquisition, the, 305–309; inquisitors of Toledo excommunicated by Leo X, 305.
Interpretation of Scripture, a wise general rule for, 130.
Irenæus, St., on the Gospels, 173; on the Catholicity of the Church, 259; on her apostolicity, 270; on the primacy of Peter, 340; on the Roman See, 343; expostulates with St. Victor, 346.
Isis and Osiris, 211.

Jacobites, 278.
Jacob's prophecy, attempts of modern Jews to elude, 162.
Jansenius and Calvin, their errors on the supernatural state, 47, 48 (note).
Jeddoa and Alexander the Great, 124.
Jehovah, this name and Elohim interchanged, 127.
Jerome, St., 340, 349, 350, 353.
JESUS (see Christ, Messiah, resurrection) fulfilled the prophecies, 169–171.
Jewish kingdom, fable of a, 163.
Jewish religion a revealed one, 103; the basis of our own, 98; its ceremonial, 122, 154; its dogmatical part not changed, 161.
Jews, dispersion of the, 171; the Jewish authorities did not try the apostles, 190; the Jews' idea of the Messiah before His coming, 213.
John, St., did not invent the doctrine of the divinity of Christ, 214.
Josephus, 118, 123, 124, 156; his testimony about Alexander the Great, and the High-priest Jeddoa, trustworthy, 167; as also about Christ's miracles, 180.
Josias, copy of the law found during the reign of, 107.
Julian the African, 132.
Julian the Apostate, 169, 175; his tribute to the holiness of the Christians, 198.

Julius, Pope, and St. Athanasius, 346.
Justin, St., 173; was not the first to teach the divinity of Christ, 224; on the Catholicity of the Church, 259.
Justinus, 125.

"Keys of the kingdom of heaven," meaning of, 333; not given to the Church, nor to the other apostles, but to Peter alone, 333-335.

Lactantius, 132, 158.
Lake dwellings, 145.
Lampridius, 179.
Law, the new, 158-160.
Leo, St., quoted, 337; reference to, 349; Council of Chalcedon, 348, 360.
Levites; 107, 109, 118, 121, 160.
Liberalism, 375-377; Liberal Catholics, 377-380—their fundamental error very like Manicheism, 379.
Liberius, Pope, 357.
Lipsius, 137.
Llorente, untrustworthy, 309.
Luther, and the "Epistle of straw," 314—and "faith alone," 318.
Lyell, Sir Charles, 145-147.

Macedonians, 250.
Mahomet an impostor, 99, 100; sets too great store by external observances, 100-101; fruits of his system, 101; why it spread so rapidly, 101, 102.
Maistre (de) on sacrifice, 97.
Malachias, 168.
Manasseh, 106.
Manetho's chronology, 135.
Marathon, stone arrowheads at, 142.
Marcionites, 250.
Martyrs, their number and sufferings, 193, 194.

Materialism, and the life-principle, 28; and the human soul, 29-32; the outcome of Protestantism, 302.
Matrimony, laws on, 365, 373.
Matter not self-existing, 11-15.
Maximus, St., on the Pope, 350.
Menes and Noe, 136.
Mercury, the first, 136.
Mesmerism, 67-69; not natural, 69.
Messiah, promised, 155; why not acknowledged by the Jews, 156, 191; expected by them and by the Gentiles, 156-158—and eagerly looked for at the time of Christ, 165; is come, 162-168; Divinity of the, 207-226.
Metaphysical causes, theoretically rejected, practically admitted, by infidel scientists, 10, 11.
Mexicans, their tradition of the deluge, 149—of a Redeemer, 211.
Ming-ti, 157.
Miracles, definition of, 58; possibility of, ib.; constancy of the order of nature, 59, 60; moral certainty about miracles excludes doubt, 60, 61; the illiterate may be competent witnesses, 61, 62; contemporary miracles, 62; unbelievers' fear of miracles, 63; the plea of unknown laws of nature, 63; God does not change His mind, 63; miracles a certain proof of revelation, 63; necessity of testing miracles, 64; the true test, 64-66; false miracles can always be detected, 66, 67; miracles necessary, 66; miracles of the Pentateuch, 114-125; Gospel miracles, 179-183; gift of miracles in the Church, 265; this gift a test of the true Church, 267; Pro-

testants cannot solve objections of unbelievers against miracles, 267, 284; "Popish" miracles—Lourdes, 283, 284.
Moigno, Abbé, 137, 139, 147.
Monophysites, 290.
Monotheism the primitive religion, 6, 84–87.
Montanists, 250.
Moses, the only prophet recognized by the Samaritans, 106; his Egyptian lore, 109, 133; his descriptions confirmed by pagan writers, 117; his disinterestedness, sincerity and simplicity, 117, 118; but few links of tradition between him and Adam, 127.
Moulin-Quignon jaw-bone, 143.
Moustier, stone implements found at, 142.
Mysteries, 52, 53; what is known in mysteries, 54; contradictions of such as reject them, *ib.*; supernatural mysteries not contrary to reason, 54, 55; their usefulness, 55, 56.
Mythical interpreters of Scripture, 182.
Mythology, 77–82.

Nabonassar, 134.
Name, the Holy, of God claimed by Christ, 217.
Natural state of man, the, 45, 46, 92.
Naturalistic interpreters of Scripture, 182.
Nature's order constant, 3; this constancy does not exclude miracles, 59, 60.
Necessity, moral and physical, 77.
Neo-Platonism, 78, 196.
Nestorians, 250, 278, 290, 347.
New Testament, 204.
Nicolaitans, 250.
Nile, deposits of the, 146.

Nomine Christiano deleto, 194.
Notes or properties of the Church, 271, 275–291.
Numinius on Jannes and Mambres, 125.

Obligations of Christianity the real grievance of unbelievers, 56.
Ontologists and the supernatural state, 48 (note).
Oppert, Jules, 152.
Optatus, St., 260, 340, 350.
Oracles of Paganism, 74.
Origen, 173, 353.
Orinoco, 150.
Orphic poems, 86.

Pagans, confirm Mosaic account, 117, 118; admitted Christ's miracles, 179; their traditions about a God-Redeemer, 210–212.
Paganism a school of vice, 80, 81; it is the issue of unbelief, 82.
Pagan philosophers, baneful influence of, 84, 87, 88; their hatred of Christianity, 197.
Page, Mr., on dogmas, 42.
Pantheism, its vagaries, 21, 79; its unity is confusion, 22; its Christian expressions, 51; traces of it among the Hindoos, 85.
Papias, 349.
Passion of our Lord, its circumstances foretold, 171.
Paul, St., did not invent the doctrine of the divinity of Christ, 214.
Peat formations, 145.
Pelagians, 250, 278.
Perfectibility of man in the moral order, 82, 83; the theory of primitive ignorance and moral progress, 83–88.
Persecution, conduct of fanatics contrasted with that of martyrs

under, 199; foretold by Christ, 261, 264.
Persians, 77.
Peter, St., the visible shepherd of the whole flock, 233; promises made to him, 237; power conferred on him, 239; he lives in his successors, 242; his primacy, 324–339; his successor in the primacy, 340–349; writes from "Babylon," 349.
Peter de Luna, 289.
Phœnicians, 77.
Photius, 347, 354.
Physical causes cannot all be laid hold of by the senses, 11, 18.
Plato, 85, 87.
Pleiades, 138.
Pliny on Berosus, 133; Pliny the Younger on Christianity, 195, 224.
Polycarp, St., on the Doxology, 223.
Polyhistor, Alexander, 148.
Polytheism not the primitive religion, 6.
Pope, the (*see* Peter); infallibility of, 350–362; the deposing power, 366–369.
Pope Joan, the fable of, 288.
Porphyrius, 175.
Prehistoric times, 139.
Presbyterians, 326.
Primitive civilization, 84–87.
Primitive religion was monotheism, 6, 84–87.
Primitive savagery, theory of, 83–87, 147.
Protestantism, spread and rappid decline of, 200, 201; cannot be the Church of Christ, 278; does not convert pagan nations, 280; cannot claim unity, or catholicity, or apostolicity, 290; how Protestants may make acts of faith, 299 (note); Protestantism leads to Materialism, Positivism, Socialism, Communism, etc., 302; on its own theory it cannot vouch for the purity of the Bible, 312; Protestants must believe in their individual ministers, 319; on the Protestant theory, Christ ought to have revealed to his apostles the advantages of the printing-press, 321.
Prophecy, definition of, 73; possibility of, 73, 74; its value as a proof, 74; pagan oracles not real prophecies, 74, 75.
Psalms of David on the Messiah, 212.
Ptolemy, 134.
Pyramid of Cheops, its bearing on chronology, 137-139.

Quakers, 297, 310, 320.
Quaternary formations, 140.

Rationalists, their dislike for prophecy, 166; their shifts, 168; their inventions, 176; they refute one another, 183, 285; their views on the Gospels, 214.
Rawlinson, 152.
Reform, in the Church, there can be no dogmatic, 270, 273, 277.
Religion, definition of, 38; religion and the duties of life, 41.
Renan, 170 (note).
Resurrection of Christ, 184-192.
Revelation, its possibility, 51; its moral necessity, 77-82, 91; given from the very first, 93; its existence proved from its necessity, 94,—from the common consent of mankind, 95 · man is not free to choose what he pleases in revealed doctrines, 248; Christ has afforded us the means of knowing his

revelation, 249 ; to reject one revealed truth is to impugn God's veracity, 253.
Reversibility, doctrine of, 97.
Revue des Deux-Mondes, 143.
"Rock," meaning of the metaphor, 330.
Rougé, Viscount E. de, on the Books of Hermes, 86.
Russians, how they make proselytes, 281.

Sabaism, 80.
Sabbatic year, the, 123.
Sabellians, 250.
Sacrifice, the rite of, points to a primitive revelation, 95-97,—inexplicable otherwise, 96, 209; animals used for sacrifice, 97; the New Sacrifice, 160.
Saints, always to be found in the Church, 265, 282.
Samaritans, their version of the Scriptures, 104, 106, 107 ; their hostility to the Jews, 106, 116.
Sandwich Islanders, conversion of the, 280.
Sargasso Sea, 151.
Savages, do not civilize themselves, 84; primitive savagery, 83-87, 147.
Sceptre of Juda, the, 164.
Science, Infallibility not opposed to, 301.
Scotland, uprising of the coast of, 146.
"Search the Scriptures," 321.
Sects, union of, 251, 253 ; their common hatred for the Church, 286, 290.
Semi-Arians, 208.
Sensitive knowledge alone admitted, in order to the denial of God, 3.
Sepp, Dr., on Berosus, 133.
Septuagint, the, 104, 130, 132.
Sergius and Pope Honorius, 359.
Seth and Joth, 136.
Seventh day of rest, the, 129.

Seventy weeks of Daniel, the, 164-166.
Sibyls, 157, 158.
Six days of the Creation, the, 128-130.
Skulls, shape of human, 144.
Smith, George, on pyramid of Cheops, 137.
Society, revelation necessary for, 91.
Socrates, 85, 87; Socrates, the Christian, 346.
Soul, its simplicity, 29-32 ; spirituality, 32, 33 ; immortality, 35, 36.
Spanish Inquisition, the Church has nothing to do with the, 309.
Species, fixity of, 6.
Spiritism, its phenomena, though often not natural, are not real miracles, but prodigies due to the devil, 71 ; known to the ancients and at present in the East, *ib.;* our explanation not unscientific, 72 ; the reason why infidels deny this spirit-power, *ib*.
State, relations between Church and, 363-380.
Stone ages, 141.
Suidas on Berosus, 133.
Sun-worship, 80.
Supernatural, hatred of the, 42; definition of natural and supernatural, 43, 44 ; man's supernatural state, 46-49; Calvin and Jansenius on the supernatural state, 47, 48 (note).
Susa, castle of, 168.

Tacitus, on the Sabbatic year, 124 ; on the crossing of the Red Sea, 125, 157 ; on the multitude of martyrs, 193.
Talmud, the, admits Christ's miracles, 175, 179 ; teachings of the rabbis about the Messiah, 213.
Taurus, 138.

INDEX.

Temple, the, 165, 167, 168.
Ten Patriarchs, the first, and the first ten kings of Berosus, 133.
Ten tribes, the, 105.
Tertullian, 173, 179, 194, 195, 204, 225, 259, 270.
Thébaud, Father, on primitive traditions, 87; on early Catholicity, 259 (note).
Thebes, meaning of, 136.
Theodoret, 346.
Tiber, its appellatives, 141.
Tiberius proposes to place Christ among the gods of the empire, 179.
Toleration, as distinguished from agreement in religion, 251; its limits, 371.
Toth and Seth, 136.
Trance, the death of Christ could not have been a trance, 184-185.
Troy, 143.
Tyndall, on life, 25; on the potency of matter, *ib.*

Unbelievers, modern (*see* Rationalists, Infidels, *and* obligations of Christianity).
Union of sects, 251, 253.
Unitarians, 208; a favorite cavil of theirs, 221.
United States, the Church in the, 377, 379.
Unity of a society requires oneness of authority, 255, 293.
Unknowable, God is not the, 19.

Valentinians, 175, 250.
Varro, 87.
Vatican Council, 361.
Vedas, monotheism of the, 85.
Victor, St., and St. Irenæus, 346.
Virgil, 138, 157.
Virginity praised by Christ, 265.
Vishnu, 148, 210.
Visibility of the Church, 203-205, 304; of her authority, 255.
Vulgate, the, 131.

Wady Magharah, stone quarry at, 142.
West, Schism of the, 289.
Worship, definition of, 38; it must be both internal and external, 38-40; social worship, 40; social worship presupposes revelation, 91.

Xisuthrus, 149.

Y-King, 86.

Zend-Avesta, monotheism of the, 85; its tradition of the Mediator, 210.

www.ingramcontent.com/pod-product-compliance
Lightning Source LLC
Chambersburg PA
CBHW050850300426
44111CB00010B/1199